Rumour and Radiation

Sound in Video Art

PAUL HEGARTY

Bloomsbury Academic
An imprint of Bloomsbury Publishing Inc

B L O O M S B U R Y
NEW YORK • LONDON • NEW DELHI • SYDNEY

Bloomsbury Academic
An imprint of Bloomsbury Publishing Inc

1385 Broadway	50 Bedford Square
New York	London
NY 10018	WC1B 3DP
USA	UK

www.bloomsbury.com

BLOOMSBURY and the Diana logo are trademarks of Bloomsbury Publishing Plc

First published 2015

Library of Congress Cataloging-in-Publication Data
A catalog record for this book is available from the Library of Congress.

ISBN: HB: 978-1-6235-6413-1
PB: 978-1-6235-6269-4
ePDF: 978-1-6235-6668-5
ePub: 978-1-6235-6769-9

Typeset by Integra Software Services Pvt. Ltd.
Printed and bound in the United States of America

Rumour and Radiation

CONTENTS

ACKNOWLEDGEMENTS

Thanks to Ally Jane Grossan and all at Bloomsbury for their amazing work and support.

Thank you to the following galleries and artists for their invaluable assistance, access to works, images and interest: Marian Goodman, New York, White Cube, David Zwirner, Hauser and Wirth, Gary Hill, Bill Viola Studio, Christian Marclay, Ryoji Ikeda Studio, Ryan Trecartin, Fitch Trecartin Studio, LUX, Electronic Arts Intermix and to all who gave permissions and access to work.

In my more immediate world, thanks also go to Graham Allen, Bernadette Cronin, Pat Crowley, Billy Foley, Gary Genosko, Greg Hainge, Martin Halliwell, Michael Hoar, Mollie Anna King, Vicky Langan, Melanie Marshall, Irene Murphy, Colette Nolan, Brian O'Shaughnessy, Mick O'Shea, Romain Perrot, Declan Synnott and Yu Wakao.

For all her excellence, warmth, formalist focussing and not forgetting proofreading, I dedicate this book to Sarah Hayden, with love.

LIST OF ILLUSTRATIONS

Introduction: How Video Works and How It Sounds

This is not a love song
This is not a love song
This is not a love song
This is not a love song
This is not a love song

JOHN LYDON

I have learnt to distrust memory.

This unreliability made its presence felt when I synaesthesized a soundtrack for one of the major works by one of the world's most accomplished video artists and now successful film director Steve McQueen. I saw the work *Deadpan* (1997), the remake of a Buster Keaton short where a wooden house falls down around the protagonist, in the Turner Prize show of 1999, possibly in London's Institute of Contemporary Arts (ICA) in 2001, and I think not in Musée d'Art Moderne in Paris in 2003. I don't know at what point this began, but by sometime like 2009, I had decided that this silent film carried a powerful, all-conquering soundtrack. The video shows McQueen framed in the house, which then collapses, the downfall echoed, heightened, expanded, exploded by multiple angle shots, multiple cuts, shifts in perspective and the sense of infinite falling, around the static, barely flinching form of the artist. In my mind, the soundtrack is still there, but, even after closer inspection in the Marian Goodman gallery, and no matter how hard I looked or listened, it really did not feature the sound of timber thumping, from many perspectives, into dry ground. Unlike early cinema, or indeed videotape, *Deadpan* really was silent, yet somehow conveyed loudness.

It is tempting to start excavating this absent sound, but this can happen later, in the quiet or silenced parts of otherwise audio-filled video spaces. It would also be tempting to begin probing the perception of images, perhaps working through senses of time, sound and image, following Gilles Deleuze, Maurice Merleau-Ponty or even Henri Bergson. But if this book is about perception in a range of forms, it is not an attempt to either find an essence for it or to identify an essence and see how that plays out in the context of video installations. Perceptions in this book will have to remain at the level of suppositions based on close readings of what the works do and how they structure relations between screen and viewer. But accidentally, this mistaken perception of McQueen's piece does signal something about video art, and that is that we take its sound as a given, just as we do in cinema (hence the public excitement upon the release of the new 'silent' film *The Artist* in 2011). The more video art spreads through galleries, the more it is disposed for public, group perception, the more it is as much about hearing as it is seeing and the more we do not hear this, at some deeper level. Video installation has made listening in galleries normal. While I will shortly be trying to piece together what exactly video art consists of, how it works and what are its borders, for the moment, I am going to assert that this was not the case when video art first lit the rooms of galleries. Even now, single-screen, monitor-based works often come with headphones to protect the gallery and those who do not want to listen, even if they would like to glimpse those works.

Video did emerge from avant-garde music and sound use (as well as performance and conceptual art), as Holly Rogers points out in her recent book, *Sounding the Gallery*, on the early, multiple connections between experimental music and music in experimental art contexts both working as seeding grounds for video.[1] In a very direct sense, video occurred in parallel with developments in other arts, including sound (not least the sound of TVs, rolling film, rolling tape), in shows by Nam June Paik and Wolf Vostell (both showing video for the first time in 1963, in the Parnass gallery, Wuppertal), and also in tandem with performance in general, in line with minimalist sculpture and in association with more popular art forms, such as rock, cinema, festivals and television.[2] The influence of John Cage, the connections Paik had with music and performance are often cited, and Fluxus itself was keen to feature sound in its (measured) assault on artistic propriety. Chris Meigh-Andrews notes that 'developments in experimental music and avant-garde film practice [overlap] with the development of video art' (*A History of Video Art*, 4).[3] Nick Kaye devotes most of a chapter to Paik (along with Cage and Fluxus), as 'the emergence of "experimental television" in North American the early 1960s was closely bound to the new musical practices that emphasized an opposition to notions of the innate singularity of *the medium*' (*Multi-media*, 37).[4] There are those who question the priority given to these overseminal moments, such as Martha Rosler, discussed in detail in Chapter 1, but there seems to be shared understanding that music as well as sound are always present, from the start, in and around video art. Yvonne Spielmann says it clearly: 'video is the first truly audiovisual medium' (*Video: The Reflexive Medium*, 1).[5]

This in turn suggests that video art is far from silent, but is capable of being, as well as using, sound art. Furthermore, video art is not one medium at all, but inherently some sort of multimedia access point or strategy. Arguably, if this is the case, we could refer to Dick Higgins' idea of 'intermedia', where media boundaries break down in forms that do not simply coalesce into new ones. This would account for the difficulty in defining video art, or delimiting it. This first sense of video art as intermedial will be important here, but has thus far been very much in the background compared to the dominant concerns with the technology of video, on the one hand, and the social/political potential it held in its early phases, on the other.

Holly Rogers also notes the intermediality of video art, but takes it in a different direction to that which I intend here. For her, video art combines video and music, and it is in this combination that 'video art-music' is intermedial – it is between genres but maintains a connection between approaches that continue within the new form (see *Sounding the Gallery*, 2, 8, 41). For me, Higgins suggested something stronger, and that is that intermedia is a new form that no longer refers back to the 'parent' forms from which it budded. More accurately, it is not even a medium, but something existing or functioning diffusely between media forms, a work that 'fall[s] between media' ('Intermedia', 49).⁶ Higgins cites Duchamp's ready-mades as being 'truly between media, between sculpture and something else' (49). He also refers to the work of Philip Corner and John Cage as 'explor[ing] the intermedia between music and philosophy' (50). He specifies that the term does not refer to mixed media work (52), and that ultimately, the inbetween-ness solidifies into recognizable new media (52). Therefore, this new 'intermedia' is a more open version of a medium, and retains the capacity to arise outside of generic categories. The viewer has a different experience due to the novelty of an overall effect, and this newness continues to develop in the form of multisensorial, space-shaping and space-deconstructing video installation.

Wulf Herzogenrath, Meigh-Andrews and Kaye, all join with the vast majority of contributors to the significant collection of writing on video art, *Illuminating Video*, edited by Doug Hall and Sally Jo Fifer in 1990, in valorizing both the contribution of portable video technology to art and how this access is somehow about democracy.⁷ This collection occurs at a strangely important juncture, compiling the past thoughts on video just as video installation is going to sweep away the contemporary pertinence of the bulk of the ideas expressed in it. So the reader is pummelled with notions of the 'freedom' that artists obtained with first the Portapack video in the late 1960s, and then much more portable machines in the 1980s. I do not wish to labour the omnipresence of this angle on video, so let us take this example from Deirdre Boyle as paradigmatic:

In 1965, the Sony Corporation decided to launch its first major effort at marketing consumer video equipment in the United States. The first 'consumer' to buy this still rather cumbersome equipment was

Korean artist Nam June Paik, who produced the first publicized video documentary while riding in a taxi cab in New York City. ('A Brief Summary of American Documentary Video', 51)[8]

Paik gets his founder-status confirmed; machinery's determining role in freeing up the artist is confirmed; the importance of democratically produced documentary is affirmed; video's connection to corporate inventiveness is hinted at. The use of video is not only seen as an aesthetic reaction to contemporary society but as something inherently political, and essentially caught up, in the spread of mainstream media. Indeed, the media helped video artists to make work, via cable, and/or regional TV. Sony itself helped early video artists Frank Gillette and Paul Ryan, via Marshall McLuhan's Center for Media Understanding at Fordham, New York.[9]

Predominantly, though, the view of artists and critics has been that video art sought to challenge media institutions: first by putting production in the hands of the public, as opposed to a centralized, sanctioned group of cosseted staff producers; second, this production comes freighted with a belief in immediacy, in real time. This works both in the form of the socially conscious documentary on 'the streets' and in TV installations which incorporated the viewer via a combination of camera and TV screens (such as in the work of Peter Campus); third, the presence of artworks within the TV system would break up the monopolistic rule of conservative programmers, revealing the paucity of the usual fare on offer; fourth, there would now be no need to even refer back to capitalist institutions such as state-run corporate media. That these perspectives cannot all work at once does not mean that the late 1960s and 1970s did not see a general, even a generic, sense of the revolutionary nature, or at least potential of video. To quote John G. Hanhardt,

> television, through its management by corporate monopolies or state-run systems, had become a seamless hegemonic institution. [...] yet the body of post-1965 video art was profoundly influenced by the work of a few artists who had appropriated the television set as icon and apparatus in the years preceding 1965. ('Dé-collage/Collage', 71)[10]

Many of the authors in *Illuminating Video* would agree with the main point, without necessarily wishing to be beholden to the same extent to Vostell and Paik, and in fact some critics would seek to move early video away from its techno-aesthetic and concentrate more on its social-critical capacity. Boyle talks of the various underground media operations in the United States in the 1970s and Marita Sturken argues that the focus on machinery could go 'to the extent of negating video's use as a social tool' ('Paradox in the Evolution of an Art Form', 105).[11] In fact, the dominant idea seems to be that the very act of doing something with TV, or using TV as a monitor, was inherently critical. Of course TV was often subverted – in Paik and Vostell's cases, TV becomes an authentic visual object, capable of being displayed in its own right rather than claiming to be merely a transparent transmitter of content (while in technical terms acting as receiver). In 1969, Jan Dibbet's piece *TV as a Fireplace* was broadcast on German TV (Cologne-based WDR [Leigh-Andrews, *History of Video Art*, 21–2]). It was an echo of Paik's *Moon as First Oldest TV* (1965), a multi-screen installation of film of the moon, as, in both cases, something you could watch without the framing of the programming of broadcast TV had been brought into representational, electronic form. In the case of *TV as a Fireplace*, the domestic is estranged, as the TV image of the fireplace sits uncannily in not quite the right place, in a home setting. These examples show video as a high-tech *arte povera*, lifting a phenomenon to re-place it more or less intact, but not quite in the same place, a very gentle recontextualization. This kind of strategy, as well as the later experiments that would perform political art, whether abstractly or explicitly (Abramović and Rosler, respectively), is one side of the critical capacity of video, but still, for some early critics (and practitioners), this is not enough – video needs to be the mobile social agent it could be, or is dreamt to be.

Video would not just be a tool for artists, whether exploring aesthetic and philosophical questions (of identity, for example) or making social documentaries. The new machinery, via radical media interventionist groups, would encourage 'production instead of consumption, neighbourhood TV, video for therapeutic use in schools, in therapy and in games' (Herzogenrath, 'Video Art and Institutions', 29, writing of the German situation in the 1970s). The continuum of politically relevant recording and playback actions runs from these directly social (institutional) uses, through political comment and statement, all the way into documentary making or even exposing the working of media themselves, ensuring that 'video as a medium more than any other has addressed historical, national, civilization-related, urban and social conflicts', as Sabine Maria Schmidt claims ('At the Right Place at the Right Time?', 37).[12] Prefiguring relational art's claims, the use of video itself can then be seen as necessarily political: 'From the 1970s to the mid-1980s, using video stood for a claim to the social and political function of art' (Dieter Daniels, 'Video/Art/Market', 43).[13]

To summarize, we have competing utopian models: the first, techno-utopian; the second, techno-critical; and the third, social-critical. All these models clearly come from the period of social turmoil and the privatization of protest as official revolutionary movements lost 'traction' – the years 1965–75 – this being the period Leigh-Andrews identifies as the 'defining period of video art' (*History of Video Art*, 113). Martha Rosler summarizes this multi-utopian situation and adds a critique of the making of a video history that has sprung from male videomakers' works, in what remains one of the rare essential essays on video art, 'Video: Shedding the Utopian

Moment' from 1985.[14] Essential does not mean faultless, however, and the essay is marred by a lumpen Marxist reading of McLuhan, a very minimal level of attentiveness to Paik and some questionable claims about how the avant-garde relates to technology. Rosler outlines a messianic path for video art – one that had thus far mostly been thwarted. At the outset, video artists took a progressive position with regard to TV and video technology, with 'the early uses of portable video technology represent[ing] a critique of the institutions of art in Western culture' (Rosler, 'Video', 31). But this focus on media technologies became fixation, and ultimately a formalism based on some sort of hope that machinery itself could initiate utopia ('Video', 44–6). The formalism is a problem, argues Rosler, part of an unholy apoliticism, that combines with quietism under the aegis of Cage (46). The formalism leads to institutional acceptance (47), and 'a main effort of the institutionalized art-delivery structures (museums, galleries and so on) has been to tame video, ignoring or excising the elements of implicit critique' (33).

Leaving aside the many reductive comments Rosler makes, this trajectory of acceptance and domestication can be clearly seen, and the more apparently critical and reflexive works such as those of Peter Campus or Dan Graham were so literal, so transparently critical that they could be even more easily assimilated by institution and public alike. The pieces would not be hard to install, they could be copied, and even the live 'unreplaceable' elements of camera/monitor/mirror pieces could always have their permissive structure re-created with minimum fuss. The same can be said of sound art that only requires listening; that is, galleries find this work easy to put on, as long as it features headphones, and the public gets to listen like it does at home, on the train or on the street, instead of having to look at art. The same is even more true of political discourse in the place of art (so-called relational aesthetics). So, Rosler has spotted something important: video art is what leads the way to this readily consumable art, but, against her view, it is not through over-formalism. Rather, it happens due to what only appears to be formal play, to pre-empt Rosalind Krauss for a moment. Either way, Rosler's model of the removal of radicality through exhibition value seems to have some contribution to make as to how video art became a gallery art form. Attacking TV turned out not to be the way to any rebellion with wider meaning or effect outside of art, or outside the gallery system (Rosler, 'Video', 50). So what is required, according to Rosler, is a model of video art that begins with the social, rather than peripherally dealing with it via machine critique. This is the stronger, more feminist part of the argument here: video needs to deal with the conditions of its creation, and these are social, gendered, historicized, and not reiterate the construction of an easy sequence of canonical figures. Even at the time of writing, Rosler seems to be focussing in on only one half of the possible narrative. Unlike those writing at the time, and many others (like Leigh-Andrews and Kaye, for example), she identifies a problematic turn in the development of video, and this is always a better and more useful position than a happy, tolerant eclecticism. The emphasis on technological mirroring and subversion was only a fake messianism, for her, and the true prospect is the socialization of the medium.

If Rosler takes a critical stance on video, then Krauss provides an antagonistic one, in her essay 'Video: The Aesthetics of Narcissism' from 1976.[15] In this early essay, she posits that video loses sight of its mechanical auto-reflection, in favour of a personal auto-reflection on the part of the artist:

> For the object (the electronic equipment and its capabilities) has become merely an appurtenance. And instead, video's real medium is a psychological situation, the very terms of which are to withdraw attention from an external object – an Other – and invest it in the self. (57)

This is based on a highly selective view whereby video is mostly a device for artists to introduce themselves into the artwork, in the recording of a performance in front of camera, now presented onscreen. Krauss argues that installations can escape this trap. In his two pieces, *mem* and *dor* (both 1974), Campus subverts this problem by turning the reflectiveness on to the viewers, who find themselves disoriented and the opposite of self-present. The question of reflection is vital in this essay, as Krauss separates reflexiveness (using Jasper Johns as an example) from auto-reflection. The first is a modernist, and therefore properly experimental attitude that uses form to explore content by 'achiev[ing] a radical *a*symmetry' (Krauss, 'Video', 56). The second attitude is the narcissism of the title, and the fate of most video art, as it encourages self-sufficiency.

Sturken points instead to the 'postmodern self-consciousness' of video ('Paradox', 102), and this does show us a way to extend Krauss's point beyond the limits of her selection of artists in the essay in question.[16] For what if video is about narcissism, and what if it is caught in a trap of self-reflection that is subtly different (if not necessarily 'less' than modernist reflexiveness)? But instead of conceiving the problem as being a bunch of artists in need of Lacanian psychoanalysis, we look to the machinery, expectations of the medium and the limits of both of those, in the period leading up to 1976. On the one hand, video is caught within 'a set of physical mechanisms' (Krauss, 'Video', 52), while on the other, these are inadequate to describe, let alone account for, what video art does, as 'the ease of defining it in terms of its machinery does not seem to coincide with accuracy' (52). This is the next important insight of Krauss, one to which the shortcomings of the essay have blinded later critics, and that is, that the machinery of video art is a distraction. Even if the medium is the message, the medium/message simply is not the machine of TV/camera. Krauss wants the medium to be psychology, but this can be made less literal if we think in terms of purposiveness.

The articles by Rosler and Krauss share a rejection of technological determinism in video. Mary Lucier then extends that agreement, suggesting the possibility of an approach that would prioritize aesthetic form over content or artistic content over machine form. Lucier argues that the camera must be seen as a tool (explicitly following Douglas Davis's suggestion that the 'camera is a pencil').[17] The argument of this book will be that without formal analysis, we are not in the vicinity of art, but in the presence of the arbitrary. Content cannot live alone and be art. Where some writers on video have come adrift is in mistaking the physical container, or tools, for the form of the artwork. If that suggests the danger of a non-materialist abstraction, it is certainly one that Rosler (of 1985 at least) would reject, but one that takes us further from the hagiography of the fire-discoverers and TV-meddlers. It makes sense that writers in the mid-1980s, up to 1990, as evidenced in *Illuminating Video*, are still in thrall to then recent conceptions of video art, but none at all that writers in this century could think the same, against the backdrop of the massive variety, subtlety and formal achievement or social commentary of video of the last twenty years. This is one of the reasons this book will be tilted towards this recent period: to bring video art discourse in line with contemporary art practice, rather than being concerned about an admittedly fascinating retro-authenticity. As Dieter Daniels has pointed out, 'the meaning of video art has changed completely' ('Video/Art/Market', 45) such that the early history of the medium has little relevance to contemporary artists or those that view (and hear) the work. Why would it? – who thinks it important to think about the history of the brush when looking at the paintings of Gerhard Richter?

This changed meaning means that I am unashamedly picking out retrospective markers for that change, the moments where critics began to see and perhaps hear something other than the hum of a tweaked TV, the ping of a sine wave or the filming of some sort of documentary from an embedded position as being the sum of video art. The critiques of Rosler and Krauss open the way to a broader method of reading video (if still visual and political in focus), as does the questioning of untouchable primacy through machine discovery or of happening to be the first to have done a mechanical trick. The question of which of 'technology' or 'politics' wins as an answer to the purpose of video art, even if we restrict it to art pre-1980, is of no particular relevance other than to show that contestation of form and meaning existed at the outset. So before returning to the question of the central role of sound in video, beyond its possible genetic input, it is time to build a clearer picture of what is meant, and what I mean, by the term 'video art'.

Yvonne Spielmann outlines a more persuasive model of what video does as a medium. She argues that there has been too much concentration on the machinic element, when this was important only at the outset, and often the focus on the machine, or the tape, or the camera, held up thought (and practice). Instead, video is an authentic medium, that uses technology in a variety of ways, 'through the articulation of a specific media language and semiotic system to successfully establish an aesthetic vocabulary' ('From Technology to Medium', 55).[18] Video is, or has, an 'open structure' (56), it has an 'open apparatus' (58) and it has 'flexible and transformative characteristics' (56). This does not mean that video is simply between media, because what it does is accumulate devices (both physical and strategic) in order to become a medium. It is audiovisual from the start ('the first *audiovisual medium*' [56])[19] and quickly crosses into the digital, long before widespread digitalization (Spielmann dates this back to 1973 [58]). 'Video' is a medium that is not restricted to video in the form of tape, or playing with camera/TV reflections. It is a term that designates a combinatory medium that began with connections between performance, the exploration of audiovisual equipment and conceptual art. Video is a *relational* medium, reliant on its crossings, most specifically between audio and visual:

In a comparative examination of media forms, the predisposition of the electronic to processing and the interchangeability of audio and video streams together characterize the technical conditions that ground the realization of the aesthetic forms specific to video. ('From Technology to Medium', 69)

We have almost gone too far with this relational definition of the video medium, even though I am in full agreement with it, and it will infiltrate the book, as will the claim of audiovisuality. Taking a step back, in line with Spielmann's argument, we can find a more pragmatic, if still deconstructive, way of thinking video:

The use of video in contemporary media arts is not necessarily driven by exploration and further development of video as an electronic form. Instead the artists draw on video techniques in film (interactive cinema installations), in multiple screen installations. [...] The point I want to stress is that such contemporary 'video installations' are less concerned with video than with other media forms. (64)[20]

So now we have a form that does not really exist, except as a relational intermedial practice, and a medium ('video') that does not seem to use its own methods. But we have the processing of signals into display conditions, we have the notion that video involves installation, that it has moved beyond its fascinating yet time-bound origins in 1960s art and politics – as evidenced by its spread through contemporary media. We also have the persistence of recording and playback, with the viewer still only rarely placed in a seated, timetabled cinema context. Lastly, video is predominantly a combination of visual and auditory signals, presented as part of one piece, rather than as mutual adjuncts. This matches Dick Higgins's original conception of 'intermedia' as a type of medium that crossed between media rather than combine them into a new, resolved medium.

Video has long been an art of installation, arguably since the early days, such that its installations are a 'sculptural medium, with the television "box" as a building block or component' (Meigh-Andrews, *A History of Video Art*, 56). Torres notes that 'multi-media installation provided an existing structure into which video was able to expand (and by so doing, help define)' ('The Art of the Possible', 207–8).[21] While installation is now somewhat of a norm, one that possibly undermines the idea of medium specificity, Sturken points out that in its early days video was tucked away, and the specificity of individual works was diminished:

> in order to receive funding, museums and art organizations segregated the medium of video into departments separate from other media. This segregation meant that most exhibitions of video have been presented in a solitary context, rarely in the context of film, painting or other media. ('Paradox', 104)[22]

Written in 1990, this predates the massive spread of 'the installation', but Sturken is nonetheless already aware that video will also affect the art institution as museums did as museums wanted to encourage the new form, even if, initially, in limited ways.

The display of video art is a vital part of its structure, definition and practice. Arguably, as it becomes more 'aesthetic', it becomes more about display in its own right. I would argue, following Krauss's critique, that video has to make the paradoxical leap 'backward' into the aesthetics of modernism, or even earlier, in order to attain the critical self-reflexivity of avant-garde practice. In other words, the literalness of looking closely at TV and its institutions and viewers was not a continuation of the avant-garde, as it was reductive of aesthetic form, and veered towards pure content. Meigh-Andrews, glossing Stuart Marshall, puts it well, when pointing to the political and representational turn of video in the 1970s: 'Modernist artists working with video who sought to uncover a pure language of the medium were unable to do so as long as they excluded the issue of representation from their practice' (*A History of Video*, 235). The way in which this often avoided either formalism or storytelling was, firstly, through the consideration that representation was not simply brought in, but brought in as a problem, and second, via the intermedial nature of video, which gradually developed into the authentic structure of video art, with sound as a driving element. So instead of thinking about the authorial content of looking at the technology of video, video art moved into a mode of display, rather than pre-emptive didactic strikes on the idea of display. As Frieling and Herzogenrath observe, even from the outset, video could be about the way in which it would be presented, displayed, viewed and circulated, and not just about commentary on these ('40YEARSVIDEOART.DE', 15).

Installation introduces a different sense of space and time to the gallery – not just its dominance of those perspectives, or the slowing down of passing viewers, but the 'passingness' of viewers – as creators of installations need to be aware that people will drift in and out, miss beginnings, come back, leave and spend time adjusting their eyesight in the 'black box' rooms of contemporary installations. Instead of heightened attention, the greater demand for attention leads to a sort of structural distractedness – that is, it is not entirely by the choice or judgement of the viewer. In short, maybe there is no change in what happens in viewing, when compared to looking at painting, but there is a sense of incompletion, of being adrift, that Sabine Maria Schmidt regards as an approximation of real-life conditions ('At the Right Place at the Right Time', 39).

Christine Ross argues that video undoes and remakes time perceptions, albeit at a cost of historical awareness, including of the history of video art itself.[23] Boris Groys offers a more sustained meditation on how the prevalence of media installations works, developing the idea of video's temporal dimension further, commenting on how the length of video, whatever the length, inflects the perception and reception of pieces (and the gallery itself, or whatever location the work is shown in). Whatever the duration, awareness that there is one determines an uncertainty and also a freedom that other forms do not provide as consistently. The sense of time being required creates an obligation, but this is not due to mystery, complexity or duration as physical or mental test:

> This is not an intentionally lengthened duration of contemplation that the viewer possibly needs to 'understand' the image – as the viewer is completely in charge of the duration of conscious contemplation. Rather it is the time a viewer needs to even be able to watch a video or film in its entirety – and which can absolutely exceed the duration of the customary visit to the museum. (Groys, 'From the Image to the Image File – and Back', 52)[24]

Beyond Schmidt's sense that the gallery visitor is thrown back into the thrownness of everyday life, only in a more purposeful way, by media pieces with set durations, Groys notes that the sense of control is what makes the viewer arrive at a sense of the uncanny. It is not just colossally long pieces, such as Douglas Gordon's *24 Hour Psycho* (1993) or Christian Marclay's *Clock* (2010), that offer and remove control, but all pieces that take time, at every moment of their display. How much of any video is enough? How am I choosing? Significantly longer pieces draw attention to this permanent condition of the moving image–based installation.

This has a bearing on the reality of the work, as the unlikelihood of watching a whole exhibition, let alone a major museum's worth, of video work, undoes the possibility of video being fixed to a true essence. Groys pins this to the condition of the viewer, writing that 'the basic experience had by the viewer of a video installation is thus the experience of the non-identity of the exhibited work' (Groys, 'From the Image', 52). This makes video installations approach the condition of scored music, he continues, with the score in existence, but rarely present (53). This is presuming too much, I think, and brings his argument back to a controlling intelligence, whether of a Platonic, Ideal piece or an equally neo-Platonic Idea in the head of the godlike creator, whose work we only glimpse through a scanner, darkly. It is interesting to see music come in at this point, but the iterations of the temporality of video are endless – that is, simply, every writer mentions it. Video structures time – but it has long been an idea present in the philosophy of music that music is the organization of time through sound. Long before Varèse and then Cage came up with the idea of music as being only (or as much as) organized sound, G.W.F. Hegel had written of music as the passage and structuring of time in sound form (*Aesthetics*, 907).[25] So it would seem that video emerges from music, and ends up doing what music does, performing its essence. But Groys identifies something more interesting still, something that connects sound and video even more closely together. As so much video seems open-ended, or does not insist on constructing a narrative that demands following all the way through, the viewer adopts a position of creative distraction, or even drift, 'thus a video or film installation in a museum radically lifts the ban on movement which determines viewing these images in a cinema system' (Groys, 'From the Image', 51). This is despite galleries trying to make video more cinema-like by putting up screening times, that is, marking when the loop begins. It also changes the trajectory of a gallery visit, where viewing a picture or object, or reading text, mostly suggests completion, or at least temporary closure, as the visitor proceeds along the curated pathway. Now, a visiting balance needs to be struck, a plan made, and also a drift initiated, and maybe a less linear circuit.

This mobility of the gallery visitor is a direct partner of the perceptual mobility of video that is achieved through and by sound. Sound travels, sound is the marker of the mobility of the visitor, even if less voluntary, such as when an installation bleeds its sound over and around the dividing walls. Sound art may disrupt the retinal aspect of the gallery situation, but it is through video art that this first happens. It is through video art, this book contends, that it continues to happen. And it does this at least in part because the normalcy of having sound and image together makes us forget to consume the sound as anything other than incidental (and sometimes to invent it, to fill a gap that is not there…). It does this in another part through the strange separation of image and sound, as the image is tethered to some solid support while the sound roams, announcing that more lies ahead. It does this in still another part through video installation having become 'a pleonasm for contemporary art' (Ross, 'The Temporalities of Video', 88). In other words, the sound of video art is both here, present, and there, entangled yet separate; it is elsewhere and infiltrating here, and most of all, it is almost everywhere.

We can narrow this to the exemplarity of two pieces by Bruce Nauman, *Performance Corridor* and *Video Corridor* (both 1969). Both pieces involve the squeezing of the gallery visitor into confined areas, and the latter piece stands as figurehead for Margaret Morse's reading of the installation as an embodied space, where 'the room is rather the *ground* over which a conceptual, figural, embodied, and temporalized space that is the installation breaks' ('Video Installation', 154).[26] In *Video Corridor*, the viewer becomes a moving element of the installation, walking along a thin enclosed space to finally see his or her passage played on two monitors, and 'the visitor is enclosed within an envelope of images, textures and sounds' (153). In *Performance Corridor*, this viewer becomes a sound-making body, in mutual resonance with the wood walls. Both engage the full range of senses through an overall restriction, letting the senses bounce around and through the installation. *Performance Corridor* externalizes the mystery of the interior, as the sound of passage extends beyond the walls. Sound seems to be some sort of siren, extending outward, and then, once within the installation, it fills the sensory body with awareness of its passage that makes the installation work. This returns us to the notion of video art as relational, profoundly intermedial in how it relates to those who construct its meaning, affect and purpose as they pass. Sound is not just a carrier for some deeper ground, but a process of grounding such as that seen in Martin Heidegger's 'The Origin of the Work of Art' essay, where 'the work belongs, as work, uniquely within the realm that is opened up by itself' (167).[27] This is not simply a modernist statement about the autonomy of art, or of an artwork, but quite the opposite. Heidegger's argument is that the work brings its surroundings into being, and vice-versa, with the further addition that these both occur in the encounter of the work, as Juliane Rebentisch notes about the 'presencing' made possible for work and visitor alike in the installation situation (*Aesthetics of Installation Art*, 64).[28]

Throughout this book, I will be arguing that sound further develops this idea of a relational grounding, where sound, visuals, visitor, auditor and viewer interact with each other and the art establishment, and the expectations of video and/or audio pieces. This will happen in different ways for and with different artists. The specific strategies with regard to sound will produce alternate theorizations, some more straightforward than others, particularly where sound is presented as an accompaniment, as in a non-diegetic film soundtrack. At each point, the original connection of video art with sound will be maintained as a trace element. This refers to video art's emergence from multimedia art events and movements such as happenings, Fluxus, performance or conceptual art, but more so it connects us to video artist Steina Vasulka's dictum that 'video always came with an audio track, and you had to explicitly ignore it not to have it' (cited in Meigh-Andrews, *A History of Video Art*, 85). I do not believe, following the insights of Spielmann in particular, that this needs to be restricted to its literal content, that is, the sound of tape whirring, or audio hum from recording as played back on monitors, or the use or otherwise of sound recording in the first place. Instead, I think that just as sound art consciously switches other senses off, then when video is silent, it is so on purpose, and that we should take the presence of sound as a given. The task is to move it from being a given to see how it is given, how it is and how it works in giving (itself).

As for video art itself, I intend to offer different readings of the 'what' of video art, according to each artist or approach covered, and this 'what' will contain or be overwhelmed by sound. On occasion (Christian Marclay, Ryoji Ikeda, Carsten Nicolai), the work will be much closer to sound art, but at the core it will have a fixed visual element that has not in its turn become periphery. In other words, an arbitrary border is drawn between works that have a clear video focus, and where the sound is either dominant or only apparently secondary, and works where the visual installation complements the aural part. It is vital that the installations covered here offer some sort of trade between visuality and aurality, between moving image and sound. The relation of still image to sound may be a curious one worthy of investigation, but the illusion or 'reality' of the possibility of sound and image coming from the same recorded source and being presented as a unity is not a sustainable sensory illusion, so interesting though it may be, this is excluded, albeit the notion of apparent stasis in a moving film is not (e.g. the films of Warhol or Chris Marker).

So, video art is relational and is not restricted to the technology of the video recorder or video cassette. The specific technology, even at the outset, is only part of an already burgeoning medium. But it will still be useful to identify some more positive characteristics of the genre of video art, as seen from the second decade of the twenty-first century, rather than merely reflecting what was essentially a transitional period as being the atemporal essence of the medium.

1. Video art features the moving image as the core.
2. Video art is an installation, even in the case of a single TV/monitor.
3. Therefore, video art affects space around it, gathering space in a way that a still artwork on a wall does not.
4. Video art is a sound art.
5. Video art is an intermedia.

6. Video art partakes in what McLuhan called 'allatonceness'[29] and occupies a privileged place in the development of installation art.
7. Video art occupies a privileged place in the development of autonomous sound art.
8. Video art can be on film or video, can be coded in analogue or digital fashion and can be shot on one format, shown in another.
9. (A work of) video art is a commentary or, better, has a position or a view on the functioning of visual media, whether intentionally or not.
10. (A work of) video art also has a position on narrative, its desirability, its structure, its expectations and its potential uses.
11. Video art not only has duration; it addresses duration as a question.

In the course of this book, those features will play out and define the terrain for sound-based analysis. The earlier part of the book looks at wider questions at play in earlier variants of video art and spends much more time on film-makers and performance artists, both of whom help bring the medium into being. Less emphasis is placed on artists well covered as 'founders' of video as art. Taking a formalist position throughout, I am interested in what the artwork does, how it functions and how sound drives that overall purpose. For this reason, omissions may surprise. But there are three reasons for possible absent artists: first, they may not actually use sound very interestingly; second, the early days of video feature many works that do not make as much of sound as we might wish, and this includes artists who came from the realm of experimental music; third, more pragmatically, there is the question of access to works, which is, shall we say, uneven, for a variety of pragmatic reasons of access and control of access. Every chapter has at its core the analysis of specific pieces (hence the importance of access), and this too has limited the number of works covered, in a positive way, because each work has its function in the book, in the argument and in the developing of a theoretical model of many strands. The strands branch from the idea of sound in video to the artists, to the works and then to the playing out of sound in those works, in detail. At every level, the question is what does the work do? How does it do it? How does sound structure that process, such that it defines the perception of the viewer/listener or installation visitor?

Notes

1   Holly Rogers, *Sounding the Gallery: Video and the Rise of Art-Music* (Oxford: Oxford University Press, 2013). The term 'video art-music' is intended as a corrective to the designation video art, which diminishes the

role of music, musical sources and musical structures in what becomes known as video, argues Rogers (2).

2   See Wulf Herzogenrath, 'Video Art and Institutions: The First Fifteen Years', in Rudolf Frieling and Wulf Herzogenrath (eds.), *40YEARSVIDEOART.DE: Digital Heritage, Video Art in Germany from 1963 to the Present* (Ostfildern: Hatje Cantz, 2006), 20–33 (21–2). He cites John Anthony Thwaites as saying that 'the room [where Mr Paik sits, with his many TVs] is full of their buzzing, humming and crackling' (22).

3   Chris Meigh-Andrews, *A History of Video Art: The Development of Form and Function* (Berg: Oxford and New York, 2006).

4   Nick Kaye, *Multi-media: Video – Installation – Performance* (Abingdon and New York: Routledge, 2007).

5   Yvonne Spielmann, *Video: The Reflexive Medium* (Cambridge, MA: MIT Press, 2010 [2005]). Translated by Anja Welle and Stan Jones.

6   Dick Higgins, 'Intermedia', *Leonardo* 34 (1) (2001), 49–54. Includes the 1965 text, the 1981 update and an appendix by Hannah Higgins, available at https://muse.jhu.edu/journals/leonardo/v034/34.1higgins.html (accessed 9 May 2014).

7   Doug Hall and Sally Jo Fifer (eds.), *Illuminating Video: An Essential Guide to Video Art* (New York: Aperture, 1990).

8   Deirdre Boyle, 'A Brief Summary of American Documentary Video', in Hall and Fifer (eds.), *Illuminating Video*, 51–69. Michael Rush talks of 'a new revolution in image making' due to the Portapak in *Video Art* (London: Thames and Hudson, 2003), 7.

9   See Michael Rush, *Video Art*, 17.

10 John G. Hanhardt, 'Dé-collage/Collage: Notes Toward a Re-examination of the Origins of Video Art', in Hall and Fifer (eds.), *Illuminating Video*, 71–9.

11 Marita Sturken, 'Paradox in the Evolution of an Art Form: Great Expectations and the Making of a History', in Hall and Fifer (eds.), *Illuminating Video*, 101–21.

12 Sabine Maria Schmidt, 'At the Right Place at the Right Time?: A Brief Report on Current Video Art', in Frieling and Herzogenrath (eds.), *40YEARSVIDEOART.DE*, 34–9.

13 Dieter Daniels, 'Video/Art/Market', in Frieling and Herzogenrath (eds.), op.cit., 40–9.

14 Anthologized in Hall and Fifer (eds.), op.cit., 31–50.

15 Rosalind Krauss, 'Video: The Aesthetics of Narcissism', *October* 1 (Spring 1976), 50–64.

16 Although I am not interested in whether video is a postmodern form or not, we could posit that as a reaction to modernist autonomist arguments, the re-emphasis on the worldliness of the art pieces along with the political and personal expressions it displayed in the 1970s mean that something like postmodernism is at stake in early video, stretching perhaps as far as the 1980s. It seems a quaint question now that video installation has become so diverse and formally developed.

17 Davis, cited by Mary Lucier, 'Light and Death', in Hall and Fifer (eds.), op.cit., 457–64 (458).

18   Yvonne Spielmann, 'From Technology to Medium', *Art Journal* 65 (3) (Fall 2006), 54–69.

19   This point is echoed by Holly Rogers (*Sounding the Gallery*, 5, 18).

20   This is a point echoed by Frieling and Herzogenrath, '40YEARSVIDEOART. DE', *40YEARSVIDEOART.DE*, 12–16 (15).

21   Francesc Torres, 'The Art of the Possible', in Hall and Fifer (eds.), *Illuminating Video*, 205–9.

22   Dieter Daniels also notes that videos would be shown in a long sequence on a single monitor ('Video/Art/Market', 42).

23   Christine Ross, 'The Temporalities of Video: Extendedness Revisited', *Art Journal* 65 (3) (Fall 2006), 82–99. The emphasis of this article is that historical time of media and historical awareness are lost in installations that require big spaces, or, seemingly, if they harbour visual ambitions as to what occurs on screen (88).

24   Boris Groys, 'From the Image to the Image File – and Back', in Frieling and Herzogenrath (eds.), *40YEARSVIDEOART.DE*, 50–7.

25   G.W.F. Hegel, *Aesthetics* (Oxford: Clarendon, 1975 [1835]). Translated by T.M. Knox.

26   Margaret Morse, 'Video Installation Art: The Body, the Image, and the Space-in-Between', in Hall and Fifer (eds.), *Illuminating Video*, 153–67.

27   Martin Heidegger, 'The Origin of the Work of Art', *Basic Writings*, 2nd edition, edited David Farrel Krell) (London: Routledge and Kegan Paul, 1993), 143–203. Translated by Albert Hofstadter.

28   Juliane Rebentisch, *Aesthetics of Installation Art* (Berlin: Sternberg, 2012 [2003]). Translated by Daniel Hendrickson with Gerrit Jackson.

29   Marshall McLuhan and Quentin Fiore, *The Medium Is the Massage* (Harmondsworth: Penguin, 1967). This total environment is specifically referred to by McLuhan as 'acoustic space' (*The Medium Is the Massage*, 48), and also in Marshall McLuhan and Quentin Fiore, *War and Peace in the Global Village* (New York: Bantam, 1968), 23.

CHAPTER ONE

Expanding Cinema

In the 1960s, cinema expanded, and it did this not in terms of scale, but through an expansion of the purpose, function, form and process of moving-image artworks. Experimental cinema began (once again) to treat its form as both medium and content. As medium, cinema began to be something more than a sequence of images projected and viewed in movie theatres or cinemas. It began, in short, to leave cinema behind, if only slowly, maybe even grudgingly. This occurred under the influence of happenings, rock music, performance art, television, computer technology and counterculture-friendly philosophy that oscillated between a burgeoning technological lore and cultural prognostic and prophecy. At the same time, film looked at itself as the object of its own activity. This latter can, broadly speaking, be seen as structural cinema, while the former set of processes is more properly the realm of what Gene Youngblood identified as expanded cinema in his book of that name.[1] For Youngblood, cinema was discovering itself in the 1960s, completing a move already underway, and he writes that 'expanded cinema has been expanding for a very long time' moving away from literature and theatre (*Expanded Cinema*, 75). In other words, cinema had slowly been divesting itself of both story and visual narration based on the spatial constraints and conventions of theatrical space. This process is accelerated by technological developments that affect production *and* consumption of moving-image art – television and videotape being foremost among these. TV frees cinema, argues Youngblood (79), allowing it to establish and develop an 'intermedia network of cinema, television, radio, magazines, books and newspapers' (54). The term 'intermedia' itself takes a turn into the machinery of media, away from Dick Higgins' more radical formulation of 'intermedia' as artwork and art practice that exceeded the division of works into discrete categories. Higgins' intermedia returns in Rosalind Krauss' outline of a 'post-medium condition', to which I will return below.[2] But Youngblood is nonetheless clear that neither cinema nor its successors will be dependent on a particular form of machine – in other words, the machine is not the medium (133).[3]

Cinema expands into other media, and connects visual phenomena, thus altering its own form. Not all of these media are electrical or electronic. The happening, as demonstrated in the Exploding Plastic Inevitable (1966–67) – a multimedia collaboration occurring under Andy Warhol's aegis, and featuring the Velvet Underground. If intermedial technology first develops as an interstitial space, its subsequent expansion is lateral. Film becomes something to be used, a multimedial component, either competing or harmonizing with other activities and art works. Cinema divests itself of its home in the movie theatres of experimental film festivals. It does not leave those entirely, but it does become mobile. From projections of films at art events, concerts or clubs (like the UFO club in London in the late 1960s) to the portable video recorder, cassette and monitor, the moving image extends its reach. Both expansions echo other avant-gardes – dada, the experiments of the Black Mountain college in the 1950s and the parallel growth of Fluxus; the reason it happens in the 1960s is the revelation that cinema does not have a timeless essence whereby everything it is made from must remain the same. The expansion or dispersion of cinema is what is specifically retained in nascent video art. Meigh-Andrews may be making a simple point when he writes that 'video art can be seen to be part of a tradition that could embrace all these works [structural and experimental cinema styles]' (A History of Video Art, 80), but if we alter 'tradition' to 'transition', we can see how the connection works in the maintenance of the expansion of cinema.

Youngblood extends cinema in a further dimension – into depth. New cinema would probe the viewer's senses to stimulate reactions that would alter consciousness and displace thought from the rational and linear tracking of narration. Unlike the bulk of structural film, where film becomes a self-reflective medium, expanded cinema works inward, downward into the mind, to then bring it upward through newly experienced depths. This newly opened depth will act on the viewer as medium – 'It's not so much what we're seeing so much as the process and effect of seeing: that is, the phenomenon of experience itself, which only exists in the viewer' (Expanded Cinema, 97). As well as the use of several media, this cinema will cross the senses in order to drive new perceptions and even 'oceanic consciousness' (92). On the face of it, this is a simple variant on the various ideas of mind expansion prevalent in 1960s counterculture, but Youngblood is also talking about a medium, here at least, and also of technology altering the relation between human thought and some of its others (cultural product and world, here).

So expanded cinema traverses new technologies and cultural perspectives, without being beholden to them (while clearly belonging to a particular historical juncture). Its changing parameters make of it something multisensory – either something of multimedia or intermedia. Ultimately, cinema leaves cinema behind (49), just as TV is not chained to the machinery of its consumption, or video to its machinery of production, and through this transition runs the thread of sound. From the persistent references to 'soundtracks' (a term that suggests the secondary status of sound as accompaniment), Youngblood develops a more interesting position, arguing that in the work of Jordan Belson 'sound often is [so] integral to the imagery' (158). Belson's early work in particular (such as *Samadhi* from 1967) combines motion in both audio and visual components that swirl together as the work tries to induce the sensory awareness of the universe's structure and constant flow in a mystical harmoniousness. Further on, Youngblood notes that 'anything that can be done with sound can be done with video if the proper hardware is available' (265). He is not particularly interested in focussing directly on the role of sound in film or video but mentions it continually, indicating that it is important and also an expected presence. But it is music that dominates his thinking – either adding to the synaesthetic experience of a piece of film or serving as compositional model (214, 215, 221, all referring to or quoting John Whitney). So expanded cinema conceives of sound as something vital, and more than either decorative or narrative in intent, but within Youngblood's conception, and that of many practitioners of video art, and indeed, early video installation works such as that of John and James Whitney, it still seems to be working more as an accompaniment. The examples of Warhol's *Outer and Inner Space* (1965), Chris Marker's *La Jetée* (1962) and Michael Snow's *Wavelength* (1967) will show how centralizing the role of sound diverts these films away from cinema and into being more than precursors of video art, and instead demands we see and hear them as early versions of what the medium of video art would do.

For Krauss, though, video is not a medium, but part of the dismantling of modernism's medium specificity and medium investigation, tied into installation art, a non-form or non-medium she distrusts, referring to the 'international fashion of installation and intermedia work' (Krauss, *Voyage on the North Sea*, 56). For all the melancholy in the short book *A Voyage on the North Sea*, centred on Marcel Broodthaers, and closing on his film of that name, Krauss provides a very useful conceptualization of what happens when film becomes something other than itself, and when video art emerges to cement the loss of medium specificity, notwithstanding that the 'post-medium' that emerges looks quite a lot like a new medium, albeit one immune, in Krauss' view, to modernist critical paradigms in any positive way.

Krauss identifies structural film (focussing on Richard Serra, mentioning Stan Brakhage) as modernist in intent, reflecting on the medium of cinema (in fact its format), such that content becomes form and vice-versa (*Voyage*, 25–30). Like many of the origin stories of video, Krauss refers to the moment the (Sony) Portapak arrived as central to the ending of the explorations of form that modernism had pursued (24, 30). This machine's complicity with mass-media, and its capacity to infiltrate multimedia artworks, undid art and film alike, such that both modernist art and critique could find no further purchase:

> if modernist theory found itself defeated by such heterogeneity – which prevented it from conceptualizing video as a medium – modernist, structuralist film was routed by video's instant success as a practice. For, even if video had a distinct technical support – its own apparatus, so to speak – it occupied a kind of discursive chaos. (*Voyage*, 31)

This moment empties the possibility of any medium maintaining its autonomy – either all art works in proper realms or the whole enterprise changes shape. Broodthaers' installation work, especially the variants of his *Musée d'art moderne: Départment des Aigles*, is one agent, but video, in the shape of the incorporation of film and/or video into installations, completes the arrival of a 'post-medium condition'. The piece *Voyage on the North Sea* is a film composed of photographic stills and close-ups of different parts of a maritime painting. These are interspersed by intertitles declaring the 'page number' we are about to see. The beginning and end of the film focus on the film as film, and grainy scratchiness flickers through the film, reminding us we are not looking at stills at all. The film not only crossed borders between stills and moving images, photography and painting, books and films and modes of reading, it also crossed into a poster, a film canister as art object and a still image. Furthermore, film, including this one, would be a regular feature of Broodthaers' radical play of self-curated exhibition spaces as artworks. The 'post-medium' Kraus identifies as a sort of end to modernism can also be seen as a heterogeneous medium – that of video art in installation form (whether whole or part), but the post-medium is already underway in experimental, expanding cinema, including in some pieces identified as 'structural' (like *Wavelength*), and this against the backdrop of structural film's inward turn into the mechanics of film as a self-generating autonomy.

Perhaps the first film to operate more on criteria appropriate to video art is Chris Marker's *La Jetée* (1962). On the face of it, this should not work – it is a film, albeit largely made up of 'static' images, shown in cinema settings. But as noted in the introduction above, finding the origin of video art has been problematic, not least when easily ascribed to, say, the making of a particular machine, or a moment in Nam June Paik's life. Instead, we need to look more archaeologically, retrospectively, from a point today where video art is a developed medium (or post-medium), within which political documentary making, TV subversion or the use of tape over movie film is very much a marginal issue in terms of being radical formal decisions. That is not to deny the history of having looked at video art that way, but to maintain this perhaps legitimate fiction requires a suspension of video history since at least the 1970s, let alone from the 1990s onward. Neither am I just going to take my list of working criteria and show how they work on this or other film pieces of the 1960s. Instead, a few simple things distinguish the films of this chapter from structural or flicker film, and these are: the concentration on images as images; the disdain of camera movement, which thereby alters the dynamic of the film as object for the viewer; the use of narrative at story level as material for visual narration; the move towards multimedia, or more accurately, intermediality; and the very significant use of sound as narrative framing or disrupting device.

Marker would go on to embrace video, then digital recording formats, and questioned the construction of narrative in cinema form. Of course, this was going on elsewhere and, just like expanded cinema, had been present from the start of cinema. The point is that this is not a precursor, but part of the beginning of the process of a developmental form (not format). In terms of its form, *La Jetée* declares itself a ciné-roman, echoing the format of the photo novel, a genre based on taking real-world images and making a narrative book from them. As a genre it took off in Italy and then France, later to get more widespread renown in the form of picture novelizations of major science fiction films of the 1970s and 1980s, but perhaps the ur-form it takes is Georges Rodenbach's 1892 Symbolist novel *Bruges-la-morte*.[4] In this book, the narrator falls under the spell of images of Bruges, driving him to a tragic and inevitable murder as place, people, dream and real collide. In *La Jetée*, a picture is at the heart of the plot narration and the film as narration – the image of a woman at the end of the pier at Orly airport, later revealed to be the image of the moment of the protagonist's own death. This image creates the possibility for the use of images to travel in time, or arguably for time itself to function. This ciné-roman is made entirely of stills and dissolves between them, except for one moment (18.45), where the movement of its second most important figure, the woman met by the protagonist in his past, emphasizes the hybrid and noisy encounter between formats that makes this film intermedial. Not only that, but the significance of vision itself as content is shown, as these few seconds show her moving from dream to waking, lucid seeing.

The film is more like a score (and the score of Trevor Duncan did precede the final version), polyrhythmic, with the fundamental time loop the paradoxical ground. On top of this is the escalation and diminution of changes between images, as well as the different pacing of what can best be thought of as movements within the film. But the image is not the only focus, for the soundtrack of *La Jetée* is absolutely vital, not just in providing a more linear structure against and on which the images can play but in sound leading the narration. The soundtrack is a curious mix of sound effects (most notably in the form of jets taking off), processed sound (in the shape of what could be heartbeats), which underpins the experimentation phase of the film, choral music recorded at very high volume, which anticipates

Kubrick's use of György Ligeti's *Lux Aeterna* in *2001: A Space Odyssey* (1968), whispering and muttering in German, orchestral music, birdsound and a narration external to any of the (unnamed) characters. Of course, an interesting soundtrack does not make something either sound art or video art – but its integration into narrative structures and disruptions in same does – as we are pushed into a realm where there is not a core element surrounded by adjunct and accompaniment. Janet Harbord writes, of the important centralizing force of sound in the film, that

> Marker's use of sound lets in a leakage of various kinds of noise – sounds that are excessive to communication, unruly and often ruled out for that reason. To include them in the sound design of the film, in addition to their unintentional presence in the narration, suggests that noise is meaningful, affective. (*Chris Marker, La Jetée*, 92)[5]

The whole works as a suggestion of synaesthetic experience: this should not be taken as necessarily indicating a harmonious and simplistic union of affects, as Marker's film is much too noisy for that, recalling the still-recent development of *musique concrète*, where found, captured or recorded non-musical sounds could be organized to make something akin to music. Where the image part of this film varies in speed of change (the camera never moving within or above any shot), the sound part is much more disrupted and full of swelling noise – jets, massed birdsound, multilayering of heartbeat sound. Sudden cuts also indicate this film is a project of a disruptive avant-garde, and that the story is a structural part of a whole, not its purpose or ultimate explanation. At the very end, as the protagonist completes his loop in time, the music returns us audibly to the beginning of *La Jetée* only to fade – echoing not just the sounds but the fade-in of the beginning: the sound loop is complete.

Andy Warhol's early films largely eschew narrative, relying instead on the image creating a viewing narrative – for example, in *Blow Job* (1964) or the *Screen Tests* (1964–66). Long duration films such as *Sleep* and *Empire* (both 1964) overwhelm the possibility of development through their length. *Empire* combines many of Warhol's film strategies – the static camera, facing New York's Empire State building, removes the drama of authorial vision; as Douglas Crimp notes, the grain of the film becomes one of the major visual elements of the piece ('*Our Kind of Movie*', 137)[6] – while film as medium is also being denied. What is the medium here? The building? The turning of the Earth from day into night? Light? While film is made visible, this is not a film about its own medium – instead it is a refusal of format – a kind of non-mediality (not the same thing as something being unmediated, which may nonetheless have been Warhol's point of interest). In a perverse response to Marker, Warhol's *Empire* is about moving pictures (moving film) becoming static, only to move again at a different pace. The length stimulates a viewing where seeing diminishes in favour of a more amorphous experience. According to J.J. Murphy, Warhol uses 'temporal duration to create transformation' (*The Black Hole of the Camera*, 3).[7]

This is a film about viewing, about the image, and, despite largely being shown in cinema settings, has been installed as a piece (e.g. in Tate Modern's 2002 retrospective) – one can drift in and out of physical engagement, becoming both more like an object and more mobile as a result. The duration of the piece invites both a ritual-like immersion akin to spectators performing durational body art, and its opposite – a wilful inattention.[8] Murphy further notes that there has been too much attention paid to Warhol's longer, static, apparently unedited films, to the detriment of the loosely planned psychodramas featuring Factory visitors and associates, and also the pieces more obviously akin to video art (*The Black Hole of the Camera*, 10). If the extreme duration films and single-shot pieces represent one facet of expanding cinema, then another comes in the guise of participation in multimedia events such as the Exploding Plastic Inevitable, where Warhol films merged with performance, music and other visuals. Beyond these, there are also the sound films that were projected onto multiple screens while being shown as stand-alone pieces. The most well known of these is the multireel *Chelsea Girls* (1966), to be shown on two screens, and given the unequal length of the reels, and instructions about when to begin the sound parts, in theory no two showings can be the same. But the piece that can genuinely be identified as video art is *Outer and Inner Space* (1965), a film featuring double-screen projection, and within each screen, the display of video. Edie Sedgwick is filmed on video; this plays while she is filmed again, along with the monitor screen. This doubling is then redoubled, as the same situation prevails on the second screen. On both screens, Sedgwick listens to herself, slightly out of her range of vision. The video version seems much more serious, even oracular, as the profile head talks continuously, occasionally smoking. The version of her that sits next to the monitor talks and smokes continually, occasionally distracted by what she says. For periods, the video part changes texture/quality – first, in the left-hand screen as we see it, the image distorts, with Sedgwick's face revealed as compositional object as it takes on new contours and sizes. Shortly after, the second screen shows the video image of Sedgwick perform a sort of analogue glitching – this time more in the form of the vertical hold being disrupted. Tape-produced haloes appear, less destructive than in the first instance on screen one, but as distorted. While this distracts the Sedgwick sat next to the screen, it is the video in which Sedgwick sneezes after around twenty-five minutes that really disturbs her, and for the viewers, this sneeze operates as a culmination of the distortions underway in both sound and image tracks.

Murphy claims that *Outer and Inner Space* 'is considered to be the very first artist video' (*The Black Hole of Camera*, 160), or at least one of the first (251). It certainly uses videotape, it uses the installation of it (within the film), it reflects on itself as medium that is not simply film and, finally, it is projected in a way that is more like an installation than the single-screen presentation that contributes to clear-eyed assessment of a film's progress.[9] Its status as origin or precursor is less interesting than its place in a continuum of the growth of video art and, in particular, the role sound plays in this development. The sound alters and distorts in ways similar to the images, and image quality, but never in perfect parallel. The sound emphasizes, models and, on occasion, drives the 'discrepancy between outer and inner space' of its several layers (Murphy, *The Black Hole of the Camera*, 157). For Crimp, 'the film's sound is thus a sort of noise' ('*Our Kind of Movie*', 79). The noise of this piece is what structures its content and also withholds it as something clear and fully assimilable, other than in terms of its formal experimentation as such. But sound is not the noise of the film, as that would make it something extraneous. Instead film (and indeed video) is the noise here, and sound becomes the primary force. The sound, other than the explosive sneeze, is relatively smooth, as Sedgwick's voice takes on a mantric, mildly minimalist character, heightening the effect of the single camera (which periodically changes zoom focus).

If the zoom in *Outer and Inner Space* is somewhat arbitrary, and constitutes part of the improvised flourishes of the film, then the same cannot be said of the forty-five-minute zoom that is Michael Snow's *Wavelength* (1967). A single room is shot from a raised, distant position, and the shot gradually (but often jerkily) zooms in, ultimately closing in on a photograph of waves, into which it dissolves. The bulk of the film (all of it after the first few minutes) also features a rising sine wave, which mirrors, maps or even drives the zoom. In a statement on the film, Snow declared that the sine was a 'total glissando while the film is a crescendo' (Snow, 'A Statement on *Wavelength*').[10] This is far from all that occurs, in this oddly busy take on minimalism: the precisely discontinuous zoom, fractured by edits, changes in film stock, application of colour filters, changes in levels of daylight and the jittery 'motion' of the zoom shot. The same is true of the sound, which moves on numerous occasions to 'sync sound', or, more usefully, in Michel Chion's terms, 'diegetic sound', that is, sound that emerges from the events being depicted. The most notable of these intrusions (paradoxical because they should be what is intruded on by the sine wave) accompany the 'four human events' of furniture moving, listening to the radio, a man dying and a telephone call relating the presence of the dead man in the room. These are the occasions where human occupation of the room occurs, and the sound overwhelms or even entirely displaces the sine wave, which nonetheless shows its ineluctability by always returning, and even accompanying, developments in the diegetic sound.

The 'wavelength' refers both to light and sound, and is rendered parodically literal in the dissolve into waves at the end, and the film suggests all manner of complex philosophical positions, as well as possible comments on the state of artistic production of the time.[11] Snow was, and remains, fascinated by sound and its imbrication in the visual and quickly moves to audiovisual installations, a practice he has maintained to this day.[12] In the meantime, writers have recognized the importance of sound – Elizabeth Legge not only tracks the changes in the soundtrack but also explains that it is 'as if the seen and the heard were being converted into one another' (*Michael Snow, Wavelength*, 12) and that the closing-out of the dissolve is joined by the sine wave leaving human aural perception behind. It is important to note the concatenation of visual and aural – the sound is not an accompaniment to the 'real' action, and is even more of a driver of narrative than in Marker's film. The human events not only feature harsher, 'real' sound but are prefigured, launched by sound. Sound has a privileged relation to the real, in fact, as it connects to events 'beyond' the room/screen/lens. Occasional punctuating sounds of traffic and external activity indicate that there is a world beyond, and the ways in which two of the 'events' develop indicate the crossing between different layers of, or angles on, the real.

The first event opens the film, as a set of shelves is brought in, suggesting that people are moving in and this is the beginning of a narrative based on the habitation of the room shown. But content, like the shelves, is only ever supplied in ways that suggest or comment on narrative as a practice. The shelf-moving begins in sound, sound that comes from beneath the camera position, from behind 'our' vision. This does have narrative value as it prefigures the central sound event of the film and what should be the defining action – the death of someone. But the narrative has removed itself from within the film, that is, from storytelling as something to be observed from without the film. Instead, narrative itself is being observed (Legge, *Michael Snow, Wavelength*, 47), and the changes in the film, the changes in state, which include the four events, are indicators of *Wavelength* being the 'definitive statement of something' even if the 'what' is very much up for grabs (19). The thumping sounds of the shelves being brought in show the reference point that is the real beyond, while also indicating the constructedness of the film as something that gestures to outside, as well as gesturing to itself as the entire world with everything else become epiphenomena. The second intrusion of diegetic sound undermines the connection to diegetic sound, as two people come in, switch on and listen to The Beatles' 'Strawberry Fields Forever' (which song has strong claims to having the first promotional video) on a radio and then leave the room. Instead of this being part of the background to events, it is the event (an event we know not to have happened through a Warhol-style appropriation of happenstance).[13] It is not background; neither does it hover above the sound of anything else.

The third event is most interesting in terms of the value of sound in *Wavelength*. The sine wave mounts in pitch, the room changes colour rapidly, and then the sine wave is obliterated by crashing thudding sounds along with those of smashing glass, possibly looped and played twice. At the conclusion of this over-riding cacophony, a man stumbles into the room from 'behind' our viewpoint, and collapses dead a long way into the room (further than we are in the filmed space, as located by the camera position). His movement is what reinforces the 'where' of the sound – he acts as supplement to its original force, while it too is cast as supplement to events that lead inward to the room and murder. For Legge, this passage preceding the event implies a mounting tension (13), and this does indeed seem to be the case. But as the camera moves 'on', it quickly moves beyond the body, just as the sine wave settles back in, and the event loses its potency, almost being wiped out retrospectively, losing any tension-building from sound or event. Annette Michelson is keenly aware of the importance of sound and its relation to 'offscreen', and writes that 'the crescendo of the sine wave will modify our perception of the sound within and beyond the loft'.[14] But the sine wave is not the only relational device, as it is caught within its own sound relation to that which disrupts it. The sine wave establishes the connection to a phenomenological view(er), and the other sounds work through the structuring of that view: the clattering that announces the murder is offscreen, and offscreen is not the just the outside of shot, nor is it the beyond of the film, but in indicating both, an interstitial, liminal space of 'offscreen' is constructed and shot through. I would argue that Snow has used sound in *Wavelength* to establish the philosophical and aesthetic complexities that have been observed over the years by critics, but perhaps not so much heard. With this film, cinema is not so much expanding, or even looking to its future, but actually chiselling away at the form of cinema, announcing the beyond that is the sound-driven intermediality of video art, with the first and third narrative moments of *Wavelength* the specific metonymic harbingers.

Of the many different positionings of sound ('in' the film, of the film, outside but connected, outside), it is in the most McLuhan-influenced terrains of video/film that sound, mostly in the form of music, is the furthest from diegetic, while at the same time most in search of an ultimate fusional capacity. Where the performance events in the Factory or the UFO club sought to create a multimedia environment, and other video/film artists attempted an enlarging of the film environment, the late 1960s saw a range of film-makers that tried to harness the power of sound to make their visuals a pathway to a cosmic awareness. John Whitney, James Whitney, Jordan Belson and Ture Sjölander all took lessons from Kenneth Anger and Stan Brakhage but understood the cosmic message as an emanation of technology and therefore one that could be directly constructed in front of the viewer. The sound would work as counterpoint – even if on occasion ultra-directly (such as in Pat O'Neill's 7362) to enhance the visual experience. In the case of overtly 'mind-altering' films, the music would work as other that would heighten the sensory experience (the synaesthesia Youngblood talks of often in *Expanded Cinema*) precisely through being separate, through being another sensory source. Having started as other (i.e. as accompaniment), music in Whitney, Belson or Sjölander becomes fusional – breaking down the overly alienated parts of socially induced consciousness.

Ture Sjölander produced what can be thought of as one of the first video art broadcasts, in September 1966, with Swedish TV showing his collaboration with Bror Wikstrom, *Time*. In 1968, his 1967 work with Lars Weck, *Monument*, was also shown on TV. Both works use the distorting capacities of a tweaked, distorted wobble and warp of what many years later we might think of as glitched TVs, opening a path that Nam June Paik had explored and would divert into often-silent TV installations. While both pieces by Sjölander continually show distorted images, the sound is constant – the use of avant-garde jazz (free jazz in the first, harsh proto-fusion in the second) sufficing, it would seem, to indicate malleability of the form of sound without need of further manipulation. Both would bring the video installation into the home, with TV transmuting from material through objecthood and finally content and form. *Monument* shows a host of contemporary figures, communications technologies in use and metamorphic hybridizing through TV distortion. The present is shown as a flexible reality subject to change and distortions from all ideological perspectives. The sound combines a harsh type of early jazz rock with voice recordings and sound effects (often of communications devices in use). The voices include Hitler and The Beatles, illustrating not only the flexibility of media and its capacity for propaganda or publicity but also the historical, non-innocent spread of the media. For *Monument*, the media 'is' all – every idea, every part of culture. The piece does not work too well for the twenty-first-century viewer – its choices too obvious, and its play with TV structures of imagery too monolithic, such that it seems very much *of* the media of the time, instead of diverting or commenting on them. Despite this irony, we have to recognize what was going on for the media theorist-practitioner: first, he was using media as source, machine and content, and then he was combining this in the final form of the piece. In so doing, Sjölander identifies the reach of the new media age, and the role of music in the same. The Beatles dominated the global media in the late 1960s – the first time that such a thing was possible. This is the important thing, not the potential (misguided) critique of a group whose work at that moment (such as 1968's *The Beatles*) far outstrips Sjölander in avant-garde terms. Similarly, the docile role allocated to music is not just about highlighting the visual narrative (or visual play, in the case of the Whitneys or Belson) but about the role of music in contemporary culture. The 1960s is the first time that media, cheap home technology and affordable music units (the vinyl 45) meant that music was everywhere, an almost autonomous part of the burgeoning mediascape. So it makes sense to see it as something that could wrap around visual elements, reflecting internally the new social environment of Western societies of the time. Lastly, music in *Time* and *Monument* takes a distance from the visual element in order not to comment but to represent the content in parallel to the image's abstraction. In other words, the use of complex jazz is about the state of culture today, and how to look on it critically, creatively, while the images are about technology and culture. The separation of the music allows it then to work as accretion of commentary.

Sjölander develops this combination further in the epic *Space in the Brain* (1969, shown on TV the same day as the Apollo 11 landing on the Moon). The music, by Hansson and Karlsson, though, has become even more of a mood-setting, or accompaniment. The film uses extensive NASA Moon mission footage, framing it with shots of woodland (with birdsong) and of human eyes. The second part of the video, from about seventeen minutes on, consists of a sequence of electronically generated warped, coloured, metamorphosing forms.[15] *Space in the Brain* closely parallels the 'stargate' section of *2001: A Space Odyssey* (designed by video artist John Whitney), in seeking to combine space exploration with the discovery of inner space. Technology (in the making of both pieces) uses technology as material to inspire consciousness expansion. As noted earlier, for Youngblood, this is a vital element of how he conceived 'expanded cinema', even if for later audiences this seems less convincing an argument for its radicalness. The role of music as mood enhancer is also a reduction of what is going on in the use of sound in early video art as an integral part of its presentation. Perhaps the issue is one of avant-garde positioning – the more ambient Sjölander work not functioning as any sort of redefinition, in formal terms of the possibilities or failures of an art form. Nonetheless, this is precisely what shows a sort of prescience in *Space in the Brain*, where avant-gardeness has less purchase than a sense of connectivity or affect, in a premonition of relational aesthetics. Instead of critical analysis, a process of defocussing reflection is induced. It also connects to an aesthetic that is not one of the film festival or gallery visitor. Instead, it is an arguably more profound countercultural statement about forms that, in refraction, offer seeds of radical change (space travel, 1960s jazz as it bifurcates into new forms). Form is subservient not to a mission, but to thematic content that will then perform its inspiration through rejection of formal or conceptual work on the part of the viewer. If the works by Marker, Warhol and Snow show the beginnings of how video art will work with sound and move towards installation objects, then those of Sjölander point to what TV will do with music and video in the 1980s, as, after initial flirtation by TV channels with video art expressly made for TV, it will be music that sets the pretext for visual experimentation in that medium. The different layerings of sounds and varying priorities accorded them in 'expanded cinema' will continue resurfacing through the entirety of what will become established as the medium (or post-medium) of video art installation.

Notes

1   Gene Youngblood, *Expanded Cinema* (New York: Dutton, 1970).

2   Rosalind Krauss, *A Voyage on the North Sea: Art in the Age of the Post-Medium Condition* (London: Thames & Hudson, 2000).

3   Given the insistence on the 'medium' of television or of video itself, both in early video art and in many texts analyzing that period, it is refreshing to find that Youngblood had no such preciousness in terms of what would effectively be a misunderstanding of what a medium is or does, when considered as a contextualized process, only part of which may be the empirical hardware or machinery. A further example, going very much against the grain of didactic video art, is his statement that 'the television set is irrelevant to the phenomenon of television' (*Expanded Cinema*, 78).

4   Georges Rodenbach, *Bruges-la-Morte* (Paris: Flammarion, 1998).

5   Janet Harbord, *Chris Marker, La Jetée* (London: Afterall, 2009). Some of the noise is more prevalent in the English-language version, where the narration comes across as being heard over a transmitter.

6   Douglas Crimp, '*Our Kind of Movie*': *The Films of Andy Warhol* (Cambridge, MA and London: MIT Press, 2012).

7   J. J. Murphy, *The Black Hole of the Camera: The Films of Andy Warhol* (Berkeley and Los Angeles: University of California Press, 2012).

8   eldritch Priest writes of nonattention as a purposive strategy in *Boring Formless Nonsense* (New York: Bloomsbury, 2013), 139–75.

9   A further illustration of this disruption in cinema is the split-screen photography of early 1970s cinema, or better still, the four parallel screens of *Timecode* (Mike Figgis, 2000).

10 'A Statement on *Wavelength* for the experimental film festival of Knokke-le-Zoute', cited in Elizabeth Legge, *Michael Snow, Wavelength* (London: Afterall, 2009, 1).

11 Legge's *Michael Snow, Wavelength* supplies an excellent overview of these possibilities, not least in the recognition of the range of work that has appeared (see 18–19, and 81-2n.34–38).

12 On the transition from film to installation and the mutual interaction of them in Snow's work, see Kate Mondloch, 'The Matter of Illusionism: Michael Snow's Screen/Space', in Tamara Trodd (ed.), *Screen/Space: The Projected Image in Contemporary Art* (Manchester: Manchester University Press, 2011), 73–89.

13 See Legge, *Michael Snow, Wavelength*, 24.

14 Annette Michelson, 'Toward Snow', in P. Adams Simey (ed.), *The Avant-Garde Film: A Reader of Theory and Criticism* (New York: Anthology Film Archives, 1978), 172–83 (174). Originally in *Artforum*, vol 9 (June 1971), 30–7.

15 Version consulted is the '2012 edition', available at http://vimeo.com/45111052, accessed 14 April 2013.

CHAPTER TWO

Bruce Nauman and the Audiospatial

Bruce Nauman made his first video pieces in 1968, which would form a clear continuum with his film work – from his point of view they represent a pragmatic choice, enabling him to make longer pieces.[1] More interestingly, they represent an extension of sculpture, in the form of the monitor in the gallery, and a conduit for the still-nascent form of performance art. The monitor that displays a performance places a solid object in the gallery space and, in so doing, combines the material machine with the content of the recording. This in turn doubles the sculptural aspect of Nauman's performances of repeated, simple, yet demanding actions. Contrary to Krauss' suspicion of the narcissism of 'post-medium' of video that would be too focussed on an individual artist as subject, content, object and rationale for an artwork, Nauman de-emphasizes the presence of his self through cut angles (often his head is missing, or he is shot from the back) and the defamiliarization of a body seen in repeated action, such as *Bouncing in the Corner no. 1* (1968). In this piece, a sideways Nauman drops into the corner of his studio, the precise angle and sound of contact varying continually, in combination with an uncanny refiguring of the body as sculpture in motion – just as Richard Serra achieves in his video piece *Hand Catching Lead* (1971) – praised by Yve-Alain Bois as a deforming, formless work in the *Formless* exhibition, curated by Bois and Krauss, with accompanying book.[2] Nauman is a 'post-medium' artist in the simplest of senses – he is not restricted to one pre-existing medium, and in the late 1960s, he makes sculptures, films, text pieces and sound works. He further added neon works, photography and multimedia installations to this array of practices. Beyond a wide-ranging artistic pragmatics, though, in his early works, video is itself a post-medium, or intermedia, where sound, vision, sculpture and reflection on 'what a medium is' converge.

Nauman has always been interested in the potential of sound to act as an art piece – one early work is just the sound of his voice in a room empty other than the speaker that conveys it. *Get Out of My Mind Get Out of This Room* (1968) presents those words and nothing else, the tone changing in a properly tragic reflection on the borders between subjects – the auditor is both called on to leave and called upon as listener to attend to the internal workings of the mind as expressed audiospatially in the room.[3] This intimacy based on a holding-apart is unusual in his work for directly calling upon the auditor, but not unusual in other video work inflected by performance, such as that of Vito Acconci, Chris Burden or Marina Abramović. Acconci uses his voice to emphasize the troubling intersubjectivity of being addressed in part of a performance in his *Theme Song* (1973), a sleazy yet prophetic take on trying to make sexual contact through a video autoportrait. Abramović uses sound powerfully in the video piece *Art Must Be Beautiful, Artist Must Be Beautiful* (1975), where she recites the title while brushing her hair – the latter sound also clearly audible. As the piece goes on, the brushing becomes more painful and it is through sound that this is conveyed. Like Nauman, she too was interested in performative, non-musical use of sound, notably in her performance in *Rhythm 10* (1973). Here, Abramović stabbed knives between her fingers until she cut herself. Having recorded the sound of this act, she replayed the tape and restaged the exact sequence of the knife's progress.

Really, though, what I want to emphasize is that Nauman is only incidentally part of a continuum of video/performance art. His reticence to be a performer of subjective situations, even of loss of self, is evident in the purposive banality of actions of the early film and video works (walking, bouncing self, bouncing balls, stamping). Not all of the pieces are so content neutral, as seen, for example, in *Violin Tuned D.E.A.D.* (1969). The status of sound changes, according to whether it is 'incidental' or part of the title, as in the violin pieces. What I want to demonstrate is that sound is integral to Nauman's video pieces – not just important but a central component, and it is precisely the seemingly secondary nature of the sound that makes it interesting (as opposed to it being an added soundtrack). Several of the early films and all the videos feature sound as part of their making, a function of the recording process – it is 'just there'. Nauman asserts that both film and video were methods of displacing the need for live performance and a way of presenting such 'as it happened'. He says that the camera was 'just in order to record [...] I was doing straightforward recording of an activity' ('Bruce Nauman', in Janet Kraynak [ed.], *Please Pay Attention Please*, 163).[4] Nonetheless, the rhythmical nature of the videos is heightened by the emphasis present in the sound part.

Nauman was well aware of the work of minimalism in all terrains, and arguably more inspired by musical minimalism than the objectness of its built works. His interviews are liberally seasoned with references to his attachment to Philip Glass, La Monte Young, Steve Reich and Terry Riley (see *Please Pay Attention Please*, particularly 245–6), whose repetitive exploration of infinitesimal change seems to have suggested a methodology for his videos as well as his other installation work. Nauman also looked towards composers such as Béla Bartók and the pioneering free improviser Lennie Tristano (see *Please Pay Attention Please*, 206 and 320 respectively). These repeated claims of musical influence surface directly in the violin piece of 1968, but also indicate the importance of sound as a temporally structuring device – minimalist music was the first music, other than some experiments by Erik Satie and John Cage, to take its structuring of time as mission – even more than Cage's time pieces, like *4'33"*, which are more about emptying musical time for sound to happen, for musicality to begin again.

Nauman would maintain the sound portion of his video recording as a vital marker of rhythm, and this sound would also spatialize the monitor installation. The installation is not neutral, as 'you also have to deal with the fact of the equipment, the monitor and the television set in the space' (*Please Pay Attention Please*, 262).[5] The effect of the sound of the video piece is to extend the reach of the monitor-based piece, just as minimalist sculpture works in an 'expanded field'. Krauss developed this idea (from Robert Morris) in order to argue for sculpture that could expand back into the realm of critical meaning, such that 'the expanded field is thus generated by problematizing the set of oppositions between which the modernist category *sculpture* is suspended' ('Sculpture in the Expanded Field', 38).[6] Given the range of artists she cites, including Nauman, minimalists and land artists, it is clear that Krauss sees this as a positive outcrop of the drive of modernism when applied to sculpture that had lost its modernist focus, a very particular type of 'postmodernism' (a word she uses here at arm's length [41]). But the field of expansion is not just one that reconfigures complex relations of location, culture and form in diagrammatic connection (37–8), as

> within postmodernism, practice is not defined in relation to a given medium – sculpture – but rather in relation to the logical operations on a set of terms, for which any medium – photography, books, lines on walls, mirrors, or sculpture itself – might be used.
>
> Thus the field provides both for an expanded but finite set of related positions for a given artist to occupy and explore. (42)

One of the ways in which video art functions as this 'expanded field' sculpture is in its introduction of time, change and, therefore, process. This is not to say that these things do not occur elsewhere, but it is in the display of video pieces that this process is brought out in full and rendered literal – particularly in Nauman's works, and especially when these are based on rhythms, as they often are. So *Bouncing in the Corner no.1* (1968) shows the frail human body encountering the sharp wall angles of the studio corner, displayed laterally, occupying the centre of the image. The sound varies as Nauman applies more or less force to his fall – working through some newly human-centred Newtonianism – and this creates a complex sound situation: Nauman tries to establish a more-or-less constant pace to his action, in order to make it 'bouncing'. But the physical body, like the physical universe in general, cannot supply either predictability or energy to maintain predictability. Instead, the certainties of gravity (illustrated here through a 90° refraction from the expected direction of the force) are counterbalanced by endless microvariations. This is present most explicitly in the sound of the video.

Bouncing Two Balls between the Floor and Ceiling with Changing Rhythms (1967–8) explores microvariation and controlled improvisation, with both of these ensuring that the thrown balls structure a kind of musical improvisation with Nauman as (sometimes dissatisfied) conductor. The studio is more obviously in play in this piece, as is Nauman, as he prowls the room. It would be easy to be distracted by the 'action' part of the pieces, instead of the revealing of the time-based production of art in the form of chosen and/or wilfully aleatory geometries. Also beyond the action as such is the structuring of the piece as time achieved by the arrival and passing of sounds that build into a seeming whole as the listener shuffles sounds into a sequence of events connected in and as time. Where Abramović will later listen for the inevitabilities of rhythm, and the fatal aspect of its interruption, Nauman expands the already-expanded work of minimalist sculpture and music into a set of works about rhythm. For Brandon LaBelle, rhythm is in fact the structuring that comes from the spaces between beats, pulses and notes:

> the percussive in this regard is not so much the hit but the subsequent surging of energy surrounding it, inward and outward, as rhythms that align certain skins with others. This energy both supplies the body with dynamic support while diffusing its borders toward a field of shared sensation. (*Acoustic Territories*, 141)[7]

Rhythm is the in-betweenness of the time of the beats, and, more than this, is the way in which subjectivity understands itself through understanding time ('rhythm [...] directs a relation of self and surrounding and breaks down their separation' [141]). This may not be conscious, but it is an ordering underway in what phenomenologists such as Martin Heidegger would call our 'thrown' existence, where Being is a process of turning away from the truth of Being, and its necessary ending in death. Nauman constructs a sequence of rhythms through sound that draw the viewer/auditor into a rhythmical relation to the space and piece. This builds outward from his repetitious physical activity, through the video monitor, into a space defined not just by the screen flicker but also by the echoing reflection of his interaction with the studio, as in the 1968 film *Stamping in the Studio*. Here, Nauman pounds his way around the studio, using shifting meters (or even 'non-meters') to time his movements. The seemingly spontaneous variation builds into a model of chaotic complexity – that is, it is indeed structured rather than free-flowing. The complexity lies not in its variation but in its rhythms that cluster into patterns – in ways strongly reminiscent of Steve Reich's percussion pieces such as *Drumming* (1970–71) and *Six Marimbas* (1986).[8] Where Reich's pieces play off multiple actors moving in and out of phase, it is Nauman that moves in and out of phase in direct connection to the viewer of the piece, who comes and goes at unspecified times, thus making the starting point of any individual perceptual narrative open to extreme variation. Robert R. Riley writes that in this piece (and others), 'Nauman engages his body as subject matter in works that quantify space and measure time' ('Bruce Nauman's Philosophical and Material Explorations in Film and Video', 182).[9] The body, just like the potential endurance element, is subsumed into a stronger phenomenological working-through of space as a relational construct featuring sentient beings and their actions.[10] In fact, we can go further than Riley and think of Nauman's videos and films building a space-time that is both perceptual and sensual – given the difficulty of avoiding the rhythms that track lines of flight upon which the viewer/auditor coalesces as a seeing/listening presence.

Stamping in the Studio is not just an exploration of sound as something beyond hearing (i.e. as part of a wider 'rhythming'), it is also the experience of sound as something less than autonomous. The sound of this piece, just as in much, if not all, of Nauman's video output in the late 1960s, is not independent; it is a reasonably faithful transcription of one set of wavelengths produced in the recording of certain movements. But sound does separate itself off in order to be heard – which it often will be in the process of the auditor approaching the monitor, at which point he or she becomes a viewer, and the sound may seem incidental, or purposeful to the point of seeming to be something added-on. The sound is not, initially, a simple part of the work: it floats off, the deterritoralizing force of the work bouncing off the gallery walls. Once fixed by its connection to the visual, it risks becoming secondary to it – the performance, the geometry, the use of materials (in the video), the use of materials (as the video) and the filming strategy – all can take over. As they seemingly take over, this is precisely where the sound settles in as if it has never been separate, as if it was always already 'just' part of the piece. This is what Nauman's film and video work of the late 1960s announces, the settling into identity of sound and vision in the one piece, as a result of the different parts initially separating. So video art is not a self-same practice or product, but one that has a built-in exploration of deconstruction, a built-in flow between identity and multiplicity.

When Nauman introduces a musical element, such as an instrument, as in *Playing a Note on the Violin While I Walk around the Studio* (1967–68), or *Violin Tuned D.E.A.D.*, it is tempting to see another layer in the mirroring of the video works, as they come to reflect on the process of music, on process as music and on how music relates to concerns of the visual arts, such as rhythm, tone, performance, technique, improvisation and a hundred other potentials. So Nauman tries to shut these down when he uses music. In the second phase of those pieces, Nauman sets up the camera so he is shot from behind, as he bows the violin monotonously, yet with continual microvariation. Just as with minimalism, this is music with most of the musical conceits stripped away, in order to allow the rhythms or basic structures of all music to emerge, almost like Platonic forms. This is where Robert Pincus-Witten's definition of Nauman as 'Post-Minimal' makes most sense.[11] *Violin Tuned D.E.A.D.* empties minimalism of the conceit of purifying music through concentration and slow phasing. Even the Velvet Underground's sawing and chopping carries more mission than this, and so in this piece Nauman hacks away at minimalism, replacing it with the nothingness of a stasis that fails to be even that. The monumentalism of minimalist music and the heroics of rock are blocked in this unrelenting simplification of music and its performance into an audiospatial device.

It might then make sense to read *Lip Sync* (1969) as a comment on the failures of pop music, an end to the utopian breakthrough of radical youth-oriented music and culture, as the practice of miming the action of singing to a song, usually one's own, on TV music programmes or music videos is revealed as a sham, an alienation. Nauman's voice intones the words 'lip sync' as his mouth moves out of synchronization (or vice-versa). His head, upside-down, wearing headphones, fills the shot. But again, this is not a piece made only of potential narrative content or connotation. Its presence on a screen means that the sound and vision play off each other in a distorted space-time where the referent (what a sign refers to) never catches or matches the real against the backdrop of our expectation that it will. Instead, the physicality of the process of vocalizing – exactly what is rejected in lip syncing – is emphasized, and the sound element *as content* falls away, to be replaced by the defamiliarizing device of asynchrony and sound as form.

This rhythmical structuring of space and time returns in the 1990s twin-screen installations *Think* (1993) and *Work* (1994), part of a series of works that use and abuse language as post-minimalist tool. As Ben Borthwick notes, it is Nauman's use of the body as rhythming device that makes the connection ('Catalogue Entries', 135).[12] Both pieces consist of the one word repeated while Nauman jumps into shot. Both use two monitors, with the second screen being an inversion of the first. With *Think*, Nauman's closely shot face is upright in the top screen, while in the lower monitor, his head dives away. So here the Nauman head buds in and out of itself. In *Work* this model itself is inverted, such that the upright Nauman head jumps upward to the central point, and the second head thumps downward to messily not quite merge. The repetition, combined with the jumping, emphasizes the materiality of the words, expelled through a Nauman breathing apparatus that is already otherwise engaged. Writers on Nauman converge on the importance of language, with slightly different angles – so for Michael Auping, Nauman uses language as an exploration of communication as an activity ('Metacommunicator', 8); Emma Dexter emphasizes the power of language, when isolated, or deviated from standard use, to not just be material but to materialize spaces within which auditor/viewers move ('Raw Materials', 19); Kraynak insists on the power of the knowing use of the speech act, making Nauman a philosopher of language as and in (his) practice ('Bruce Nauman's Words', 36 and *passim*).[13] In the case of *Think*, the repetition of the word 'think' causes it not only to lose its proper morphology in its situated enunciation but also to change status from being an injunction to being a suggestion, a possibility and an observation. As Nauman bounces in and out of himself (in and out of his head, visually speaking), the command to himself is made absurd as in respecting his injunction to himself; he makes it lose its potency in the absurdity of jumping and repeating the word, in the place of thinking. So language here is already more and less, becoming less, and changing its possible signification as part of an art piece. The sounds of feet hitting the floor and other incidental physical sounds provide almost a second soundtrack, echoing the foolishness of a philosophy of art as pronounced at its most conceptual, or indeed meta-conceptual, in the form of the word 'think'. But *Think* has not yet finished working, because the dynamic induced by Nauman's movement and the loss of sense in the speaking of the word 'think' stretches out to the viewer. So to the previous movement of undoing of sense, of removing the portent of thinking, is added the injunction to the viewer to reflect on the foregoing undoing. Better still, it does not, or cannot, make the viewer 'think about art' or 'the nature of language', as instead, she or he will be caught in a ping-pong movement of competing absurdities, prevented from completion – just as the two Nauman heads cannot meet, barred by the line of the monitors from congealing into a happy conflation of signifier and signified perhaps.

Work seems to do something very similar – it has the same repetition of the word, such that it loses its consistency. It has the same shouted injunctive quality, the same dissipation over the course of a loop also informed by the 'external' clatter of Nauman's jumping (Borthwick, 'Catalogue Entries', 132). The same sequence of instruction to himself, followed by the display of the piece extending that directive to the viewer, ends in making a not-quite complete loop where 'Work' will not be acted upon. Whereas, it has been, for there is a work entitled *Work*. The further address of this piece is 'work' itself, presumably including artistic work, and 'the' work that results from 'work'. Here, not only is process emphasized, such that the 'work' becomes 'the' work, but in turning on itself work (to work) is work (making work) is the work (this made work) is the work (work) of/for the viewer. If *Think* is intersubjective, and prevented from mind/body dualism in its vigorous peripatetics, then *Work* raises the stakes to consider the relation of communicating and auto-communicating subjects to technological awareness and working of the world.[14]

These pieces, as well as many others already witnessed, confirm the importance of language, which also features in works of many other genres/ methods used by Nauman. But, I would argue that the video pieces enact a troubled relation to language, using it in order to disrupt it, and in fact make it less language than voice – not even a speech act, but an act that comes in the place of speech. In *Think* and *Work*, as in *Thank You* (1990) or *Raw Materials – OK OK OK* (1990), language is stripped away, even as it becomes central. Other sounds intrude, and in fact the voice intrudes on the delivery of 'proper' language. We are left with delivery as message – post-medium as post-message, maybe. Other works, such as *Violent Incident* (1986), use the voice in a more narrative form, as the sequence of incidents plays out across a panel of twelve screens (in three sets of four). The voices of both male and female actors take turns in either abusing the other or, mostly, reacting physically to the current provocation.[15] *Good Boy Bad Boy* (1985) uses two monitors of talking heads of a man and a woman, reciting a not-so-moral list of activities, somewhat like grammatical conjugation or declension exercises. The same pattern is played out over the much larger multiscreen installation *World Peace* (1996). These last two works are much more explicitly interested in the twists of language rather than in its sonic production – and this will be reversed to some extent in the audio-only installation *Raw Materials* (2004), in which they feature, along with many single word pieces. So it is not possible or desirable to underplay the importance of language, but language in Nauman's videos falls into being an element among many, the very functioning of language as communication deviated and/or destroyed, to be replaced by precisely that destroyed language in the form of sound, and also of voice.

Giorgio Agamben argues that the voice is both originary (vital in establishing the humanness of humanity) and an emptiness within the human. The voice is where signification happens, but voice itself is 'no longer the experience of mere sound, and not yet the experience of meaning' (*Language and Death*, 34) – it is in between meaning and sound, and awaits both.[16] The experience of voice in fact is the anticipation of meaning, not the meaning itself – 'the voice, taken in this way, will then show itself as a pure intention to signify, as pure meaning, in which something is given to be understood before a determinate event of meaning is produced' (*Language and Death*, 33). In drawing attention to sound, to the sound of language, Nauman broaches the voice as potential for communication, and also for its failure, because ultimately, writes Agamben, death is what brings the pure or mere voice of existing into play. True voice is empty, or for humans, an emptying (*Language and Death*, 44–5).

This emptying takes literal form in the repeated 'no' of various interconnected video pieces featuring clowns, including *Clown Torture* (1987). Two of these are used in *Raw Materials*, and it is *Double No* (1988) that I am going to focus on here. This piece is another double-stacked monitor piece, a variant of the side-by-side installation of *No, No, New Museum* (1987).[17] Both of these use the same imagery of a clown jumping, shouting 'no' over and over again. *Double No* sees the clown jumping the right way up in the bottom screen, and inverted (and colour inverted) in the top monitor. The thumping feet and repetition make this of a piece with the 1990s videos, with less direct and explicit reference to Nauman addressing himself and the public. The pathetic yet aggressive clown is rejecting something, but the combination of a character and the limited material of the language drive speculation rather than knowledge. So, one variant of 'no' is the refusal of the auditor/viewer's attempt to find meaning, and others could include rejection of clowning, the rejection of straight life by clowning, rejection of being viewed, rejection of something that led to where the clown is now, a rejection of the viewer and of the artist, disavowal of the work by Nauman and so on. The incessant 'no', though, seems more like an affirmation after a while – an acceptance of living-on in negativity, of the absence of meaning. The rejection of language in its reduction to one word of refusal brings Nauman closer still to Agamben's sense of language as an emptying device. This emptying is also the condition of possibility of language, of meaning – and the 'No' part of *Raw Materials* is identified by Dexter as central to its functioning:

> *Raw Materials* can move, with components such as *No No No No*, from the apparent simplicity of an ordinary 'No' to a connection with every 'No' ever uttered or likely to be uttered in the future, thereby becoming a 'No' that reverberates at the very edge of our universe. ('Raw Materials', 23)

Certainly, language, the voice and sound are identified and dogmatically asserted in the *Raw Materials'* installation of twenty-one different recordings played on thirty-four speakers, along the length of the Turbine Hall in Tate Modern. This piece mostly separates off the audio track from pre-existing video pieces, creating a false distinction between image and 'soundtrack', as the visual track disappears. The writers in the catalogue for the show are keen to emphasize Nauman's play with materiality in producing this perversely minimal work. Vicente Todoli writes that 'The Turbine Hall is empty but its entire space has, paradoxically, been filled with acoustic material' ('Foreword', 7);[18] Dexter notes that the title itself announces this play, rais[ing] one of the paradoxes of the work, which is that the chief elements from which it is composed – sound, speech and space – are all intangible and supposedly immaterial, yet the work materialises speech and space together into one entity. ('Raw Materials', 19)

Both are correct in identifying sound as a solidifying force. The sound waves structure the space in the most material way, but also something more happens, which is that beyond the literalism of the air movements is the perception of a location defined by the occurrences within it. The Turbine Hall thus becomes a forcibly altered space, perhaps more itself than when other artworks redefine it. Why would this be? Sound draws attention to the subject's locatedness, making it a prime force in installation as an artwork that viewers move in/around/through, rather than objects that stand in front, above and before. The multiple sound sources of *Raw Materials* ask of the gallery visitor that they move amid a space that is hosting art, but where art seems absent. Instead, a sonic path is mapped out, one where the sounds alter constantly as the visitor moves along. Dexter writes that 'bands of audio clarity […] criss-cross the width of the space, between which are areas of barely audible or inaudible sound' ('Raw Materials', 19). Furthermore, the whole is underpinned by a persistent drone that echoes the building, reinforcing the spatial intent of the piece. I do not remember the hum element intruding, but the variations in cones of sound were certainly apparent.

Yes, *Raw Materials* is about the structuring of space through sound – but in 'stripping away' the visuals (curiously, Dexter refers explicitly to the audio being stripped from the visual ['Raw Materials', 19]) to bring out the audio part of video pieces, it is as if Nauman lost track of the very audiospatial process that so often defined the original pieces. The building became a non-visual equivalent of the vision track of the video work (non-visual because the piece consists only of the speakers and texts, and instead of the building providing a new focus, the shape of the piece draws attention to the building, the hall as emptied container). I am not sure the piece does much with language. As above, I think we need to see Nauman's rendering of voice and language as something a bit like a speech act, but one where the act has replaced speech as a carrier of meaning. Voice, text and language are all explicitly impoverished in *Raw Materials*, perhaps here more than in any other piece.

Shown in parallel to *Raw Materials* was the more demanding yet also seemingly casual *Mapping the Studio I (Fat Chance John Cage)* from 2001. In this multiscreen piece, Nauman's studio is shot at night time, a room with the artist absent, removed rather than simply not there. Nauman records his absence, the silence broken by traffic sounds, external animal cries and occasional appearances of cat or mouse. Shot over a few months, the scene also changes as a result of daytime activity by the absented artist.

The screens fill the gallery room, turning the display area into a space into which the studio bleeds (where the single monitor pieces bled outward). Arguably, many video installations do this – but it is Nauman that identifies the process of spatializing as a central part of the content of video work.

Notes

1   See Nauman, in a 1970 interview with Willoughby Sharp, in Janet Kraynak (ed.), *Please Pay Attention Please: Bruce Nauman's Words* (Cambridge, MA: MIT Press, 2008 [originally 2003]), 111–54 (124).

2   Yve-Alain Bois and Rosalind Krauss, *Formless: A User's Guide* (New York: Zone, 1997), 136–7; originally shown and published as *l'informe: mode d'emploi* (Paris: Centre Georges Pompidou, 1996).

3   The continued narration means that we continue hearing a room as voiced, unlike in Alvin Lucier's tape piece, *I Am Sitting in a Room* (1969), where multiple re-recordings of his taped voice create a sonic rendering of spatialization.

4   'Bruce Nauman, January 1972', interview with Lorraine Sciarra, in Kraynak (ed.), *Please Pay Attention Please*, 155–71.

5   'Interview with Bruce Nauman, May 27 and 30, 1980', interview with Michele De Angelus, in Kraynak (ed.), *Please Pay Attention Please*, 197–295.

6   Rosalind Krauss, 'Sculpture in the Expanded Field', *October* 8 (Spring 1979), 30–44.

7   Brandon LaBelle, *Acoustic Territories: Sound Culture and Everyday Life* (New York: Continuum, 2010).

8   Peter Roehr, who died in 1968, explored repetitive minimalism to a phenomenal degree of obsession in sound and also in a variety of visual and audiovisual forms. He specialized in taking small snippets of film, mostly from advertising materials, and constructing loops from them in highly rhythmical form. His wall-based works used a similar aesthetic, for example, taking a single picture from Volkswagen car brochures and presenting multiple copies of it in grid-like structures. Perhaps unusually for someone so interested in repetitive form, it is that interest in itself that dominated over the choice of medium, such that the medium could even be said to disappear, as opposed to the intermedia practices outlined here in the case of Nauman.

9   Robert R. Riley, 'Bruce Nauman's Philosophical and Material Explorations in Film and Video', in Constance M. Lewallen et al., *A Rose Has No Teeth: Bruce Nauman in the 1960s* (Berkeley: University of California Press, 2007), 171–89.

10 Nauman explicitly rejects the possible significance of bodily (or viewerly) endurance (see Kraynak [ed.], *Please Pay Attention Please*, 248).

11 See Constance M. Lewallen, 'A Rose Has No Teeth', in Lewallen et al., *A Rose Has No Teeth*, 7–115 (15).

12 Ben Borthwick, 'Catalogue Entries', in *Bruce Nauman – Raw Materials* (London: Tate, 2004), 130–41.

13   Michael Auping, 'Metacommunicator', in *Bruce Nauman – Raw Materials*, 8–17; Emma Dexter, 'Raw Materials', in the same volume, 18–23; Janet Kraynak, 'Bruce Nauman's Words', in Kraynak (ed.), *Please Pay Attention Please*, 1–45.
14   These are questions to which Martin Heidegger's thought still supplies us with complex reflections of great value in understanding what exactly technology is. See, for example, 'The Question Concerning Technology', from 1953, in Martin Heidegger, *Basic Writings*, ed. David Farrell Krell (London: Routledge, 1993), 311–42. Translated by William Lovitt.
15   For Nauman's 'score' for the piece, see Kraynak (ed.), *Please Pay Attention Please*, 96–7.
16   Giorgio Agamben, *Language and Death: The Place of Negativity* (Minneapolis: University of Minnesota Press, 1991 [1982]). Translated by Karen E. Pinkus with Michael Hardt.
17   Borthwick untangles the connections and how they work in the new installation ('Catalogue Entries', 132–3).
18   Vicente Todoli, 'Foreword', in *Bruce Nauman – Raw Materials*, 7.

CHAPTER THREE

Body as Screen

When the body came directly and explicitly into art, video was there – as a key part of documentation of live performance, but also a refraction device to bring out the disjunction of the importance of being present and the impossibility, or at least, serious unlikelihood, of physical presence for most of the actual public. More pragmatically, on the one hand, performance artists such as Abramović, Acconci and Chris Burden took video as a way of recording acts that set out to frame the complex border between public and private through the playing out of extreme or subversive physical acts and behaviours. More formally, video performed a self-undermining of the authenticity of performance, as guaranteed by liveness and attendance by viewers. Two competing models arose for analyzing this situation, neither of which is fully adequate. First, for Krauss, and as noted in the Introduction, the 1960s saw a range of art strategies that brought the artist inside the frame of the art work, and for Krauss, this showed a failure born of narcissism, a failure that signalled the arrival of postmodernism.

Against this, Rosler claimed that video worked as political, committed, properly vanguard art because of its inclusions. It incorporated many voices, actions and communities that had had little or no participation or reflection in modernist formal play, even at its most performative. This is probably true to a large extent, but such work does not extend or build on the formal work of modernism through a purposive use of sound and, when at its most representational, represents simple aesthetic conservatism – the return of content to the exclusion of other factors. On the other hand, if we look more closely at Krauss's complaint, there is a glaring problem: the so-called 'narcissistic' presence of the artist was very often highlighting the hitherto absent artist – most notably, women. Further, not only had social context been at least minimized in modernist criticism, but the artist as embodied and contextualized subject had been airbrushed out (this not so much a product of modernism but of the European art institution, where once the artist is a private, individual creator, in a new secular, non-aristocratic world dominated by what Walter Benjamin terms 'exhibition value', so is he perhaps a product of modernity).[1] The gradual change away from this, via dada and Futurist performance, Fluxus, Yves Klein and the extravagantly invested painting of abstract expressionism, took hold as strategy combining form and content in performance and video.

With performance art, the body and artist would not just be inside the work, but one would inform the other as content turning into form and back again. The performance would use the body as tool, in a sort of shallow Cartesianism, but as the body becomes more of a formal object, the controlling consciousness slips away into heightened embodiment – an embodiment that is mediated – perhaps even intermedial, when presented (precisely *not* represented) through the format of video. Sound is absolutely essential in this process, at one stroke removing the prioritizing of one sense over others for artist and viewer alike. Instead, the multisensoriality of the real world would be introduced into performance video to heighten the implied presence of the often-suffering artist/body. From that starting point, gendered physicality, with its implied resonance with how gendered identities and behaviours play out outside of art, gradually comes to be more formally complex, less real in one way, but arguably more effective in its critical intent. This progress can be tracked through the works of Acconci, Burden and Abramović through the work of Joan Jonas, culminating with Dara Birnbaum's explosive Wonder Woman.

Chris Burden's *Through the Night Softly* (1973) stands as an exemplary work in his series of physical challenges and durational pieces. This one was designed with video and TV in mind. Burden drags his body, with his arms behind his back, across broken glass, on a Los Angeles parking lot, for two and a half minutes and it seems a lot longer, raising the idea of duration as something more than 'a long time'.[2] Burden had the idea that a ten-second segment would be shown on a Los Angeles TV station, and unlike Sjölander and video users of public broadcast TV in the USA, Burden would not frame the action with any discourse; it would instead nestle among the advertisements (five times a week, for four weeks).[3] In the video, Burden holds his arms behind his back and crawls, diagonally, from 'back right' to 'front left', until his head passes the camera. It is not a long piece, but is about duration – it is not, claims Burden, about blood (hence its being filmed in black and white), but it is about some sort of violence. It is not about gender, but there he is, in his underpants, crawling and making vocal sounds we presume to be male. The drag looks painful, and perhaps tells us something about the human condition, like the swimmers in mud in Samuel Beckett's *How It Is*.[4] Or something about the struggling male condition, dragging his poor body over broken glass, a relic traversing remnants.

We hear the body impacting on glass and concrete, painfully shifting shards of glass as it goes. The sound makes it clear that the glass is a sort of interstitial space, a membrane that connects one material to another, and Burden is trying to either break this unwanted membrane or expose it as being more porous than we might imagine. Meanwhile, he grunts and gasps as he goes, not too loudly, but constantly, as his body describes a to-and-fro rhythm as it undulates along (due to the arm clasping). This pendular motion, much more explicit due to the scraping sound, sets up a reference to bodily rhythms, to ways of processing the world as structured, all through the irony of this seemingly unnatural auto-aggression. But this is not a penitential journey – that we see neither end nor beginning of the movement in frame means this is more about signifying a permanent condition, whether psychological, political or ontological. Only the vocal reactions indicate the presence of human culture amid the glass, amid the built and the destroyed. The voice is above all patience. With that, it can work as a second measure alongside the pitch and yaw of the Burden body, a physicalization of the idealized consciousness (speech) as it becomes mere voice.

Burden's work in the 1970s was heavily focussed on pushing his body and experience of time, and is perhaps highly literal, if not necessarily masculine or macho in intent. An oddity of early performance art is that the presence of the artist body within the work makes gender, or better, sex, something in play, but in terms of gendered behaviour through physical testing, it would be hard to differentiate a masculine testing as opposed to a feminine one. Arguably the making of the body into material, of making it *this* body, in *this* art, for *this* moment, is already a putting into play of gender. This is, of course, open to debate, and again, what I am interested in here is the play of audio and visual components in the realization of a nowness, albeit recorded, that can be vicariously experienced via video. It would be interesting to see if presence itself is gendered – and I do not mean any specific presences, or experiences of being as a man or as a woman, but rather whether presencing is in any way gendered, but it is the hearing of this question, as well as how we see it, that will assist in defining telepresence or tele-absence in the case of performance art as structured in and across video.

Vito Acconci developed a strongly assertive and sexually aggressive practice in his early 1970s performances and videos, wherein he explored sexual and interpersonal dynamics. This aggression ultimately led to a parodic and somewhat flaccid masculinity, where his actions and attempts to dominate met with failure, suspension or angry isolation (Amelia Jones refers to his 'pathetic masculinity' [*Body Art*, 132]).[5] From the outset, he was also interested in language and sound – coming together logically and obviously in a strong emphasis on the male voice, his voice, in many of these works.[6] Brandon LaBelle brings out the vital role of sound in Acconci, focussing on two pieces, *Seedbed* (1972), where he lies hidden under a raised platform in a gallery, masturbating all day while reciting his fantasies through a microphone, and *Claim* (1971), where Acconci sits blindfolded at the foot of a set of stairs, holding a metal pole, ranting about how no one should approach or he will attack them.[7] Although sound catches the attention of LaBelle, and he notes the video monitor at the top of the stairs in *Claim*, he does not develop the idea of Acconci's distance as something specifically mediated through live footage of sound and image on that screen. Both LaBelle and Jones underplay how sound acts as part of mediation, even as they observe its presence as part of performance. Jones is interested in the mediations performance art uses to bring out or deconstruct subjectivity, noting on several occasions the mutual dependence between visual document and live action in performance, and in her chapter on Acconci, she refers to how media double back on the physical element:

> The body art project initiates an 'infinite chain' of supplements – the body 'itself', the spoken narrative, the video and other visuals within the piece, the video, film, photograph, and the text documenting it for posterity – all of which work to produce the sense of the very thing they defer. [...] Rather than confirming the metaphysical coherence of the body-in-presence, the 'body' in body art exacerbates its own supplementarity. (*Body Art*, 105)

Inclusion of the voice as supplement illustrates how far Jones wishes to move from the possibility of authentic self-expression or realization through body art (even if she does believe in the value of psychoanalytic reading), but specifically forgets that many of Acconci's performances do not occur in transparent ideal form but exist through the very specific format of video or film on a monitor. They are designed, in other words, to close off the prospect of the self, except as always already mediated. The media is not an incidental add-on, for all that I agree with Jones' argument entirely – it just needs to go further and retain her own earlier exhortation about photographic documentation and body event needing each other and generating referents one for the other (37) and extend this to being an integral part of video performance art (as opposed to video recordings of performance events). Where LaBelle has sound as mediating device, without referring to the devices through which it mediates, Jones has everything but the medium of video as mediating device – video disappears in the play of materials, events and discourses mobilized by Acconci.

Let's return to *Claim*'s inversion of surveillance, where Acconci is holding off invaders but is hampered by lack of vision, and the presence of the warning sign of the monitor showing his readiness and obsessive preparedness for violent defence. The video is all that will be (was) encountered, like some of Abramović's works, and the ranting, punctuated with pipe bashing against the stairs, conveys something less than heroic precisely because of the distance established through the video. Why is this man lurking at the foot of the stairs, ranting and raging? Already we can see how Acconci takes a form of seemingly blatant masculine power and pushes it to exaggerated and self-defeating lengths, and this is conveyed through the distancing of the monitor. What now remains is the video, as if half of the performance has survived (as opposed to this being documentation of a transient event). In *Pryings* (1971) with Kathy Dillon, Acconci struggles to force her eyes open, stumbling about a room, pushing her hair out of the way, pushing at her, tugging her around, hoping to help ease her eyes open. Jones here makes no reference to the video, nor does the shuffling sound of their awkward, almost abusive encounter feature in her analysis – where, for me as a viewer, at least, the sound is the index of failure and aggression that slowly draws attention away from the eye-forcing that seems doomed to progress without completion – the narrating of the failure is in the desperate mutual shuffle sounds.

In many pieces, Acconci focusses visual and aural attention on his face and mouth, and we can track connections through three of his works: *Open Book* (1974), *Turn-On* (1974) and *Theme Song* (1973). In the first of these, Acconci's face fills the screen, his mouth dominating, and he speaks a monologue about openness. He does this without closing his mouth to make the sound of consonants, and as his mouth dries out this fails, so he also has to speak of how he fails to always be open. The effective removal of consonants makes language a realm of difficulty, a place where language itself, or communication, is what is conveyed. The visual focus also reduces the personality of the speaker. Any intersubjective relation here is just about communication, free of a 'what' or a 'who'. Instead of this approaching some purity of communication, the distancing device of the forced way of speaking as well as the piece being a video work, rather than performance presented live, contribute to making communication fruitless, a collapsing monologue about the possibility of communicating: Or eh o-i-i-i-y o oh-u-i-eih-ing. *Turn-On* sees a more flamboyant and seemingly predatory male turning on his viewer, in between bouts of humming soundtracky mood tunes to which he shakes his head. The viewer sees the back of his head, filling the screen, at these points, the screenful of hair giving way to Acconci's full face as he talks of having 'to face you' but not being ready, or not having anything prepared (he is also talking reflexively of the piece itself, and his work, and as it goes on, there are more and more mentions of 'me'). The 'turn-on' is multiple – an apparent sexual turn-on (in Acconci's character's mind) underlying the turning around to face the viewer, while also representing the violence of turning against someone (as shown and sounded in the physical turn that is accompanied with the ranting, cajoling, chatting of the speaker who posits himself as the unwanted encounter).

Theme Song is almost free of aggression, except that Acconci continues to demand physical and visual attention, albeit gently. He lies on the floor, his face occupying half of the screen, and tries to talk the viewer/addressee into a romantic encounter. Insofar as there is a narrative, it is clear that the viewer is already 'back at Vito's place'. As he talks about his loneliness and his loveliness, he smokes cigarettes and punctuates his talk by playing cassettes that play snatches of songs. Half of his monologue takes off from the lyrics of those songs. Acconci plays songs from The Doors, Van Morrison, the Velvet Underground, Leonard Cohen and others, ending with a bit of Kris Kristofferson's song 'Me and Bobby McGee' – whose keyline is 'freedom is just another word for nothing left to lose'. Acconci's appeal for love and sex is completely tied up in the playing of music, as the bohemian yet not too outré selections show his sensitivity, intelligence, coolness and even some vulnerability. His joining in with the songs starts out as an attempt to show just how much the songs make him feel, but they end up lost in a slurry of approximations, as Acconci turns back to his central theme on the basis of lyrics from whichever song is played. The regular thumping of the tape switches also 'breaks the mood' over the thirty-three-minute seduction period.

The question might be why these pieces are not just audio works? It is a form he was interested in, after all. I think it is because it would not show the foolish, aggressive hopefulness of the desiring Acconci, and would come across as less spontaneous. But the pieces are structured, prepared to some extent, and mediated – so it would seem important that Acconci heighten the audio pathos (or lower it further) with the use of the visual supplement, which emerges alongside the audio from what seems a live and unedited performance. It is the multisensorial experience of Acconci that conveys the limp aura of flattering masculinity – with impressions playing off one another rather than acting as incidental by-products. It is clear that the audio part is essential, likewise the visual, of these video pieces, and the simplicity of the ideal aims of a performance is mediated out of meaningfulness by Acconci's play or, as LaBelle has it, the 'displacement of presence' is what we end up with (*Background Noise*, 109).[8]

Other than the potentially determinist reading based on the biographical biology of a performer, it is not obvious that performance art can be defined as either female or male – and arguably body art of the more extreme kinds is an attempt to posit a world outside of gender, especially when it deals most directly with it. Or not. But gender is in play and the sex part of sexuality is heavily in play in performance; to switch to an ostensibly female version of mediated video performance, I want now to consider again Abramović's 1975 piece *Art Must Be Beautiful, Artist Must Be Beautiful*. Unlike Acconci, Abramović displays a suffering female body as representing gender normativity – in *Art Must Be Beautiful*, she brushes her hair with two brushes, roughly, while restating the title many times, often revealing the pain of what is supposed to be a normal everyday (female) activity. Abramović not only makes visible the social expectation of female beautification and its undesirable consequences (presumably indicating the psychological rather than the physical trauma of hairbrushing) but makes it audible too. For all that the piece seems badly dated and obvious today, the interest lies in its play of audio and visual: it is in the audio, in the voice, condemned to repeat its auto-instruction, that we see Abramović's subjectivity as something under threat, as something subject to complicity and as something that can be asserted or taken on positively, in a reversal of power relations. Abramović's voice is an overcoming of the task it sets itself. The picture too is an important mediation: not only is Abramović performing to the camera (as opposed to many of her other works which insist on her bodily presence along with that of an audience) but she is looking slightly off-camera at what I take to be, or to represent, a mirror. In setting up this set of reflections and framings, we can return to the 'art' of the title – Abramović's naked body reflecting a history of female representations in art history (again, this was a more significant position to take in the 1970s), and that this too is another reflection of women seen as primarily body. This body is a speaking one, even if constrained to a dogmatic mantra, and as it acts, it interacts with the sounds of machinery (brushes) penetrating Abramović's hair. The sound of this relation is what drives the voice that is both complicit and rebellious (through what Jean Baudrillard would describe as 'hyperconformity').[9] If we compare this to *Theme Song*, we can see and hear Acconci mastering technology, by presenting it as his to share, where Abramović presents brushing, art, camera recording and even her own body as tools of which she has been dispossessed. This is not a simple product of each work's intent, but a direct result of the use and outcomes of the sounds produced.

Like Acconci, Abramović is interested in the sounds that emerge from performance, or even sound in its own right, and as with many involved in performance and video,[10] there is a complex play of presence being worked through in the use of sound and image – the combination adding up to a sense of 'thereness' of an event, but giving way (in some works) to a more interesting, critical and formal use of those audio and visual registers. Carolee Schneemann took up the bodily and specifically erotic exploration of subjectivity in the late 1960s and 1970s. While she is more recognized (mostly via photographic documentation) for her physical performances and an interest in the present moment of embodiment, she also worked through video, adopting a more 'processed' approach on *Plumb Line* (1968–71). Focussing on the 'dissolving' relation between a woman (herself in the film) and a man, Schneemann mobilizes direct interventions on the film, rapid changes between single and multiple, mirrored images, and a soundtrack that rarely touches on what is going on at that moment in the film, while heightening the sense of oppressive tension. The piece combines what looks more or less like holiday footage, with many shots of the face and torso of the male, mostly still, but interspersed with some moving footage.

The film begins and ends with film burning, and with the title – but the soundtrack is both different and made audible *as* soundtrack at the end. So, at the beginning, there is the sound of a projector, a small percussive sound, which gradually increases in volume before giving way to machinic sounds, such as creaking, hums, vocal sounds, including speech, and the sound of a cat (which sounds like a baby looking for attention).[11] The changing image dynamics are driven by colourized sections and a rhythmical return to the man's face, while the soundtrack becomes tougher, with Schneemann, at one point, recounting a mental removal from the world, shocked out of it. Serra and Ramey note that 'this emotional outpouring is as confrontational as Schneemann's physical nakedness in her earlier work' ('Eye/Body', 118), and this confrontation is played out further in the soundtrack – at the end, not only does the multiple sound continue over the repeated opening, but it is stopped and started, and slowed down – echoing what happened to music in the middle of the piece, and emphasizing that this is where control is an issue, and, ultimately, asserting itself through direct intervention. This completes the process whereby sound and image have been relating discordantly throughout, and the disjunction means that sound and image are mutually non-diegetic – they do not fit in the same space, but do refer to each other in the way they grate along. The emphasis on the male body as object and as a form of politically aesthetic resistance is directly echoed in the control of sound, where instead of traditional (or expected) domination of the visual, the sound comes to be the resistant force. The presence of the female voice is part of this, but a more critical move occurs formally when this voice operates as part of a self-reflexive disruption, revealing apparently present subject individuals as caught within multiple processes of perception and action.

In a piece as repetitive as it is fragmented, Joan Jonas sets an even higher bar for a formalist feminism with her video piece *Vertical Roll* (1972). In this piece, based on a filmed and vertically glitching TV monitor image, she displays the female body as partial, disrupted, withheld from solid identity. In placing herself in the frame as the object made subject, Rush argues that the piece 'amounts to a loud proclamation of the body's (especially the female body's) presence in the work of art' (*Video Art*, 87). As Meigh-Andrews' summary of the piece makes clear in some detail, *Vertical Roll* is about movement (and emerged from a longer performance, entitled *Organic Honey's Vertical Roll*,[12] both actual [diegetic] and conflicted [the stuck screen, the cuts, the glimpses of body]). The body in fragments, the presence of the female artist body, body as subject and object – the content seems clear – with the method a way of combining those purposes. But it is the sound that completes the work – starting with Jonas tapping a spoon on the screen (from the viewer/listener's perspective) and then fading into a non-diegetic version, there is a relentless pulsing, which turns this piece into a perverse version of minimalism. The disrupted, disorienting image is further displaced by the percussive rendering of aural consistency.[13] This in turn signals Jonas' own second breaking of diegesis as she leans in towards the camera near the end of the piece, in front of the monitor it is recording. From a feminist perspective, this would seem to reiterate the possibility of female presence – of an actual whole woman, and one who is an artist, shaping material, and transcending it in a visible and audible (the spoon) self-reflection.

Vertical Roll is more interesting than that – the fragmentation is not merely a replication of 'Woman' as a collection of fetishized objects, even with the inclusion of 'beauty' poses, dancing legs and moving 'parts'. Instead, we do not have to see the arrival of Jonas-complete at the end as a kind of too-easy conclusion; rather it can be seen and heard as an assertion of the value of diverting fetishism into fascinating, ritual body play. The dual forces of the divided body and unitary rhythm establish a Burroughs-style exploration of the secret identities behind conspiratorial control. Arthur and Marilouise Kroker draw precisely this conclusion from looking at photographer Francesca Woodman's multiple takes on her own (disappearing) body, compared to the commercialized fragment fetish of a Capezio advertisement featuring a distorted woman's body with shoes on each limb, and yet more placed on top of them ('Theses on the Disappearing Body', 33).[14] It is Jonas' deviation and manipulation of the fetishizing that has been rendered banal and normative that push the formally grounded critique of *Vertical Roll*.

Not all early work concerned with gender in video stuck to the affirmation of women's presence in art, and in society. Nor would it have to be direct, pragmatic and discursive. Arguably more powerful as critique was the highly formalist approach of pioneering appropriation work *Technology/ Transformation: Wonder Woman* by Dara Birnbaum, produced in 1978. Yet again, the sound is vital to the work, and that aspect has been somewhat neglected by critics. This piece takes as its material elements of the TV series *Wonder Woman*, which ran from 1975 to 1979, and was based on a DC comic serial launched in 1941. Diana Prince would transform, through spinning, into the scantily clad, tiara'd eponymous superhero. The costume's colours broadly suggested the American flag (its 1940s origins being clearer in this regard), and the need for a superhero to be wearing revealing clothes suggested that if women were to join the ranks of superhero crimefighters, they would still have to be 'sexy'. Birnbaum took the transformative moments and turned them into repetitive, rhythmical sequences that highlighted the gender stereotyping of the series. Christopher Eamon writes that through the combination of repetitions and the 'hyper-sexualised disco soundtrack [...] Birnbaum emphasizes the deployment of female sexuality in the media. Both ironic and humorous, the work attacks and disarms the unacknowledged myth-making process inherent in the narrative' ('An Art of Temporality', 83).[15] Michael Newman glosses this idea when he notes that 'the secretary passes through an explosive moment to assume agency, but notwithstanding remains trapped in a fetishistic costume' ('Moving Image in the Gallery Since 1990', 104).[16] Both of these accounts have found a new story to replace the narrative that has been fragmented, and have lost sight of the method of the piece, let alone what it sounds like (the sexy disco song comes after the repeated shots of Wonder Woman). Meigh-Andrews offers much more detail, identifying the full sequence of shots and stating that the editing strategy 'entirely eliminates the narrative from the original TV series, leaving only the fantasy element' (*A History of Video Art*, 172), but still we get a story to replace the lost one – a consciously feminist story as opposed to the illusory freedom that obscured the many underlying stereotypes about women's behaviour and roles.

There is much more to *Technology/Transformation: Wonder Woman*. First, its cutting does not just remove narrative but shows us its impossibility: this wonder woman mostly never arrives, held up in multiple explosive changes, as if dwelling in transformation as opposed to the predictability of end-driven narratives of rescue and redemption. In this piece, when she does save the hapless male character, we still do not get to the conclusion of the battle. Prior to this, the film begins in explosive fire, the booming of Diana Prince's change standing alone – a material power beyond even her control. These give way to numerous takes of the change into Wonder Woman, interspersed with some running. Aurally, we are faced with explosions alternating with hints of the theme tune, and in one great moment we hear into the future, to Christian Marclay's *Crossfire* (2007), when we hear and see bullets pinging off her shiny bracelets, held in dynamic battle pose. One sequence shows Wonder Woman in a room of mirrors, loudly scratching out a break to jump through – a reflection on media, a reflection in gender, in a 'changing room', but also the breaking through of the veil of illusion. POW! She's through and into rescue mode. But the concentration given to the cutting is not just about reflection but also about the role of fragmentation, the role of the cut-up in acting as a critical reflection.

Birnbaum does not stop at an easy critique of 'women in the media'. Wonder Woman is not just given agency but sexuality – the song 'Wonder Woman in Discoland' reiterates her sexuality, and her becoming sexual – sending the viewer back to the continual explosions as a move from orgasm to jouissance. Instead of coming to the rescue, she is coming, which makes this video a direct response to the 'narcissism' Krauss saw in video art. Birnbaum takes her literal self out, thus removing the possibly overliteral presence of the artist, in favour of an emptying, or a shaking-out of existing, fictional material riddled with gender 'issues'. From this comes a loud yet not open-ended feminism – the looping undermines any claim to fixing a problem, while the explosions that end the section that is based on clips reiterate a sort of eternal return of occupying a moment that cannot be dwelt in.

The formalist approaches to gender, physicality or sexuality seen towards the end of this chapter are certainly more satisfying in critical philosophical terms, but clearly not as obviously functional politically as more narrative, symbolic or psychological works might be. My point is not about the goodness or success value as such, but how sound and our listening inform perceptions of gender in video art, where sound has been 'seen' as peripheral or incidental – a soundtrack perhaps worthy of comment, but not capable of working as part of the formal strategy of the work. This is what I have tried to bring out in the sequencing of this chapter, traversing a continuum from self-presenting performance works for video to the early appropriation work of Birnbaum, as shown in the authentically iconic *Technology/Transformation: Wonder Woman.*

Notes

1 See 'The Work of Art in the Age of Mechanical Reproduction', 218–20.
2 On this idea of duration, see Henri Bergson, *Time and Free Will: An Essay on the Immediate Data of Consciousness* (New York: Harper Torchbook, 1960 [1889]). Translated by F.L. Pogson.
3 For Burden's ideas on this piece, see his commentary on and around the early 1970s videos on *Films and Documentation, 1971–1974*; available at http://www.ubu.com/film/burden_selected.html.
4 Samuel Beckett, *How It Is* (London: John Calder, 1964).
5 Amelia Jones, *Body Art: Performing the Subject* (Minneapolis: University of Minnesota Press, 1998).
6 On the importance of language in Acconci, see Craig Dworkin, 'Fugitive Signs', *October 95* (Winter 2001), 90–113.
7 Brandon LaBelle, *Background Noise: Perspectives on Sound Art* (New York and London: Continuum, 2006), 108–22.
8 For Dworkin, even Acconci's body becomes 'one element in a chain of medial technologies' ('Fugitive Signs', 109).
9 Jean Baudrillard, *In the Shadow of the Silent Majorities* (New York: Semiotext[e], 1983), 47. Translated by Paul Foss and John Johnston.
10 See, for example, Chrissie Iles, 'Cleaning the Mirror, Marina Abramović, 1995', in Caleb Kelly (ed.), *Sound* (London and Cambridge, MA: Whitechapel Gallery/MIT Press, 2011), 187–90.
11 For more detail, see M.M. Serra and Kathryn Ramey, 'Eye/Body: The Cinematic Paintings of Carolee Schneemann', in Robin Blaetz (ed.), *Women's Experimental Cinema* (Durham, NC: Duke University Press, 2007), 103–26.
12 Meigh-Andrews, *A History of Video Art*, 158–9.
13 I suspect it is more disorienting when filling a large screen than when centred on a monitor as a single-screen installation.
14 Arthur and Marilouise Kroker, 'Theses on the Disappearing Body in the Hypermodern Condition', in Arthur and Marilouise Kroker (eds.), *Body Invaders: Sexuality and the Postmodern Condition* (Basingstoke: Macmillan, 1988), 20–34.
15 Chris Eamon, 'An Art of Temporality', in Stuart Corner (ed.), *Film and Video Art* (London: Tate, 2009), 66–85.
16 Michael Newman, 'Moving Image in the Gallery since the 1990s', in Corner (ed.), *Film and Video Art*, 86–121.

CHAPTER FOUR

Gary Hill, Seeing Language

Many early video artists incorporated sound and voice into their works, with varying degrees of purpose and attention to sound itself. I have sought examples of how the sound, the hearing and the presentation of those voices might form part of an essential approach, reading or understanding of how we read video. The fact that video is a sound medium (unless consciously removed) should quickly dispense with the erroneous belief that a soundtrack is somehow merely a secondary, additional part, as opposed to being an integral part of the process of making video. Gary Hill renders this multiple 'track' nature of video more explicit, using voice, sound, language and visuals as alternating devices. He takes on the process of the making of video work that incorporates sound and vision in highly conscious, philosophically informed fashion, and makes this process itself the content of much of his work. In so doing, this process is used to examine perception, states of being, spectatorship, listenership, subjectivity and the way in which these are formally and socially constructed.

For Hill, language becomes a privileged means of exploring sound (and vision). With language, humans have always already formalized their communication – given it structure, capacity for meaning and expression. Language is there to be heard and to be seen, and like Derrida, Hill refuses to privilege one communicative strategy over another. It is easy to misunderstand Derrida's injunction that 'there is nothing outside the text' (*Of Grammatology*, 163) in this regard.[1] This statement stands as an exemplary expression of his philosophical position about the world being constructed of oppositions – oppositions which in fact relate opposites intimately and necessarily, such that they influence each other constantly. So, the 'text' referred to can be the textfulness of spoken language – what would a language be without structure, and the capacity for shared understanding? Nothing. So what underpins oral communication is writing – a writing where meaning is made, beneath and beyond the literalness of the inscribed word. The 'outside' of the text could be construed as 'the world' – but how do we know this world? Through previous experience, through categories provided by societies for us to inhabit and at particular moments in time: the world is coded, or, effectively, it is not. Later, I will also refer to Giorgio Agamben's sense of language itself as a border condition between life and death, and human and animal, but to begin with, the proximity of Derrida's thought to that of Hill is what is important. Hill is himself deeply interested in French theory – as well as Derrida, Maurice Blanchot's work feeds into much of his art practice – sometimes directly and explicitly as in the major piece *Incidence of Catastrophe* (1987–88), which is based on Blanchot's *Thomas the Obscure*.[2] In this chapter, I will concentrate on how Hill develops an audiovisual theoretical style that puts into play questions of how being, perception and language work together through voice, writing and the sound of language and its absence, and also pay particular attention to how he develops these ideas in his earlier works.[3]

Hill is interested in sound and language – and how language comes to sound or resound. His work takes words so literally that they become not only content but a second layer of form – with language itself as the second-layer content. This is then explored to examine how language structures our experience and vice-versa, so many of his pieces in the 1970s and 1980s feature texts that are spoken, as well as written works, often presented in ways that undermine their narrative cohesion. Language works as a metonym for the (video) work itself, as it too is there to be seen, heard, construed and processed. In Hill's early works based on video manipulation, where sound plays a key part, it is as if we encounter the emergence of language (obviously this entails not only the deconstructive time of 'the always already' but simple hindsight based on our subsequent knowledge). It is hard to ignore the possibility of language itself being nothing other than an emergence from sound, a stochastic evolution rather than a set of decisions. Critics have noted the importance of sound in Hill, but they have tended to stay close to sound that is linguistically significant, or where significance is at stake through language and voice. Stephen Sarazzin identifies many occasions where language is both at work and at stake, and also discusses how language and image relate, but does not move outside of those ideas (see his essay 'Surfing the Medium').[4] Jacinto Lageira goes further, and although privileging the immediacy of voice, makes some interesting points about how voice appears in Hill's videos, hinting at the importance of the recurring idea of emergence:

> It is not a question of making verbal what is mute in Nature through speaking instead of things and objects, since the appearance of voice in their midst marks the insuperable distance between the naturalness of what is and its perpetual reformulation through our words. [...] The voice has to turn into sonorous matter in order to distinguish itself from or oppose itself to the world *almost* on the same level, for visible matter responds to phonic matter [in Hill's artworks]. ('The Image of the World in the Body of the Text', 31)[5]

This is a very good starting point from which to consider the use of voice, language and sound, and while it privileges voice as an immediate expression of an unproblematic, factual real world which seems to have autonomous existence, it gives a clear sense of how voice and world intertwine via human sound as well as human meaning.

George Quasha and Charles Stein extend the title of one of Hill's early works, *Electronic Linguistics* (1977), into a guiding principle for the explorations conducted in the shape of his work in the late 1970s and early 1980s. They write that language can be 'understood through the terminological lens *electronic linguistics* [and] irrespective of whether a particular piece uses text, in particular instances his work inquires into the nature of language as intrinsic to art-making through electronic/digital technology' (*An Art of Limina*, 66).[6] The piece is itself quite simple, as simple yet amorphous images come into being and disappear, shapes form, sounds rise and fall in line with those changes (i.e. in tone, intensity, volume), in a more-or-less musical fashion, emerging from seeming formlessness. As with much of Hill's work, it is hard to tell whether sound leads image or vice-versa – and it is clear that the two are to be maintained as other to one another, intertwined in deconstructive pairings – that is, instead of simply surmounting that question, we are brought to it, as sound and image remain distinct and therefore continual contributors to properly intermedial work, as opposed to merging in sensorial unity. *Electronic Linguistics* posits that language, or better still, writing, emerges – and it does so visibly and audibly, on the basis of language that is always already there – that is, in the shape of coding/programming. This in turn refers back to a conception of the world as codable that relies on linguistics that emerges from human languages. *Equal Time* (1979) separates voice and image more – as two sets of patterns move towards each other in the centre of the (video-recorded) computer screen, and two voices flatly recite separate self-referential stories (about movement in and across a room), meeting in the centre and joining to recite for a short moment in chorus and then diverging again. For Quasha and Stein, it is in this piece that we begin to see Hill's interest in the status of the viewer/listener (*An Art of Limina*, 106) – who has to work to follow and understand the separate soundtracks and will likely fail – thus becoming more aware of this activity as process.

This brings us perhaps too neatly to *Processual Video* from 1980. In this piece, a white bar rotates to the same rhythm as a flat intoning voice, recounting the changing position and perception of a third-person protagonist. As the bar rotates, changing dimension and direction, we see glimpses of flickering separate, shorter white lines, suggesting distance, and moving shapes. As the piece begins with such 'flickering' lines and the statement 'he knew the ocean well. He grew up there and observed the waves daily', the viewer is led into the belief that the lines on the screen represent the story visually. The narrator then tells of a trip to the mountains, of flying, of movement in general, of lines, of geometry, of machines and of spatial division. The direct narration is troubled by the simplicity of the moving line (actually not a line, but different sections of screen line coded white in each shot), leading the viewer to move away from reading the line as representation and instead to reflect on abstraction. A century of abstract art has made viewers casual about the idea of abstraction, with it increasingly being seen as synonymous with an absence of direct, content-based referentiality. But the story itself, as a way of processing the world through symbols, words and speech, is as much, if not more, of an abstraction, as it hides its process of abstracting. Unlike the line, which literalizes it – in the same way as Mondrian's early pictures gradually divest the landscape of its details and splinter it into lines very much like the 'sea' here (see particularly *Pier and Ocean* from 1914). The rotating bar then becomes a holding point around which abstraction (the transfer of world into meaning, into communicable forms) operates as explicit process. The bar itself can also be read as signifying the line between signifier and signified, referent and sign, representation and real, speech and writing and so on.

The presence of the speaking voice is important in that it introduces the human body as a vector for mimesis, representation, abstraction and meaning. It also undermines the claim that any one human can make to being an individual creator *ex nihilo*. Not only does the voice move along with the white line(s) on the screen, as if both are trying to map the phenomena of challenging complexity, but also does it become just one element of many that contribute to the viewer's internal processes of re-creating a story – a story which undoes itself, from the clear, establishing introductory narrative to the closing 'Within limits, he enjoyed long distance driving and travelling light', where travelling light is exactly what the viewer has likely been neglecting in favour of representational (abstracting) habits. In fact, had the viewer gone immediately to the abstraction and self-referentiality of *Processual Video*, that viewer would have missed the processual part, the work that undoes itself as the bar turns. So it is vital that the voice provide an anchor, and act as a turning bar around which the visuals operate.

In *Happenstance (one of many parts)* from 1982–83, the voice acts as a guide, beginning by announcing the sounds and shapes that go together, like a self-referential children's programme that could be called 'Doing Things with Words and Shapes'. This piece is much more playful and, as its title indicates, is about contingency, albeit in highly composed form – such that the contingency is content rather than a producer of 'true' visible or audible material within the final piece. As with many of Hill's pieces, *Happenstance* features a more-or-less rhythmical narration (reminding me of the vocal delivery of Pink Floyd's Roger Waters), where content is displaced into a series of self-reflexive moves. Just like the voice, the piece uses image shapes, video-processing animation, written words and letters, music and sounds, all in an ironically multimedia style. In other words, these forms interact with each other as if constituting a unity, but in fact living up principally to the main maxim of contingency: 'Things. Things are going to happen.' Words and images fall away constantly, while the words partially, sometimes misleadingly, connect with the spoken part. The voice itself can be subject to alteration, for example, through a vocoder for the phrase 'cross my heart, hope to die', and for that reason, this piece is not looking to Hill's voice as a reflection on embodiment or the performance of the artist's own involvement. It seems more like an acted voice, a vocal role, such that the voice becomes one element among many, just one thing that happened to be used. This objectification of his own voice had been developed in *Soundings* (1978), and simple though the piece is, it develops an interesting line on the status of the voice, and of speech – as these become separate.

In the works considered above, the voice plays a pivotal role in situating artist and viewer as embodied auditors. The voice is strongly identified with Hill while also operating as an uncanny vocal operator, speaking in musical rhythms (explicitly summoning 1960s musical minimalism as a resource), flatly, and with little purpose other than to communicate a sense of 'hereness' to varying degrees. In *Soundings*, the visual focus is on a loudspeaker, which is spun, burned, covered in sand or water, pierced with a large nail, while we hear Hill's voice referring to itself as 'mine'/his ('my voice', 'the skin of myself', 'where I voice from'). The voice is often distorted, processed or, as it submits to attack, lost, muffled and altered. Voice is rendered physical, paradoxically, through a proximity achieved from its removal from the bodily source (as Dyson discusses when addressing telegraphy, telephone and recording throughout *Sounding New Media*). Instead its object status is confirmed through its emergence from a machine ('where I voice from') in the form of the loudspeaker, in this piece, and not the hands that come into frame, nor the body of Gary Hill.

The speaker itself is both sound producer and receptor – is it just a transmitter? It is better, perhaps, to conceive of the speaker being 'mere transmitter', as telling us something about the supposedly authentic presence of a human voice, which in turn can only transmit in order to be heard or understood. In fact, the repetitive phrases suggest a speech that loses all meaning – becoming what Agamben thinks of as pure voice (*Language and Death*, 73).[7] For him, humans may have speech, but it emerges from animals' sense of voice in terminal vocalization – which achieves itself as voice at the point of death (45). The animal voice operates at other moments, but it is voice only – where voice is nothing but 'I am speaking', like a paradoxical Cartesianism (33). Humans take this and develop systems of thought or representation and imagine that voice is a carrier of self-conscious presence (Aristotle's *pneuma*) rather than a trace of voice as awareness of being and the possibility of non-being, and nothing else.[8] There are many potential problems with Agamben's imagined 'animal voice' – not least the idea that there is such a thing as 'the animal', but we can at least partially justify his view if we take 'the animal' as being that which is retrospectively constructed as the non-human, once humanity 'emerges' from animality. The key point is that within speech lies the trace of voice, which is individual to a physical animal, human or otherwise, and voice is what we have here in *Soundings*, a voice which merely exists, amid contingent events. Hill's hands, which drop sand, pour water or spin the speaker, are the development of technology, of culture – the hands speak and carry meaning. The voice is or is not, simply, in brute formlessness.

There is a continual tension between voice and speech through Hill's works, including, as we shall see, pieces where there is no vocal speech, such as the multiscreen *HanD HearD* (1995–96), where each image in the multiscreen installation shows the face of a person staring at one of his or her hands. The slowly moving images contain no voicing, but we are, I think, invited to see expression occurring – not in the form of sign language as such, but with the palm of the hand as the site of communication – the place where nature can transform into culture, non-language into language and touching into transforming. The title indicates an attentiveness, so that listening can *work*. Hill is careful to specify that silence can be a meaningful sonic intervention, as in *Tall Ships*, the 1992 installation made of large-screen projections of people advancing to the viewer, when activated by the presence of the latter. Here, Hill is explicit, 'even after I deleted the speaking, I considered the sounds important: I imagined filling the space with silence'.[9] The sound is there as an absence, part of the unsettlingness of the piece, where there is both welcome and potential for unexpected proximity. The removal of the sound trace makes the advancing figures less like a depiction of real people in a real multisensory world. Like all videotape recording, sound needs to be removed for there to be silence, so what is experienced is precisely the sense of something missing.

Sometimes text and sound can both overwhelm, and this is the condition of being we find in *Incidence of Catastrophe*, a visual reading of Blanchot's 'novel' where Hill particularly works through the section where the main character reads himself into a story about himself, echoing the protagonist's revelatory stumbles into worlds where language is the object. So in terms of literary influence, much of the early work inhabits a realm close to that of French *nouveau roman*, or late modernists like William Gaddis, but *Incidence of Catastrophe*, in making its excessive gloss on Blanchot, ventures into the more absurdist terrain of Jorge Luis Borges and the crossover between existentialist literature and literary theory. This knotting of avant-garde strands is why Quasha and Stein make a point of maintaining the French word *récit* for Hill's work – a category much favoured by Blanchot. This term conveys the idea of something being recited, where the 'what' is not perhaps the most important element. In Blanchot, the telling is also not of great importance – with the result that what remains is precisely that – the remains of literature – something close to the voice that underpins speech – or the place writing can go once freed by the words that fulfil their task in being read and thus being passed over, or surpassed. Ironically, one of the best ways of conveying this filling and emptying of language is to step back from the working or drive of *Incidence of Catastrophe* in order to track the non-narrative (or narrative that undoes itself) as a sort of progression, and, while navigating its 'facts', consider how it unravels and what role sounds play.

The piece begins with roaring waves, working away at a sandbar. This is not the epic destruction of a tsunami, nor is it the solo wave that can be dramatized in surfing. Rather, this is the relentless yet ever-changing tidal flow of water, altered by its encounter with the shifting sands, tugged by a distant force of gravity. The text of Blanchot's book begins to appear, as the loud sounds of the sea become muted and electronic sounds take a more prominent position. Sounds of paper being handled, turned or marked become louder. Not for the first time in Hill's work, the hand becomes part of sound, writing, reading and communication. The book too comes alive as a sounding object. The microphone is held very close, exaggerating small sounds and making them communicate rather than being audible only to those who would perhaps live as insects inside the book. The hands are not just adjuncts of the eyes, as, later when we see the central protagonist, played by Hill, reading, it seems also to be about the posture, the complete bodily involvement in the act. Or it is about the performance of reading, such that it is not a means to an end, or even a means in itself, but an endlessly altering, emanating process. The sounds go from natural to more processed, at every stage (even the sounds of the water on sand), making the process of recording, or reading, both audible and visible.

The book moves to the centre of activities, and it is loud, an object that dominates all around it, especially its reader. The text of the book and the sea combine in this opening five-minute sequence: the water sounds drop in and out, changing tone and presumed source, or distance from source, the text drifts in and out of readability, with the viewer's eyes grabbing words as we are moved above them. The water stays out of reach, unstoppable, forming a whole that is full of all possible details, thus offering an illusion of unity to its reader. This is the illusion that whacks into Hill at 5.10: text as ocean and ocean as culture. It is not that straightforward, because content or no, we could stop now if that was it, in a sort of mystical revelation. *Incidence of Catastrophe* and *Thomas the Obscure* both withhold such illumination. Instead, we have the sense that it may be there, as the thing withheld, that at the same time can overwhelm. So, instead, we should imagine the sea and the text as washing over each other, colliding with and eroding one another, only to form new shapes, which in turn are fated to disappear, re-form in or from formlessness (figure 4.1).

FIGURE 4.1 *Gary Hill,* Incidence of Catastrophe *(1987–88). Video (colour, stereo sound). U-matic; forty-three minutes fifty-one seconds. Image courtesy of the artist.*

In the build-up to seeing Hill, we see fingers on the book, but also feet in water – is it a sign of evolution? A reference to Bataille's idea that the big toe is the fulcrum between nature and culture and therefore must remain hidden?[10] At the very least, it must be a take on the attempt to understand, to process, through the body, through touch – which mirrors that of the fingers on the book. Hill initially plunges into (shallow) water, only then to be hit by the roil. After this, he can stand back to try to assess the text of the sea. This will prove as awkward as the attempts of the microphone to read the text up close result in bashing sounds, also in this opening 'scene'.

Undeterred, the protagonist continues to meld with the book, and now it is through dryness he struggles – dry twigs as he struggles through dark woods, the crisp flicking of pages, while in the distance, electronic sounds and water provide a backdrop – a space of aural memory. The images of running in the wood could be seen as a dream, a mental image summoned by the text, or the text itself, but that would be a hasty separation of real from non-real: the text, the woods, the sea, the protagonist, the camera, the book and the fingers that personify reading in the piece so much more than eyes, all these phenomena merge in communication with one another, there can be no precedence and this is indicated precisely, and in complex fashion, in the interplay of sound and image. This dry phase brings the protagonist to the outside of the shed, seemingly exhausted, with the camera viewing him from inside the building, to a form of 'nature ambience'. Then we/he/

the book move inside, where Hill arises from bed to be seated in front of the book, to be booted out of linear time into an accelerated jump format, as he is seen in time-lapse, hunched over the text. Both flicker. In the lead-up to this, the pages turn by themselves while ever-louder processed recordings and water sounds fill the aural interior of the building (as mind, as true content, as memory?). This all stops when Hill cuts himself and examines his bloody finger.

There then follows a three-minute, three-part section dominated by audio. In the first part, the protagonist runs towards us/the camera, held up at each move, as the loop of him running moves forward, but partially recursively. We hear the sound of an unnaturally strong echo of his shoes – at a literal level, this just indicates a studio, or inside, but this breaking of the illusion of real sound actually signifies a space outside of normal space. Hill's character seems to be in a state of panic here: he is both running towards and away (i.e. in the spiralled loop). This sequence ends with a shot of a stylus caught, and so repeatedly clicking, in the groove of a vinyl record. So what we hear is the sound of reading, rather than content. The camera then pans around a room where the protagonist reads the text. From here, we begin to see objects being brought along a corridor, loudly dragged. Hill sits down to read, exhaling audibly. The ensuing dinner scene, with its dialogue moving in and out of phase, seems to be shown as content, but this will be disrupted as he arrives in the room, greeted as an unwanted intruder who has unexpectedly displaced one of the company. Once he has been asked 'have you swum today', the company stops its conversations, many of which seem to be recounting the experience of the protagonist. After some time, the individuals speak brief phrases or words, out of synch, slowed down or otherwise distorted, alternating with shots of the waves eating at sand. The party closes with Hill's character stumbling backward and pulling off the contents of the table, only for him to be washed over by superimposed waves once more. One sentence stands out, said three times by a dinner guest: 'inundated with sight and sound'. In this film, where the borders collapse between image and real, metaphor and that which would be metaphorized, such a thing is possible. It is more likely, I suspect, that the inundation comes from the text – as source of citation and source of imagery both audible and visible. The inundation occurs precisely in the absence of 'sublime' content – the sensation emerges from the fullest of language, which is only language, but also language as all, as the ocean and woods.

From here on, the video takes a sacrificial, or even an abject, tone – a period of obscure ceremonial and disjointed activity in the post–dinner party room, including a female corpse on a table, takes place amid the clattering drag of porcelain. A book sits on the dead woman's back, its pages flicking. The scene ends with a reprise of the dramatic removal of the table's cover, and as he falls, Hill plunges into deep water, and the sounds of water fill the piece – the text as ocean and vice-versa again, a literal rendering of the inundation mentioned at the dinner. This must not be taken as any kind of baptism – it is at once too perverse, too primordial and too textual. It is an always-already of immersion into some other state. This is emphasized as shots of the protagonist in water alternate with shots of him tossing and turning on a bed. Maybe it is a dream, but it is one that makes the bedbound version retch as if he has inhaled significant amounts of water. Boundaries become increasingly irrelevant, compared to the movement in or out of water and texts – emergence and immergence. As Hill's character runs water into the sink, water covers the pages of the book (to the sound of processed recording of water), sounding somewhat percussive, like a ferry churning water as it passes. One final retch – abject emergence – brings us to the painful last section where Hill, having been washed up by the tide (water roars across sand), lies on a floor, naked and talking some kind of pure (i.e. nonsensical) language, for which the sound and mouth are out of synch, while the walls give way to huge claustrophobic pages of the text. The passage of the pages of the book emits a deep rumbling sound, not that different to the deep water sounds (that return once more over the closing credits). Barriers may have gone, or at least ceased to have meaning as barriers, but resolution or realization on the part of the protagonist is withheld. That he is being poked with a stick for much of this closing section indicates a search for meaning, prodding him to tell us what he has seen, or heard. But all we have is his failure to respond, his failure to become one with the text and sea. Perhaps he has become none.

Hill's interest is not only in sound but in how it combines, drives, assists, betrays, reveals and covers the transmissions of language and the meaning of language as well as meaning within language. The voice is something that seems to slip outside, and Hill realizes this in video work that is both audio and visual, mirroring the play of rival media in human communication and how they require each other while being specifically not the same as one another. The unique place his work from the 1970s to the 1980s occupies is due to its explicit working-through of problems that have emerged in modern and late modern writing and theory, predominantly as explored by French writers. In so doing, Hill scratches at the idea that video is an empty medium whose role is transmission of meaning, and also moves on from the criticism that video is a 'post-medium' without reflexive formal capacities, and the answer, as is mostly the case, lies in the status of video as intermedia.

Notes

1   Jacques Derrida, *Of Grammatology* (Baltimore, MD: Johns Hopkins Press, 1976 [1967]). Translated by Gayatri Chakravorty Spivak.

2   Maurice Blanchot, *Thomas the Obscure* (Barrytown, NY: Station Hill Press, 1988). Originally written in 1941, first translated into English in 1973, by Robert Lamberton.

3   Yvonne Spielmann explores the connection Hill makes between electronic and verbal language and linguistics in *Video: The Reflexive Medium*, 108–9.

4   Stephen Sarazzin, 'Surfing the Medium', in Robert C. Morgan (ed.), *Gary Hill* (Baltimore, MD and London: Johns Hopkins University Press, 2000), 62–90.

5   Jacinto Lageira, 'The Image of the World in the Body of the Text', in Morgan (ed.), *Gary Hill*, 27–55. Frances Dyson writes of Western thinking's tendency to silence the voice, removing its sonorous qualities while attributing to it the capacity to be the site of thinking, or of presence. See Dyson, *Sounding New Media: Immersion and Embodiment in the Arts and Culture* (Berkeley and Los Angeles: University of California Press, 2009), and 20–2 in particular. Hill's work and numerous commentaries on it would seem to offer an art-based theoretical response to this aptly identified problem.

6   George Quasha and Charles Stein, *An Art of Limina: Gary Hill's Works and Writings* (Barcelona: Ediciones Poligrafa, 2009).

7   Giorgio Agamben, *Language and Death: The Place of Negativity* (Minneapolis, MN: University of Minnesota Press, 1991 [1982]).

8   For a reading of tape as an oddly living, breathing example of technology with *pneuma*, see Paul Hegarty 'Hallucinatory Life of Tape', *Culturemachine* 9 (2007); available at http://www.culturemachine.net/index.php/cm/article/viewArticle/82/67.

9   Gary Hill, in Regina Cornwell, 'Gary Hill: An Interview', in Morgan (ed.), *Gary Hill*, 224–31 (225).

10   Georges Bataille, 'The Big Toe', in *Visions of Excess: Selected Writings, 1927–1939*, ed. and trans. Allan Stoekl (Minneapolis, MN: University of Minnesota Press, 1985), 20–3.

CHAPTER FIVE

Bill Viola, Elemental Ambience

In large dark rooms, figures slowly express emotions, dissolve into water, rise into the air, burst into flames or simply vanish; bright, crisp images emerge from series of screens that seek to enfold the viewer. Such are the works (like the 'Passions' series from the early 2000s) for which Bill Viola has become renowned. Increasingly detailed and high in definition, these works attempt to summon a sort of sacred, a symbolic interaction and a sublime sentiment. While not all would agree that this is achieved, the ambition cannot be denied, and neither can the consistent application of a focussed, deep and purposeful aesthetic. The lavish images have somewhat obscured the sound component, which for Viola is essential to encourage immersion in the pieces.

Viola started out as an artist who was very much interested in the possibilities of sound as an artistic (as opposed to musical) medium. Bruce Nauman and Gary Hill both made sound sculptures early in their careers, and Viola further joins Nauman in having exhibited sound-based works as architectural experiments. Foremost among these early experiments by Viola may be *Hallway Nodes* from 1973. In this work, the visitor to the installation pushes through thick plastic door hangings and into a space that is solid with vibrations from two large speakers pulsing out sounds at the very low frequency of 50 Hz. The viewer has little to see, the listener has nearly as little to do, because it is your entire body that will be doing the hearing. The visitor enters a sculpted soundspace, and the sound goes through the body, such that we can begin to apprehend sound as something physical (vibration) and as something felt as physical in effect (vibrating body). The experience is both soothing and troubling, and ultimately disorienting when leaving the short corridor. Part of the piece is about learning, about being able to think sound other than processing it as something understood and listened to (*entendu* as French has it).[1] The piece itself overcomes any split between mind and body as the learning occurs in both at the same time, leading to a questioning of how separate or how hierarchically related those things might actually be. This comes from the two speakers resonating in an enclosed space.

It is through sound that Viola develops his sense of art as something that could communicate something of what lies beyond the everyday, whether something spiritual, physical or emotional. One of these sonic tests took the form of the sonic exploration of cathedrals and churches in Florence (also in the early 1970s), where, he says, 'sound seemed to carry so much of the feeling of the ineffable' (Viola, 'In Response to Questions from Jörg Zutter', 241).[2] This capacity of sound to spatialize something like the sacred, to bring it into space and use space as a medium for it, is something Viola persists with to this day. The visitor to an installation is called on to become involved through several senses, but listening remains a key – even with the high-resolution images of recent works – because listening, or more accurately, being ready to hear, separately to understanding, is more central a sense to escaping rational processing of the material world than vision. Without wishing to repeat the simplistic idea that sound surrounds us and that we cannot close our ears, humans certainly spatialize through sound, that is, they have developed processing strategies to hear sound as spatial, to locate both it and ourselves. We are more bat than we think.

Viola also cites his experience of working with David Tudor on his flexible piece *Rainforest* in 1973, in which a host of objects resound, partly acoustically, partly electronically, according to random capabilities of material and actions. There are, of course, parameters, and the task of the musician improvising with natural or 'non-musical' stuff is to set borders within, around or through which a piece can occur. Viola attributes a key role to field recording, which 'forever changed my awareness of sound as a dynamic lifeforce' (Viola, 'David Tudor: The Delicate Art of Falling', 53).[3] Furthermore, Viola began to notice the similarities between the random functioning of technology and the seemingly chaotic sounds of nature: 'the world inside of electronic circuits and the world outside in the forests and rivers were revealing their common forms and underlying principles' ('David Tudor', 52). These origin stories are interesting, but not to be taken uncritically – in Viola's case, he has always made a point of sound's importance and was directly involved in a world where sound art and music sought to reach beyond the constraints of those categories. On the other hand, this cosmic significance that is lying in wait to be discovered is a disavowal of precisely how his training 'allows' this sound to emerge *for him*, and then attribute it to a characteristic of both nature and human culture.

While Viola's use of sound is consistent, it is far from unchanging – the pummelling of *Hallway Nodes* is largely replaced in recent works by medium volume ambience. Early pieces continue to employ sound as force. This alters as sound becomes part of a multisensorial environment. One thing that is a constant is that the sound element is nearly always from the same source as the image ('I do not consider sound as separate from image', he writes, in 'Statements 1985' [151]),[4] and if one is slowed down (as often happens), so is the other. In fact, the usual hierarchy of sound and image has to be totally reversed if we believe Viola's own claims, as he says that 'I began to use my camera as a microphone' ('In Response', 242). For him, this meant that the camera would not be restricted to a single point of view or vision, but be open to all that was occurring around. The visual becomes sound and, presumably then, would be at least partially led by sound, by multidirectional sensory experience. The camera then takes on a mystical capacity of its own, as it stretches beyond its initial function to capture something of a reality higher than merely what would be put in front of it, as chance opens up the field of view.

One such chance was the discovery of the way that water reflected images, thereby expanding the notion of what can work as a screen; in *He Weeps for You* (1976), a tap drips steadily, and a camera films the drop; the viewer is caught on the surface of the pendulous water and becomes part of the projected wall image. We could be distracted into thinking about this piece as a reflection on viewing, or the functioning of video, but Viola is presumably more interested in something more mystical, hence the title, which to my mind signals the Christian religion's martyred god, Jesus, his suffering on behalf of humanity, his sorrow for their fall and so on. Certainly, the title is an expression of pity, so how does this relate to the viewer (who is the addressee, as the viewer becomes the 'you' through being incorporated into the piece)? Does it connect to another Christian eye message – 'there are none so blind as those who will not see'?[5] In which case, Viola extols us to see the world to lessen some sort of pain at not being seen.

Given Viola's generalized rather than sectarian mysticism, it would be more likely for him to consider nature as that which consoles, and thereby encouraging a return consolation in the form of the viewer's attention. But the drop is not just to be seen, whatever its message or its 'affect', but also to be heard, as it drops its water onto a microphone pad, which then projects the sound through amplification. Partly, Viola has already told us the answer: you cannot switch the sound of the world off, anymore than you can definitively close your eyes to its sight. Either would be a renunciation of humanity as something located (or evolved) within the world, not separate from or above it. The volume of the resonating thud of the water is consonant with the magnification of the image of the end of the tap, the water and the reflected image of the viewer. The interaction, though, on the other hand, is limited to the play of seeing and being seen in the visual image. Instead, the room is what Viola terms a 'tuned space' ('He Weeps for You', 42).[6] The room becomes a sort of container, with sound guiding the visitor to become a proper viewer (self-reflective), and a proper auditor (self-reflective), so the sound does not fade, but completes the loop between person, room and elements within the room.

We can see and hear the development of Viola's holistic worldview in his relatively difficult work *Anthem* (1983). Those accustomed to the more celebratory ecstatic videos of the last twenty years will perhaps wonder at the neutral portrayal of industry going about its business, interspersed with shots of nature (early on), medical operations (past the middle of the piece) and a girl waiting and then screaming in Union Station, Los Angeles. Gradually more shots of detritus and dereliction emerge, as the film tracks a movement similar to the 1982 film *Koyaanisqatsi* (directed by Godfrey Reggio, soundtrack by Philip Glass). However, the path to potential destruction is less obvious in Viola's piece, unless we consider operations and body scans (uterine, brain) to be something unnatural and undesirable. Viola's work has a didactic element, but he is content in *Anthem* to posit only an ambiguous critique. Scenes of everyday American life pass by, industry carries on its activity night and day and this is certainly no utopia. The opening shot of the flag of the United States waving in slow motion in front of full-block buildings already says as much. Although Viola will later go on to use slow motion to connote seriousness or otherwise unremarked truths about humanity, nature and the universe, in *Anthem*, its use is an implicit critique of contemporary society. Instead of a song-based anthem, we hear a wordless scream slowed down, played back at various frequencies, only at one moment playing at recognizable human pitch. First, we have a scream instead of a celebration, so the obvious yet appropriate reaction is to see this as a complaint, an expression of pain. But the slowing down alters this entirely – it becomes more meditative, and the sound often suggests other mammal life forms – whales, seals, wolves and dogs. It thus seems a richer communicative act, and a way of humanity re-establishing its place as part of the natural world as opposed to (what we take to be) its current alienation.

The sound of the girl's scream, mutating across species, levels, pitches and durations, is an assertion of humanity's physical condition – and part of this is to live within the current industrialized society, as shown in the technical interventions on the human body that are also shown. These are not shown as triumphs but expressions of fragility – a body cavity held open to reveal a beating heart, an eye stretched to be treated and so on. The scream is not one of rage but the vindication of what it means to inhabit material, yet soft, temporal, bodies. On several occasions in the first eight minutes of the video, we see the girl whose screams we already hear, visually slowed down, preparing to make her sound. Only then, for the last three minutes, do we see her open her mouth to produce sound. Certainly, the sound and sight of someone screaming in a cavernous space does not signal contentment, but as we hear and watch the precise strategies adopted by Viola in how sound and sight combine (e.g. we never hear the machinery, traffic or crowd hubbub that would signal an overload of urban industrial life), we are tempted to think 'machines + scream = howl against society's woes'.

A similar, suggestive narrative technique underpins one of Viola's major works, *The Passing*, from 1991. Featuring pictures of himself, his then young child and his dying mother, this is a very personal, yet symbolic approach. The liminal states are conveyed principally through the appearance and sound of water and the sound of breathing. The slowing down of sound and image conveys the gravity of the subject matter, clearly connoting significance, meaning and profundity. In slowing down the 'action', not only are the viewers given more time to reflect on specific images, as well as on the development of the piece, they are also given a personal take on the meaning of things that is designed to supersede one individual's concerns. In other words, Viola's elemental symbolism is carried by the vehicle of slow motion, in order to attempt a type of universality. Unfortunately, this does also mean that his work can come across as clichéd, too beautiful or even reductive of the epic themes he wishes to cover, as the visual detail overwhelms a potential experience of the sublime in favour of an enraptured consumption.[7] *The Passing* presents us with three stages of life, along with much underwater imagery of immersion. Viola's mostly sleeping face is shown periodically in close-up, with his breathing high up in the audio mix. This breathing supplies the organizing core of the audiovisual narrative – the point of view is actually auditive, as the breathing moves with the camera, whenever Viola is on screen, and persists after many of those shots. It is a video that on the surface recalls Hill's *Incidence of Catastrophe*, containing a central protagonist around whom events occur, possibly in some other dimension. Here, though, there seems to be a clear divide between screen-Viola's experience and those events, as screen-Viola captures events while sleeping or experiences something beyond a dream while in a gentle trance. Even real events are distanced in this way, if we take the example of the underwater camera that espies the child on the beach or running through the shallow edge of the sea, tentatively leaving its domain of water – but the piece as a whole closes with Viola shown laid out on the seabed, indicating that this is his realm, away from the other events.

Water sounds, slowed, punctuate the video, but instead of fragmenting the piece, these act as unifying forces, recalling the womb, the debt to the mother and to nature. Water also acts as medium for sounds (again, slowed down, merging with the sound of water itself) – the linking condition, then, is the liminal state of being in water, or being away from air – hence the importance of Viola's loud breathing (in contrast to his mother's visibly difficult breathing, and ultimate absence of breath) as a vital force of consciousness and even animality (as opposed to say commentating on what we see). The urban footage, however, is also mostly silent – connecting it to the shots of natural locations – so, unlike *Anthem*, this piece reflects on natural and urban environments as genuine human dwellings, bringing our focus back to the shots of what I take to be the mother's house.

Water cascades through Viola's oeuvre. Water features as a reflective medium not only in *He Weeps for You* and *Migration* (1976) but also in the more narrative *The Reflecting Pool* (1977–79). In the latter, a pond lies in woodland, occupying the bulk of the screen. Water sounds lap the ears, and after a minute, a man approaches the further edge of the pool and leaps, with a battle cry. Instead of falling, he simply stops, suspended in midair, above the pool, for about three minutes. In the meantime, the water continues unruffled. The lack of a break in the water is made visible by the smooth persistence of the soundtrack, drawing attention to the unchanging water. In fact the image track has separated off, and is a loop showing the unbroken reflection of overhead foliage, which is then disrupted by something that causes ripples to flow out across the pool (from under the man's suspended body). As he slowly fades, we see figures 'reflected' in the water while not being visible outside of it. A light crosses the water and then a naked man emerges and vanishes again, only to re-appear walking off into the wood. Something has occurred, but it remains enigmatic – but what we see are themes that will crop up amid torrents of water in later works: origins, reflection, illusion, rebirth, the spirit world and, above all, water as a border rather than an 'other'. The water might be complex in *The Reflecting Pool*, as it does not exist either as a discrete world or a reflection of this one, but it is neither threatening nor a synonym for death. Viola's water is not held apart from airbreather humans (figure 5.1).

FIGURE 5.1 *Bill Viola,* The Reflecting Pool *(1977–79). Videotape, colour, mono sound; seven minutes. Photo: Kira Perov. Image courtesy of Bill Viola Studio.*

Water flows less ambiguously in other works: in *Arc of Ascent* (1992), a man arises out of water (albeit a reversed image of a man diving), as seen again in much larger scale in *Five Angels for the Millennium* (2001); in *Emergence* (2002), a man arises in flows of water from within an altar; in *The Raft* (2004), a group of people is attacked by floods of water, and in *The Crossing* (1996), one screen shows a man who enters a wall of water and then disappears, while the other shows the same event set in flame. All of these works use water not as reflection but as carrier of meaning or as something that structures human experience. All occur in slow motion, and so the sound of water is deep and rich in many frequencies – and more a bringer of calm rather than terminal danger – danger and/or death is present but surpassed, in these audiovisual ambient stories.

If we take *The Raft* first, then water appears as intrusive border, with the capacity to cross a membrane we did not notice to be already present (i.e. the border marking the absence of air). A line of ordinarily dressed people is shown in a slowly moving tableau, filling most of the screen horizontally, while not forming a physically deep group. A sense that this piece comments on Géricault's *Raft of the Medusa* (1819), itself already a visual allegory of the vices and decrepitude of society, will provide the feeling, at least, that this group seems 'representative', or better still, reflects society in its various categories, or even humanity as a whole. From both left and right, jets of water drive the group closer together as they stumble under the force of liquid. Society collapses, and even as the waters disappear, the sense of survival is now altered by the knowledge of the fragility of social unity and purpose. Perhaps the water is a force of enlightenment, driving awareness through its exposure of the reality of 'the human condition'. Even as the water attacks, though, the sound is more soothing than overwhelming – the slowness taking away from empirical narration and making the water a symbolic or signifying element. The presence of so much sound shows that while water is some sort of outside that can cross into the inside of human living, it is also something that is everywhere, only temporarily withheld. Other possible, more political readings of the dousing of civil protest are undermined by the slow-motion sight and sound.

The various emergence pieces, where submersion is turned into protean immersion (on screen), play out dramas of entering and leaving worlds. Water has been used by the religions of many cultures to act as a rebirthing device – liquid is the 'other' dwelling element brought closer in ritual at key significant life events, and in this sense, water resembles blood. The human body is full of water, of course, and many of its parts are residues of earlier sea tetrapod living (including hearing through adapted gills). But mostly we want this liquid kept inside, functioning in some sort of internal exile, kept away as if it were other (in 2007, Viola actualizes this internal sea in *Ocean Without a Shore*, where water apparently floods from bodies on giant screens) (figure 5.2).

FIGURE 5.2 *Bill Viola,* Ocean Without a Shore *(2007). High-Definition video triptych, two 65" plasma screens, one 103" screen mounted vertically, six loudspeakers (three pairs stereo sound). Room dimensions variable installation view, Church of San Gallo, Venice Photo: Thierry Bal. Image courtesy of Bill Viola Studio.*

Viola's use of water is about all these varied human interactions with it, often all at once – this allatonceness being precisely the quality water and the sound of it in torrents that Viola wants to harness momentarily. *The Crossing* is the most complete of these liquid narratives. Both the fire and water panels suggest death, but also its overcoming through incorporation – so even immolation is to be understood here as immersion. A man approaches from afar, and as he does, he comes to sheets of cascading water (slowed visually and audibly). He steps into this waterfall, which increases in force, shielding, enfolding and imbuing him, until, as the water slows, he is gone. The 'crossing' seems to be a crossing into another world – the spirit world after death (more explicitly in the parallel fiery process), but instead of a dead body, there is none. The body has changed substance, becoming one with the respective elements. So rather than see the walk to fire or water as earthbound life, and the torrent as the passage into death, we should see (and hear) the sheets of water or the engulfing flames as life – life as a consuming, passing place where all and any narrative is possible. In more religious mode, maybe we can see and hear the soul approaching the water or fire to be embodied and dwelt in a while before heading off to a *bardo* or some such holding area. Lisa Jaye Young writes of how Viola combines body and soul, as 'he presents his viewer with a visual reference to the body and spirit as a fusion of two states of consciousness' ('The Elemental Sublime', 69), although I would add that this is a fusion that is an ongoing process in Viola's way of showing us passages, liminality, as opposed to final resolution.[8] Young notes a further fusion between what is being shown and the state of mind of the viewer, through 'images that conjure up the nascence of visual perception' (70), and to this we should, of course, add the onset of audition.

Water is transition, an endless movement. In this it is no different to any chemical phenomenon, but what it carries for humans is the possibility of rendering this movement visible and audible, as Viola does. It does not just mark transition, but also dwelling, because of its volume, and the way it fills screens and speakers with such a wide range of sounds. The noise of water thus becomes something calming, that can bathe the human, and so works at least as much like a sensory deprivation tank as a womb – letting the conscious mind drift towards a lost amnion, one version of which would be the physical womb.

Douglas Kahn writes of a change in the use of water from being a thing signified (in classical music of many eras) to being a thing present in the music of John Cage and Fluxus exponents such as George Brecht. Kahn identifies the former as 'discursive water' (*Noise Water Meat*, 246).[9] Viola's water is certainly part of a story being told, but it is actual water that is being mobilized for suggestive narrative. This water is then transformed into sound material, where the sound can be part of what is very composed audiovisual work, without itself becoming music – so, as with many video artists, we cannot say that Viola's works have a mere soundtrack, as the sound is more *integral* to the way in which the pieces are designed. In fact, with Viola we have to consider the opposite direction of influence, partly through his own background and early work, but more directly we can look at the work he provides for Nine Inch Nails on their 2000 'Fragility' tour (*And All That Could Have Been* DVD), where sound is the explicit source of the visual construction.

Viola provided three pieces which acted as backdrop for one section of the concerts on tour. While the combination of Nine Inch Nails' industrial rock and Viola's more tranquil sublimity might seem odd, it is for a sequence of tracks that are the most reflective: 'La Mer', 'The Great Below' and 'The Mark Has Been Made' – the titles alone suggesting the possibility of a connection with Viola's water-based liminal spaces. Viola himself talks about the 'eye of the storm' in the concert, and how this section, helped considerably by his videos, provides a counterpoint to the crunching power angst of the band in the rest of the performance.[10] Three screens transform from light sources into screens, and track paths across rippling water, a female figure moving in them ('La Mer'). For 'The Great Below', Viola continues to parallel the lyrics, starting out with craggy islands sat in a still sea, which then begins to move into a rolling wave. As Trent Reznor declaims 'I descend from grace', we see an upside-down suspended man rise and burst water into a slow-moving explosion. 'The Mark Has Been Made' begins to raise the intensity further, and once again Viola maps the trajectory of the song into images, as we move from greenish water (there are many changes of colour across the three videos) to a distant fire, which gives way to fiery sparks as the camera descends into the fire. As the band launch into the more anthemic 'Wish', the screens simply cut out to be replaced by multiple light bursts. It is clear from Viola's comments that he felt a kinship with the music and, visually, it is equally clear that he took a very literal approach and sought to *visualize* the songs. In turn, the videos impose a tight discipline on the performing group for the near twenty-minute section, so Viola is not totally the submissive partner here. What is interesting is that Viola's literalness in sticking to the words of the songs and musical development actually illustrates the possibility of separating away from the literal – that is, we do not have to hear the sound of powerful water events, but can abstract them retrospectively into the sounds produced by composed songs played on instruments.

Water and sound intertwine continually in Viola, the one emerging from the other, working in a spiral of suggestive empathy for the viewer/listener to commune with the piece as a sensory expression of a timeless or ahistorical human condition. Viola abstracts sound, without making it acousmatic – it retains the trace of itself even as it alters (e.g. in slowing down, or changing pitch), gesturing towards the functioning of the work as a whole.[11] Where Hill has sound, voice and visual parts as expressly separate yet linked, Viola conceives of a more holistic sensorium for his video art (an approach that recurs with Pipilotti Rist).

Notes

1   F.J. Bonnet hints at this idea, but essentially favours the popular yet somewhat limited phenomenology of Merleau-Ponty, in his essay 'Noyade phénoménologique (Notes à propos de *Hallway Nodes* de Bill Viola)'; available at http://www.vibrofiles.com/essays_françois_bonnet02php (accessed 15th August 2013).

2   Bill Viola, 'In Response to Questions from Jörg Zutter', in Viola, *Reasons for Knocking at an Empty House: Writings, 1973–1994* (London: Thames and Hudson, 1995), 239–52.

3   Bill Viola, 'David Tudor: The Delicate Art of Falling', *Leonardo Music Journal* 14 (2004), 48–56.

4   'Statements 1985', in Viola, *Reasons for Knocking*, 149–52.

5   The proverb is attributed to John Heywood, published in 1546, and refers back to Jeremiah 5:21, in the Christian Bible, which also refers to not hearing properly.

6   'He Weeps for You', in Viola, *Reasons for Knocking*, 42–3.

7   These suspicions are outlined by Chris Keith, 'Image after Image: The Video Art of Bill Viola', *PAJ: A Journal of Performance and Art* 20 (2) (May 1998), 1–16.

8   Lisa Jaye Young, 'The Elemental Sublime: Bill Viola, *Fire Water Breath*', *Performing Arts Journal* 19(3) (1997), 65–71.

9   Douglas Kahn, *Noise Water Meat: A History of Sound in the Arts* (Cambridge, MA: MIT Press, 1999).

10   For Viola's assessment of what he tried to achieve in these videos, see his commentary piece on Nine Inch Nails, *And All That Could Have Been* (2002), DVD 2.

11   Pierre Schaeffer coined the term 'acousmatic' to refer to sound that was isolated from its origin, i.e. the source would be hard to identify – see his *A la recherche d'une musique concrète* (Paris: Le Seuil, 1952).

CHAPTER SIX

Dan Graham, Stan Douglas, Laurie Anderson, Dara Birnbaum: Performing Musically

While many video artists, or those who use video, have a strong interest in music, and cite the significance of aspects of music in defining their practice, video art was reticent in treating music as material. Music tends to bring the piece into the realm of cinema, the world where sound is an expectation, not an event, so I would claim that that is why video is much more interested in sound, or the sound of music being made or being nearby (as in Nam June Paik's solo work and collaborations with Charlotte Moorman). We might also imagine that the proper musicality of video is withheld or restrained by the presence of music itself. With the advent of regularized transmission of music videos to promote individual songs in the 1980s, occasional use of creative visuals to accompany music became a sort of industry standard and allowed many possibilities for avant-garde exploration of the connection between sound and music, as well as more literal visualizations of song lyrics and themes. Later, this would return to the terrain of video art, as if a level of security is reached whereby the music can be part of a work rather than overdetermining it or becoming a mere soundtrack. Increasingly, music acquires presence within the operation of video art, and I argue that exclusion as a matter of principle would be as limiting as the idea of restricting sound art to being only an audio phenomenon. Perhaps perversely, I am going to start this chapter that concentrates on the 'appearance' of music in video works, with precisely such an exclusion, in the shape of Dan Graham's mirror and video works of the 1970s.

The mirror works are a curious and wilful distortion or swerve of Graham's strong interest in musical performance, ranging from the minimalism of Steve Reich or Terry Riley to hardcore punk, an interest which returns in full in *Rock My Religion* (1982–84). Graham set up various installations that would enforce performative interaction on the viewer, ideally situating the viewer strongly in place, aware of his or her status as observer and the observed, and explicitly 'parallel to the time-delays that Terry Riley and then, later, Steve Reich, were doing in music'.[1] Is it just an accident, or parochialism, that makes the first generation of artists working with video cite minimalist music so often? Maybe the loop, or the cycling of gradual change that seems to require a different kind of presence for listening tells us something about video as a format. As I suspect that today's video artists are not so focussed on minimalist music, we would most likely have to lump the two art forms together as part of some sort of epistemological moment, with just the one surplus idea that minimalist music is more akin to 'post-minimalist' art, that is, less dependent on a didactic phenomenology than minimalist sculpture.

Graham's early video works would not just be about seeing but would also work on 'the idea of *physiological* presence ... [a] work about the perceptual process itself'.[2] In *Present Continuous Past(s)* (1974), Graham sets up a sequence of delayed reflections, using mirrored walls, two video cameras and feedback between the cameras. Delays of eight seconds create a hiatus in time as you peer into you as part of the past, seeing the various presents slide into the past but maintained as present, as if viewing from a future a few seconds ahead. In *Public Space/Two Audiences* (1976), two groups are separated by glass, with one wall mirrored to reflect back both. Although each group can see the other, the instructions specify that 'each audience sees the other's behavior, but is isolated from their aural behavior'.[3] The mirrors and glass in these and other works locate spectators as something less than present, as they are not in control of their visions. As Birgit Pelzer writes,

> the video works juxtapose both perspective and its simulated subversion to a positional system in which it is impossible to determine distances by any infinite measure, as well as to a topological system in which all structural elements are subjected to continual deformation. ('Vision as Process', 47)

Vision is heightened at the expense of the subject: 'the eye is stripped of the presence which constitutes it in order to return to a preexistent vision which submits it to sight well before all visual centering' ('Vision as Process', 51). This still does not explain the need for silence, or silent functioning of the pieces, other than the participant spectators. First, sound would introduce too much noise where delays and feedback are involved. This would in turn make the purpose too easy to perceive and remove the initial period of disorientated defamiliarization. Anyone visiting these pieces will be making plenty of sounds and it is their full physical occupation of the space that completes the piece. Paradoxically, this is what brings the works close to the concert experience. But the concentration on vision as the only sense involved in presencing means that Graham and Pelzer, after him, have transformed the now-decentred spectator into nothing more than a giant eye, with the physical thereness transformed into looking at 'being-thereness'. This in turn means that for all the conceptual work the spectator is supposed to produce, it is only within a circuit of a visual economy of presence that it works. Maybe that is the world we actually live in, but it is a necessary blind spot in this hypervisualization designed to end controlling visions of controlled vistas.

The instructions for *Public Space/Two Audiences* suggest that Graham was onto this idea and significantly directs the removal of the capacity to hear the other group. The word 'audience' shows that this is not just about two groups of viewers, but groups specifically arranged for hearing, only to have it removed. They are also driven to concentrate on their own 'audience' (they are locked in for thirty minutes). In reducing the capacity of an audience to hear, they become less of an audience, but also more of a group – just as in the mirrored audiences for Graham's performance *Performance/Audience/Mirror* (1977). While these perversely reflecting works position viewers as joint constructors of work, pre-empting the idea of 'relational aesthetics' developed by Nicolas Bourriaud in his 1995 book of that title,[4] it is when Graham himself reflects on performance and audience as material, and brings music into video, that more developed ideas of perception through and around art objects and events arise.

Rock My Religion moves through time in ways that parallel the movements and images built in *Present Continuous Past(s)*, as music and its effects are tracked through time, but not in sequence, as a means of formally stating the ecstatic properties of music that are the stuff of the piece. The video announces its formal and content-based strategies early on, as hardcore punk band Black Flag cede to the story of Ann Lee, the founder of the shakers in the eighteenth century, in scrolling text, then in voiceover, as Sonic Youth play in the background. Multiple layers collide and cross into one another in a purposely jarring montage. At 2.34, one of the key figures of the piece, Patti Smith, appears for the first time. As Kodwo Eshun notes, Graham tries to build a story connecting radical movements by using the material 'it speculates about' (Eshun, *Rock My Religion*, 8) and replicates the formal fragmentation of early 1980s American punk (9, 12).[5] While Eshun recognizes that the story is told from a position that seeks to validate and ground hardcore more solidly (13–15), he regards the piece as a historical commentary, and that it is politically problematic. Eshun joins earlier critics (Dieter Lesage and Ina Wudtke, Benjamin Buchloh) in condemning the almost-exclusively white history that emerges from the video, as it entirely bypasses the period from the founding of the Shakers through to white rock 'n' rollers (4–6). Eshun writes that '*Rock My Religion*'s omissions of African American music could repel and attract in equal measure' and that 'its exclusions disqualify it as reliable history' (6). It is indeed odd for a video that seeks to cover the history of rock to omit black American music, especially as the normal critical narrative is of the wide-ranging and essential role black musics have taken in pushing popular musics forward. However, we should stop and think whether *Rock My Religion* actually tries to be such a history at all (despite Graham's claim that it is), and consider that it is instead a very specific reading of hardcore punk as something that recalls early Protestant movements in the combination of physically ecstatic reactions in public gatherings and a proto-Communist model of social organization. With hardcore punk as the focus of the video, then, the other elements become a knowing and purposely anachronistic and retrospective musing on where hardcore punk's purism comes from. That this tells us something very interesting about hardcore's relation or apparent lack of relation to black music is an unintended consequence perhaps, but it would be a wilful misreading of the piece as a whole that could identify this as a badly done and incomplete history that verges on racism.

Graham's interest in hardcore punk can be seen in the earlier documentary footage of Minor Threat's 1982 CBGB performance in *Minor Threat* (1982), small sections of which recur in *Rock My Religion*. In the latter, the ecstatic states of punk concerts are intercut with historic prints, footage of Shaker settlements and shots of Patti Smith and, later on, Jim Morrison, along with Native American ghost dances. Eshun identifies and closely tracks how these interrelate throughout, but his claim that punk is posited as transhistorical (Eshun, *Rock My Religion*, 13) is not matched by the situation of punk as the 'now' of this film. If anything, it is everything else in the film that floats transhistorically. Jim Morrison and, then, Patti Smith are presented as channelling the physical and excessive qualities of religious celebration (an idea much more convincingly applied by Paul Gilroy to Jimi Hendrix).[6] Smith is presented much more positively, not only as an archetypal Shaker out of time but also as the beginning of punk. Graham has certainly made some very selective leaps to position hardcore punk as resonant with earlier communal forms, and, in terms of content, the most curious thing is what it tells us about American punk as opposed to its British manifestations. While there can be no doubt that punk started with art performers like Iggy Pop, Suicide and Patti Smith, and that this all fell out of the late psychedelia of The Velvet Underground, The MC5 and so on, something happened to push punk further with the advent of the Sex Pistols and their fellow travellers and copyists, and that is the discarding of a heroic outsider position in favour of a more comic or even risible abjection. *Rock My Religion* unwittingly illustrates the unreconstructed heroism of American punk and its wish for a historical road trip of justification.

This heroic and shamanic quality is, however, undermined by Graham's cutting and overlays. Texts crop up and scroll slowly over single colour backgrounds, pieces of music, text and narration do not so much bleed into one another but scratch and scrub at each other. This and the particular style of the shots of punk gigs offer the best sense of visual and aural combining, and the beginning is a particularly strong if subtle statement of intent. Black Flag play silently on video, with out-of-synch music coming in, which then persists as the screen cuts to black. Punk is thus identified as being out of time, as breaking in to linear time. John Miller goes so far as to identify this with Walter Benjamin's *Jetztzeit*, a type of time summoned in the form of cracks or shards that disrupt 'monumental' time (Miller, 'Now Even the Pigs're Groovin', 129).[7] Sound and vision are going to slide past each other but accumulate in a way that suggests progress without becoming eschatological or homogeneous. The sliding away of sound from vision is an exact premonition of Graham's more formal argument that the essence of properly radical music is in ecstatic community. The same can be seen in the pauses in the *Minor Threat* video, where the crowd gathers into a coiled spring, ready to leap into moshing action.

In *Minor Threat*, Graham's camera is immersed in the concert to the point of being jarred into analogue glitching, resulting in bursts of colour and/or, on several occasions, what seems like a sound overload glitch. While the video is a very simple filming of one concert, even the simplicity is in tune with its subject matter, the musical performance as content and form, as Eshun points out in *Rock My Religion*. The low-grade and presumably deteriorated video is perfect for an aesthetic of do-it-yourself (DIY), of spontaneous and amateur production. I mean amateur in the sense of fan, because that is what Graham seeks here, to be part of the whirl and thump of this moshing bunch of mostly male, all white (as far as I can make out) colliding bodies. It takes a while to make out where Minor Threat actually are amid the dance-fight, and for long sections of the thirty-seven minutes, this remains the case. Ian Mackaye even has to beg for some room at one point, despite total immersion of band and public being the point. The band's music acts as a conduit for a community to come into being; the songs are its constitution and the lyrics, the defining philosophy. This is philosophy as practice – as occurring right now, physically present, with borders broken down in elective physical contact. It might surprise some that a concert consisting of an eruption of moshing at the beginning of each short song does not end in violence or injury, but that is because of the precise border rules that the crowd seems mostly to understand, having built them itself. Mackaye does on occasion check on the audience's well-being and gently admonishes them. Graham's camera is very much within the crowd (even if positioned higher up) and the definitional weaknesses of the video format help heighten the sense of immersion. Nonetheless, we do seem some characters emerge – mostly those who are close to stepping over the mark from communal activity into selfish individualistic takeovers (e.g. hogging the stage area). He also picks out individuals' faces, ensuring that we do not see the mass activity as the product of a mere mass, and in the rapid and blurred flow of movement, even brief attention to individuals is almost a move to portrait photography.

Once we have seen what *Minor Threat* does as a piece, I believe we have to take *Rock My Religion* as a work that seeks to connect hardcore's communality that is both left wing and ecstatic to other religious or quasi-religious moments in American history. The focus is firmly on hardcore punk as the thing that represents ecstatic possibility in the now of 1984, and this has to be remembered within the context of what would be a disappointing and weird rewriting of rock music, were this its prime purpose for viewer/listeners. We can also return these pieces to Graham's attempts to make participation the vital driver of the final form of the video/mirror pieces. This form is never in fact fully finalized, because the public comes and goes, and makes a scene for itself to inhabit, with the art seemingly a conduit for that. But Graham's mission is to make this art act as conduit, and therefore it is just as much about getting a public to react as, say, a painting. This mirrors the practice of hardcore concerts, which have to set the parameters (or permission) philosophically and through aesthetic form. This is not a critique of those moves as failures, but a Foucauldian reading where exposing the circuits of viewing does not remove us from power (of art or music institutions based on hierarchy) but recasts them, in ways that may well be more democratic, communal or enabling of physical release.

Where Graham attempts to open up connections through disjunctions internal to a piece, or in how a particular performance or track is played, Stan Douglas offers a more politically driven critique with similar methods. Again, a division is applied, but in a more significant fashion. This can be seen and heard in *Deux devises* (1982–83) and *Hors-champs* (1992). Both avail of modernism's defamiliarization technique of fragmentation and re-collaging, the former in a more obviously formally charged political way. In the former piece, a song by nineteenth-century composer Gounod plays, in crackly fashion, while a blank screen shows the English translations of the lyrics. In the second part, stills of Douglas' mouth and lower face accompany the song ('Preachin' Blues') by Robert Johnson, to which he mimes the lyrics. The installation is initially based on slides, with the sound being continuous. The piece divides into two, and each part is split into two. However, these divides are not the same as the first part consists of sound and text, and the second, sound and visual. But we are invited to read Douglas' mouth as accompanying text, as an echo of the first part. In other words, it is this that we read, while the lyrics and music pass by.

Part of the critique that structures this piece is the division of the art world into high and low, classical and popular and, by visual implication, black and white. For all the myriad advances and inventions made by black musicians in Western styles, let alone beyond those styles, canonical music history and musicology perpetuate the notion that Euro-white music is the canon, whatever the merits of 'other' musics and musicmakers. But that is only a first-level reading, for actually, what is happening is not just a facile juxtaposition of classical and blues, but one of presentation: Gounod's song floats immaterially, free of a visual bodily signifier (e.g. we could have seen someone playing or singing it), while Johnson's song is represented through the appearance of Douglas' own face. In this way, music of African American origin is rendered historical and material – it comes from a specific 'minority' history. Classical music has history, of course, but as the canon, it no longer needs to imagine itself in this way, and tends to conceive of itself ethereally as 'just music'. Douglas' miming face reminds us that all music is historical and cultural, not just music of black origin (otherwise there would be no value in juxtaposing the two different ways of showing the passage of the different tracks). The question of the highlighting of the historicity of black music does not limit it to being representative content, but it is a possible correction to a certain strand of modernism that would have sought to overcome difference in favour of 'the art itself'. This is the gist of Georges Lewis' argument in *A Power Stronger than Itself* and a key question posed in *Deux devises*, and also in *Hors-champs*, in which Lewis himself participates.[8]

The piece consists of two recordings of the same performance, with the two recordings playing on opposite sides of a two-sided screen. Lewis, Douglas Ewart, Kent Carter and Oliver Johnson play Albert Ayler's 1965 composition 'Spirits Rejoice', which borrows heavily from the French national anthem, 'La Marseillaise', written in the closing phases of the Revolution by Claude Joseph de Lisle Rouget. Their version slightly underplays this aspect, compared to Ayler's 1970s performance in the Fondation Maeght, St. Paul de Vence, in particular. The status of the anthem is to be a quotation, but is far from a simply musical reference. As Lewis points out, free jazz was much more widely received and commercially more viable in Paris than in US cities (*A Power Stronger than Itself*, 228). So, one entry-level idea is that this tune represents a mutual cultural encounter. A further one is the reclaiming of a revolutionary musical tradition. Neither Ayler nor this quartet fuels the anthem with the formal fury of Hendrix's 'Star-spangled Banner' at Woodstock. Despite its slightly jokily pompous feel, highlighting the nationalist hubris of all anthems, 'Spirits Rejoice' is a polite re-reading, when compared to free jazz's enormous capacity to re-interpret, as seen in John Coltrane's late bands' versions of jazz standards. So what we have is a refracted appropriation, rather than a critique.

The two recordings in *Hors-champs* offer very different perspectives on the performance. Where one 'side' is that of the professionalized focus on soloists and/or capturing where the supposedly main part of the music is happening, the other shows the peripheral activities of the band. This 'side' begins with laughing banter and shows a more relaxed image of exactly the same moments as in the first side. Players are often shown watching another perform a solo, exchanging a few words and having a rest. This second side diminishes two mythical views of free jazz, or even jazz in general – that it is the spontaneous expression of something, and that it is deadly serious for that reason. The song gets room to breathe visually, as we see the communal aspect of performance to the apparent detriment of what is deemed most important – the more complex lead lines, mostly. Thus, the second side emphasizes community as opposed to the solos, culminating in the three other players gathering to just watch Johnson's drum solo, and in the beginning of the lightly epiphanic band finale, where all four are in camera shot just before the only moment in 'side one', we see such a combination of all together. As with all group improvising music, the soloist emerges from the communal entity, and the latter returns as a unity after his work – and when this is in dissonant 'harmony' as in free jazz, this signals not the conservative return of the same but the maintenance of the other, of what Jean-Luc Nancy terms the 'inoperative community'.[9] This is highlighted in the visual, not by showing the group, but by contrasting the soloists with the non-soloists, with having both community and individual play as two sides of the same performance (figure 6.1).

Free jazz, as part of black American avant-gardism of the 1960s and early 1970s, has been closely associated with black power and cultural nationalism, and a radicalization of the civil rights movement into dissonance in art and culture.[10] The presence of black musicians in avant-garde settings of the time can be seen as a return of a repressed political in modernism, and a move to the postmodern, in terms of assertions of identity, for example, via negritude or returns to Africa. *Hors-champs* emphasizes the physical presence of the players, on black and white recordings, against backdrops rendered monochrome in turn, hinting at pre-1970 television. The presence of the group is heightened by seeing the players not playing – this shows that the music cannot be 'just music' or the simplistic modernist dream of

FIGURE 6.1 *Stan Douglas. Still from* Hors-champs *(1992), two-channel video installation with stereo sound, dimensions variable. Courtesy the artist and David Zwirner, New York/London.*

form alone. That one of the players, Carter, is white, is curious, especially as he features much more strongly in the 'second' side than the first, where he barely appears at all. The 'first' side, the more 'proper' recording, maintains that this is black music, more than the second side seeks to, thus pointing to a stress point in the assertion of black identity via black music – the risk of ghettoization. I would argue that *Hors-champs* surmounts the twin difficulties of pure formalism, on the one hand, and identity primacy, on the other, through its staging of duality. That staging, ironically or otherwise, ends up in affirming not postmodern refutations of modernism's limits, but of the black African American modernism present in free jazz and early Afrofuturism. This is because the piece works through form – it does this through the establishing of a set of dualities that undermine each other – and while this may sound to some like postmodern theory, it is not. It is theory as extension of modernism, or warping of it.

Artistic modernism is seen as dominated by the figure of Clement Greenberg and a troubling drive to purity that somehow threatened political motivation in the arts or claims of identity. In this caricature of the 'movement' and its apparent leader, we see not a suspicion of authority and order but a fear of experimentation as core value. Douglas' doubled video has no such qualm, and yet is capable of questioning the flattening of art into abstraction, into material with its material origin removed. This is done through the doubling, but also the diversion, of focus in doubling into the visual – there is only one 'soundtrack', even if the 'second' side has some chatting not present on the 'first', as the titles roll on the latter. It is also a doubled play with the late modernist object: first it is given sound – a loud, interfering and atonal sound. Then, instead of unity, it can only be understood through a combination of contrasting 'missions' on each side. Then it smoothes the low (as in low comedy) explosiveness of the performance into a sculptural object that is in the place of, instead of, an object. This is signalled in the title – it is what is outside, beyond the field, that defines what is inside, or, more accurately how inside and outside play on one another and how they differ (soloist/group; sound/vision; side one/side two; modernist/anti-modernist; identity/non-identity; community/individual; black/not black).

Laurie Anderson takes video further into performance, perhaps recalling the early experiments of Acconci, Nauman, Rosler and Abramović. Anderson is both a very established sound artist and someone who uses the then new technologies of the 1980s to expand the reach of multimedia performance – specifically, into the concert setting, and then into film, in her piece *Home of the Brave: A Film* (1986). In this work, she integrates her instrument making, technological play, video, computer animation, contemporary opera and gender play – especially via vocals. These latter had already featured in her 1981 hit single 'O Superman', surely the most commercially successful avant-garde song in terms of chart placement.

Anderson's voice shifts between male and female ranges (or what we take to be those gendered ranges) and between organic and machine, all via variations on a vocoder. Around the declaiming, chatting, singing or questioning voice(s), a concert band performs a sequence of tracks, against a backdrop of animations, computer-generated imagery and other visuals. Unlike many concerts that feature visuals heavily, Anderson succeeds, through very careful choreography, in making the various media interact on stage. In addition, the video pieces often refer to their own status – such as the use of 0 and 1 in on-screen graphics early on, which is followed by 'This Is the Picture', where the picture itself is at stake amid alternating white noise, computer commands and slogans. Video itself is brought onto the stage when it crosses between recorded material and a blank screen, which silhouettes performers, integrating them into screen flatness. Almost at the centre point of the film (c. forty-four minutes), Anderson dances in front of projected snow, allowing it to wrap around her, and immerse herself into screen-mediated reality – which is a substantial part of the lyrical concerns of the overall piece.

The world also serves as backdrop – percussions inspired by global music attempt a type of synergy that verges on over-eclecticism and dates the piece precisely to the discovery and incorporation of world music by leading Western musicians at the more interesting end of pop. The world lurks as an imaged presence that the audience is somehow called upon to read as political, even if this is done obliquely, via the suggestive critiques of Anderson herself, and William Burroughs. The world that is summoned as the new home of the brave beyond the American anthemic is a digitizing world of potential but also political and military risk – hence Anderson's continued attempt to subvert visual and vocal expectations through stage choreography, cyborg voicing and sounding.

Video forms part of *Home of the Brave*'s toolkit, but is also what unifies the spectacle into a multimedia whole (not intermedia, as video is). Generally, it is the sound within a gallery that creates a spatialized crossing between media and sensory perceptions. In this performance, it is the video part that works like this, grounding the sound as more than a sequence of tunes (sound itself is an important feature, beyond its musical use, and the mixing is very detailed). In the end, the piece, though, is the film, which, as the end credits announce, is 'written, directed and visuals by Laurie Anderson'. In other words, just like the 'pioneers' of video art, the performance is for the film – which is to be consumed, either on film, or ultimately, on video format in the home. Video itself integrates the use of video into a piece that can properly be thought of as multimedia. Where Douglas works in some detail on the form of the piece as its content, Anderson's formal play is at the level of format – the use of particular strategies or technologies sets up a structure where the medium becomes message in a way that sidesteps late modernist concerns with form. The pieces addressed above offer different perspectives on how video works inward into the form of music, and into music video as format. Each manages to establish a position on community as expressed via musical form and setting, and in each the visual element does not simply complement the audio and/or political parts, but intervenes in those to drive them forward.

These examples do little to exhaust the creative possibilities of music and video working together – and the 1980s saw a mass expansion in the format of the promotional music video, as MTV worked out that it was highly popular and cheap to flood its schedules with such programming, in turn driving the production, demand and expectation that singles that sought sales would have to be accompanied by a video, resulting in works that often reached creative levels that at least matched that of work done in video art. The video goes from being the accompaniment to being the main feature – even more so today with sites like YouTube. In one way, the dream of earlier, politicized video makers on a mission (particularly in the United States, Britain and Northern Europe) is realized through this burst of visual play, but, of course, in a much more consumerist fashion, with all kinds of problems (e.g. the difficulty of getting rap videos onto the dominant channel in its early days). Mostly, the place of the music video on TV or computer screen militates against its fully being part of video art's intermedial status – the music video simply becomes a category, like geometric painting, and it is more in its use, occasional location outside the TV, integration with other art forms or consecration in galleries that it re-acquaints itself with intermediality and the establishing of audiovisual and spatial crossing between outputs and senses.

Visual artists have exploited the format, though – we could single out Tony Oursler's collaborations with Sonic Youth and other New York-based artists,[11] or Julian Temple and Derek Jarman, without leaving the 1980s. Personally I think that the promotional music video raises many questions beyond the scope of installed video art, and it would be wrong to count videos made by established artists as somehow different to 'ordinary' videos. We should also note the use of audiovisual works by bands such as The Residents, Throbbing Gristle and Coil, and industrial music groups more generally, but they do not raise any specific question of how sound relates to visuals, as this relation is taken as a given in those contexts, and then worked upon. So, in mild contradiction to the preceding, I think we can pick out video that comments on the format of music video, especially if using found sounds and visuals, and as my exemplar, I turn to Dara Birnbaum, specifically, to two of her pieces – *Fire! Hendrix* (1982) and *Pop – Pop Video* (1980). In *Fire! Hendrix*, we hear the song 'Fire' played live, and played straight through, while the visual component/imagetrack is more busily edited. It cuts between highly mobile squared framings of a young woman watching a drive-through restaurant, and sipping at a glass of juice, and shots of people approaching, using or leaving an assortment of fast-food chains. It is shot as if it were an action film, but instead of the satisfying drama of dénouement, mundanity spreads through formalistic appropriation of drama, cutting against the sex focus of the song. Lyrics appear in subtitle form for most of the song, and, in my view, soften further the erotic charge of Hendrix's fiery guitar love. The piece ends with the slow dropping and breaking of the glass, which goes on fire, if not exactly pathetically, then at most in a pleading display of yearning.

The earlier *Pop – Pop Music* is an even more purposeful dismantling not only of music's relation to video but also of the viewing of television, as we flicker between images in a screen of simulation where all messages blur together or flatten into messageness.[12] The first part of the piece cuts between the drama series *General Hospital* and female speed skating. Both sound and visual parts are found materials, with Birnbaum's work consisting entirely of montage and framing. Like *Technology-Transformation*, the piece is set up to have a clear and developing visual and aural rhythm. The soundtrack moves from no wave-ish guitar into Donna Summer, via cuts from the sport commentary and also a few repeated lines from the drama, most notably 'He doesn't do anything he doesn't say anything', and also comments about being looked at, both from a central female character and a mostly silent male. We could fantasize a psychoanalytic feminism at play here, but even if this is what is going on, it is submerged within a more radical play of slicing into ways of viewing that would undermine such a clear-cut reading. In the second part, 'Kojak Wang', we see sequences from the TV series *Kojak* in cut-up form, again accumulating into a rhythmical collage. Shooting sequences cross in and out of dialogue and plays of masculinity as the trajectory of criminal towards realized failure plays over and over. These sections are interspersed with a woman pressing a button on a home computer, as laser beams fire into the machine. The final element in the collage, that is part two, is the shots of colour bars indicating a transmission breakdown. The whole is linked with blue computer screens with intertitles for the sections. TV, or more accurately, the domestic screen, is shown to be more complex than being a passive receiver of vision. The use of found materials suggests the potential for these images and sounds to already have been containing the explosive potential force revealed in the actualization of the cut-up, just as we may have read in Bryon Gysin and William Burroughs. *Pop – Pop Video* may indicate through its title that it is about music video, and how art and music come together in contemporary media, but it is not quite about music video. Instead, it is about what music video does – the enshrining of background, accompaniment, flow from one disconnected piece to another and forging of new and unexpected unities which may have commercial and popular success, but also contain untapped radicality to be revealed through reconfiguration. Where Graham, Douglas and Anderson sought to play with music as part of a multimedia event, becoming intermedia when located as video art, Birnbaum helps us complete the analysis through practice that video artists (such as Nam June Paik) did when reflecting on music's relation to recorded visuals.

Notes

1   Dan Graham, in Mark Francis, 'In Conversation with Dan Graham', in *Dan Graham* (London: Phaidon, 2001), 8–35 (15).

2   Cited in Benjamin Buchloh, 'Moments of History in the Work of Dan Graham', in Alex Kitnick (ed.), *Dan Graham* (Cambridge, MA: MIT Press, 2011), 1–20 (16). Graham is specifically referring to the input music has into his work.

3   Graham's instructions and diagram are cited in full in Birgit Pelzer, 'Vision in Process', in Kitnick (ed.), *Dan Graham*, 41–59 (44).

4   Nicolas Bourriaud, *Relational Aesthetics* (Dijon: Les Presses du réel, 2002). Translated by Simon Pleasance and Fronza Woods.

5   Kodwo Eshun, *Rock My Religion* (London: AfterAll, 2012).

6   Paul Gilroy, 'Soundscapes of the Black Atlantic', in Michael Bull and Les Back (eds.), *The Auditory Culture Reader* (Oxford and New York: Berg, 2003), 381–95.

7   John Miller, 'Now Even the Pigs're Groovin', Kitnick (ed.), *Dan Graham*, 129–62.

8   See George Lewis, *A Power Stronger than Itself: The AACM and American Experimental Music* (Chicago and London: University of Chicago Press, 2008), and see 33–6 on this point.

9   Jean-Luc Nancy, *The Inoperative Community* (Minneapolis, MN: University of Minnesota Press, 1991 [1986]), translated by Peter Connor.

10   See Lewis, *A Power Stronger than Itself*, 43–6 and 196–214, and also Graham Lock, *Blutopia: Visions of the Future and Revisions of the Past in the Work of Sun Ra, Duke Ellington and Anthony Braxton* (Durham: Duke University Press, 1999).

11   More recently, Oursler directed David Bowie's comeback release 'Where Are We Now?' (2013).

12   Jean Baudrillard sees this phenomenon as an implosion of the media, partly foretold by McLuhan. See, for example, Baudrillard, *Simulacra and Simulation* (Ann Arbor, MI: University of Michigan Press, 1994 [1981]. Translated by Sheila Faria Glaser, 30), and also Gary Genosko, *McLuhan and Baudrillard: Masters of Implosion* (London and New York: Routledge, 1999), 93–6.

CHAPTER SEVEN

Christian Marclay,
The Medium as Multiple

For over thirty years, Christian Marclay has worked at a variety of media, with a very firm emphasis on sound, and yet he firmly rejects the term 'sound art': 'I hate that term "sound art" [...] It's just a tool, a medium that's being used' (Marclay, quoted in Jennifer González, 'Overtures', 34).[1] Marclay is best known for his sculptural approaches to sound and music, his turntable work and his video installations. These latter will be the focus here, yet Marclay's importance in the wider use of sound in gallery contexts cannot go unremarked, and operates as a prelude to the video works. Many of the artists in this book have some sort of direct connection to music or sound experimentation. Others refer to the signal importance of particular musical moments, movements or scenes in the development of their aesthetic. Others still incorporate music or reflect upon music in or through video. But Marclay is the first to start from a position of reflection on sound in artistic contexts and reflect the world of material sound and musical production in his artworks, including video installation form.

In order to understand how someone who makes art from audio, record covers, records, cassettes, CDs, playback machines, instruments, handmade instruments and sounds of visitors in galleries; who makes sounds from films; and who pointedly emphasizes sounds in his more visual works is somehow not a sound artist, we need to muse on the anti-sound art statement a bit further. As Alan Licht points out, it is not uncommon for 'artists working in sound' to reject the term of sound art, just as video artists (see Gary Hill) eschew the use of 'video art' as it is seen as an inadequate description of their activities.[2] Partly, this recalls Krauss' assertion that video (and subsequent art forms, such as Broodthaers' multi-object gallery-scale installations) is part of a 'post-medium condition' – that is, the purpose of the artist is not limited to the exploration or exhaustion of a particular medium or, as she would have it, to the proper task of art that continues on from modernism. As I have argued earlier, we do not have to take Krauss' concluding judgement on board to note the interesting aspect of the idea of a 'post-medium', one that would be properly intermedial – that is, something like a new medium, growing in hybrid or mutant form from existing species. In the case of Marclay, the use of the word 'medium' with regard to sound is misleading, as for him, it seems to mean something more like material – as opposed to method or set of principles. To be consistent, he could well have said that sound is a material, and not a medium, in fact. The point would then be about art discourse being too lazy to come up with a proper term (imagine an art called 'colour application art' or 'paint art'. Or why not 'shape art'? It would be hard to take such a medium seriously enough to wish to work through its potential). 'Sound art' certainly does not adequately represent the presence of sound when mobilized in artworks and certainly lacks something if applied outside the gallery and into live performance spaces. 'Sound art' also fails to capture that, in numerous ways, sound is not the only element in 'sound art', just as shapes are not the only element of painting. Even when a sound piece is to be heard through headphones or inside a small booth, it still requires specific and non-incidental material, mechanical supports. Mostly, in gallery contexts, 'sound art' is far from limited to merely the aural and aims for audio purity at its peril, for then it does seem to fall into the trap of being a 'medium' limited to simplistic expression, one that actually has little correlation with public, spatially located art.[3]

So, for Marclay, 'sound art' fails to capture what something like sound art should be doing, and it unfairly ghettoizes the activities of an artist. Furthermore, 'sound art', in an oddly Greenbergian turn, also imagines a world where listening can be kept clean of all other influences. In more postmodern, postproduction terms, the listening demanded by art that features sound structures a world where listening connotes interaction and creative engagement. For Marclay, sound is rarely there by itself, to be heard in isolation from either the world or other sensory perceptions. Before he made gallery work, he was involved in performance, and very early on he moved towards the appropriated sounds of already-existing records. He, like Laurie Anderson, developed an instrument that used a turntable instead of strings as the sound-producing element (his was more like a guitar, hers a violin). Pre-recorded sounds would replace the spurious authenticity of chords, scales, harmonic or melodic progressions, yet the performance aspect of a portable sound device would be maintained. Around 1980, at the same time hip hop was sharpening itself into life, Marclay began attacking, distorting, reconfiguring and sometimes literally reshaping vinyl records. This would lead to the mass DJ-ing of *One Hundred Turntables* (1991) and also the reconfiguration of old records into new recordings. One example of this in installation form is *Footsteps* (1989), consisting of 3500 vinyl records, featuring the sounds of Marclay's footsteps and tap dancing. These were laid out in such a way as to fill the gallery space, and then visitors to the gallery would walk on them. The records were then 'complete' and released.

In some ways a more conventional release, *Record without a Cover* (1985) also looked to physical deterioration and impact for its effect. This recording of Marclay's sounds was visually completed by a description of the piece. The idea would then be that the record would gradually acquire sounds from its interaction with the world, thus puncturing the imagined purity of a hi-fi recording in favour of a more unpredictable and unmanufactured set of sounds. González claims that Marclay's works that alter vinyl represent a lowering of the vinyl form, with its precious cargo of carefully recorded, mastered and moulded sounds: 'In response to its once-precious commodity status, Marclay toys irreverently with the plastic medium' ('Overture', 34). It is certain that Marclay does not respect the vinyl record as an integral, untouchable carrier of either consumer delight or aural perfection, but paradoxically, he is adding value, as instead of a mass-produced, reasonably cheap object, what we now have are artist-modified, more or less unique pieces – whether we refer to *Footsteps*, or the cut-up, melted, stacked, jumbled and broken records of other installations, or the recombinant album artworks in the *Body Mix* series of the early 1990s. Each *Record without a Cover* is properly unique, except for those copies squirreled away by collectors into the prophylactic sleeves of other records, and those pristine copies tell us something very odd about this type of readymade. To follow the artist's instruction is to acquire for yourself an original copy, subject to the whims of its physical encounters, and thus the record eludes the control of the maker of the sounds contained within its grooves, but to ignore the instruction, and secure the vinyl inside protection, is to ensure it remains a mass-produced object, albeit through asserting your own creative control.

Much of Marclay's 'sound' work is more about the transmission methods of sound, even when he produces sounds as part of the finished piece, and the vast majority of this work is highly literal in its approach. This to me is the point: against Krauss' limited view of the prospects of the post-medium, in fact *a* post-medium can reflect on its own production, the conditions of its making, as part of its mission.[4] Rather than attacking consumerist society through physically intervening on its objects, Marclay brings back the material element that this society seeks to hide.[5] This is even more relevant today when not only do we imagine that music hides in Platonic ideal form, waiting to be released by hi-fi technology, but we also imagine it as entirely dematerialized, despite the existence of such music depending on software, machines, telecommunications and economic networks (absence of payment does not mean absence of economy). The material side is brought out not only by the emphasis on the material but through the literalization of sound's material conditions of production in brute form, such as a mass of CDs, records or tape(s). Marclay's earlier installations are doubly intermedial: first, between sound and sculpture, second, between sound and its material manifestation. But these could best be described as intermediary objects, rather than intermedia as such – for that we need to move into the spaces of the video installations.

Guitar Drag (2000) dramatizes Marclay's playing with music as sound source to an extreme degree and bellows around the gallery room it is installed in. The video is simple, but highly charged: an electric guitar is tied by a rope to the back of a pickup truck, and the sound we hear is of the guitar being pulled along the ground, through an amplifier on the back of the truck. Although I will pay more attention to the formal sound properties of the piece, it has an avowed real-world context to which it refers, and that is the murder of James Byrd Jr. by a group of white racists in 1998. Byrd was chained to the back of a truck like the one we see and dragged for up to three miles, and was killed in extreme pain. Marclay attempts to re-create the rage and suffering through the injured guitar, while at the same time, perhaps, offering an electric hymn to Byrd's memory. Certainly the intention to refer to this murder is clearly signalled and indicated as a direction of reflection for audiences of *Guitar Drag*, but for all Marclay's good intention here, the point is made only in suggestive terms of resemblance. The critique of racist violence is not made formally clear in the dragging of an inanimate object that seems nonetheless to live through its howling. We may be led to reflect that if this is what it is like for such an object to be dragged violently, then how much worse would it be for a man. Further to this, the process is made audible, rendered into sound, without the painful literalism of a re-enactment featuring actors. It is not that Marclay's protest does not work; it is just that it is not self-evident through what happens in terms of sound or vision. It is just something like the murder.

Formally, this piece is heavily laden with reference points, which, to my mind, do not outweigh the angered reflection on Byrd's fate, but certainly open up multiple lines of flight, some of which bring us back to the first authorial interpretation. First, what is the piece doing to the guitar? Marclay has played with guitars, records and other instruments before – the fate of this guitar is an extension of what happened to records walked upon or left out to be damaged. Here, it is the guitar itself that becomes material, reminding us of the material production of music through electrification, which we perhaps take for granted as a transparent tool between musicmaker and audience. The guitar itself makes the sound. Except it doesn't – the amplifier is what produces the audible sounds of the landscape/guitar interaction – as if one or both of those two took the place of the musician, and the amplifier becomes the tool/instrument. The truck can be understood as music producer – without its intervention, the amplifier will hiss in more or less predictable fashion, perhaps strong wind will create stronger sounds, but that is all. Or the truck can be conceived as the ultimate instrument.

The surprising complexity of the system established by Marclay in *Guitar Drag* suggests we need to rethink relationships of control in music or sound making, such that we need to emphasize the machine as something that is made of relations between different elements, of which videomaker, truck, amplifier, guitar, driver and ground, all interact (figure 7.1).

In the course of the 1960s, musicians began to push amplification further, looking for distortion and opening a range of sounds beyond the controllable tones of proper string playing.[6] Marclay both refers to this expansion of the soundmaking properties of the electric guitar and undermines the heroism that the guitarist acquired in the same period. For all his creativity and skill, Jimi Hendrix was a different kind of guitar hero to almost all the others – happy to stretch way outside traditional patterns of solo-ing and into much freer terrains, and, famously, using the destruction of the guitar as a source of music. It is not so much that action (as captured at Monterey jazz festival in June 1967 when he lights the guitar and concedes the soundmaking to the object itself) but the playing of the American national anthem at the Woodstock festival that *Guitar Drag* conjures for me. In a set of devastating experimentation, this piece stands out for its capacity to re-form the anthem, and to unpick its intent and structure without destroying it, such that the mass of distortion, feedback and howling summons the prospect of a true utopia hinted at but currently elided by the reality of the modern United States of America.[7] This then is how we come back through the sound of the piece to the narrative elements.

FIGURE 7.1 *Christian Marclay,* Guitar Drag *(2000). DVD projection with sound; fourteen minutes. Courtesy White Cube.*

There is still more to the piece – it has to be staged in a room, in large-scale projection form, with guitar blaring. There was a record released, peculiarly, further materializing the aleatory tones of the dragged guitar – something from next to nothing that was close in finalized form to the sounds emanating from Marclay's New York contemporaries Sonic Youth. The tying of the guitar to truck also takes some time at the beginning, parodying the tuning up or the practice guitarists are encouraged to perform. The dirt tracks have no such readying, yet their contours imprint on the strings, pickups and so on of the guitar, such that *Guitar Drag* also becomes a kind of no-wave land art, an instant, multiple rethinking of Richard Long's walks or the interventions of Robert Smithson or James Turrell.

In another rare example of Marclay using 'non-found' material, *Solo* (2008) plays out another history of the guitar, with the guitar as sex object, conduit or even participant. A young woman (played by actress and musician Tree Carr) arrives in a studio, bumps the drumkit, and the drum sticks fall. On foot of this, she sees a guitar standing upright in its stand, plugged in and ready. Slowly, tentatively, she begins to play it, at first jumping back as it responds. Slowly she takes control, her hands moving across the neck and body. She then moves to play the guitar with her whole body, starting to take her clothes off as the piece progresses. She and the guitar rub together, and sounds spark off from its strings. Once she pushes the guitar into her belt and pubis (the guitar facing her at this point), the sounds become more raucous, more the product of willed activity than something purely instinctual. The guitar takes on very obvious phallic characteristics, both in its positioning, and her movements around it. Also, this phallus is something she can take hold of and possess as hers, including very obviously as an extension of her sex as she holds it sticking out in front of her. The guitar's shape seems an explicit match for the penis, but historically has also taken on more metaphorical aspects of phallic power in being 'wielded' in order to unleash vibrating and heroic solos. In *Solo*, this part of guitar play is made clear and taken on in masturbatory form by a woman, thus changing the dynamic of the phallus as male possession. But the guitar also has more 'female' curved forms, and Carr also works on those, sitting on the side of the body, or touching the whole body of the instrument, not just its most ejaculatory neck part.

As the video progresses, connections other than guitar solo-ing emerge – such as the collaborative performances between Charlotte Moorman and Nam June Paik, where the cello is used as physical participant rather than traditional note-producing object. When Carr discovers the fx pedals, which are already set up, she moves more into the terrain of experimental guitar playing, and by this stage (8.32, more or less halfway), we have moved from seeing and hearing the interaction between woman and guitar as something naïve and incidentally revealing to recognizing the intent to produce something like free music (it is interesting to note the presence of a guitar consultant, who is Keith Rowe, of improvising band AMM, and pioneer of playing guitar in many ways not thought of by its designers). The video is not about a nude woman playing or fucking a guitar – that is the content, but not what it is about. It certainly seems to be about how the electric guitar has a sexual history, and that the sex of its fellow human performers has been likely to be dressed males, their fingers clutching their own instrument to produce runs, riffs and licks. To hear *Solo* is to hear a piece of free music, perhaps from the late 1960s or, alternatively, the taking apart of guitar we can hear in no wave or post-prog of the late 1970s and early 1980s. Now that those moves are in some way standardized, Marclay brings sex back into improvisational exploration. From around twelve minutes to fifteen, Carr and guitar are in more of a full-body rapport, Carr taking turns to receive the guitar's heft, or to return the favour and flip roles, as the guitar submits to her pounding it. At 15.40, she begins to slow her movements, and turns the tuning heads in post-play mode. At 16.30, she throws the guitar away, in a steady howl of feedback. The video ends soon after.

It is too easy to focus on the explicit display of sexual activity and the naked woman being suggestive of some sort of guitar porn – even if more honest than the repressed sexuality in fan worship of technical guitar ability. The display, and its various possible meanings or connections, is only half of the story – the very clear sound and the development of a piece of improvised music are at least as much a part of the content as Tree Carr's intimate playing with the guitar. The sound is not so much about sex but about exploration, developing a sense of what will work, but also letting go as the playing develops – in other words, a deeper sexuality more like the sacrificial eroticism imagined by Georges Bataille in novels such as *Story of the Eye*.[8] Then we can hear the destruction of traditional music as an excessive development of it, a breaking-free that comes with violence, and too often becomes academicized in the po-faced complexity of post-jazz improv music. Another part of that music is summoned in *Solo*, which is that the playing is never entirely solo, never in a void, but involved in contexts, a history of instruments, amplification, listening and tunings. Further, what we hear and see here is an exact parallel for the spontaneous presence of the improvising act: the loss of self in playing is ultimately lost as it dissipates.

In Marclay's work, this piece refers to many tributaries to his aesthetic – his own moving on from the guitar, the use of guitar in *Guitar Drag* and the references to music history, particularly rock and improvisation. Where some of the sculptures freeze sound into its material form, the videos covered in this chapter (and many others) maintain sound as essential driving force – music as sound as well as history. This mobilization of sound and music is both cause and effect of Marclay's video work – and makes explicit the phenomenon of intermediality proper to video installation, while insisting on the presence of music as content as well as structural form or guiding principle. At every stage, the materiality of music and sound production is made visible, and in *Solo*, the phenomenon of music making as physical act (or interaction) is revealed.

Sounds are also musicalized, or brought into larger structures, in the multiscreen video works – announced by the phones of the single-screen *Telephones* (1995). The piece itself consists of clips of telephone calls from mainstream films, cut together in groups – ringing, picking up, answering, hearing one side of dialogue and replacing the headset. These fragments become a musical whole of several movements, unifying disparate original conversations into coherent groupings, progressing in a newly constructed narrative. As it becomes clear that the content of the calls will remain mostly mysterious, we pay attention to other parts of the communication, the practices and machinery of mediation and communication as the new content for the collaged whole. First, even in the absence of the voice or image of the other person, the second part of dialogue and subject matters, and there is plenty for the viewer/listener to follow, and in terms of the people themselves, this consists of gestures, facial expressions, tone of voice and use of standard telephone terms as emotionally charged communication (such as shouting 'goodbye') (figure 7.2).

In the original films, these actions serve to emphasize narrative and character development as well as supplement the subject of the phone call. *Telephones* ramps up the importance of these elements, performing an analysis of telephonic tropes akin to Christian Metz's structural analysis of film which sought to remind the viewer of films to consciously note the

FIGURE 7.2 *Christian Marclay,* Telephones *(1995). Edition of 250; Video; seven minutes thirty seconds. Courtesy White Cube.*

role of all elements in a film, as opposed to consuming story, character and message.[9] These gestures are not restricted to the film world, but extend to communication in general, so Marclay is also separating out individual acts of communication (like speech acts), in order to line them up in a newly identified set of signifying activities. In those situations (outside of film activity), there is a tendency to regard the medium as transparent, and certainly the films 'quoted' in *Telephones* may have done that originally, but the sounds of the machinery are brought to the fore through the editing choices, and they become opaque once more – taking on aural texture explicitly, as well as partaking in something like a telephonic gestural, or performance. Each statement is turned into cliché once placed into the context of repetitive and mechanical communication, and perhaps shortly after that, a viewer/listener will remember that his or her own language use can be very similar to that seen and heard here, based on a limited set of stock conversational moves, and that without shared expressions there would not be any social communication.

As physical and linguistic machines combine in their functioning, media (talking, telephone conversation, film and video art) cross, raising even further the sense that the medium has become subject matter (not message alone, as McLuhan knew well), and it might be tempting to attribute some of that clarity of comment, through sound, on media, to the now archaic devices on show. All the telephones in use are very noisy machines compared to those in use today, and their sounds can stand in for a cosy nostalgia, like the recording of vinyl pops as a signifier of warmth, possession and familiarity (incidentally, this is very far from Marclay's own use of the sounds of the playing of vinyl records). But that would presume that today's telephonic devices are transparent, and transaudient. They too make noises, or movement, or heat. They do not provide the digital perfection the now-future would have us believe in. Perhaps when we ignore the continued physical location/presence/embodiment of people we will get a better sense of perfect communication, but the signs are in the other direction, as if a tech-burdened society is resisting a drive to perfection, whether through low-grade audio files or through the submarine tendencies and dropouts of Skype and similar programmes.[10] In short, Marclay's telephones are not the loud sound of yesterday compared to the shiny new of digital or cell technologies: instead they are the illustration of the noise of all media, the noise that is their material grounding.

From *Telephones*, we can trace a line, as Mark Higgs does, to *Gestures* (1999) and *Video Quartet* (2002) ('*Video Quartet*', 85, 88).[11] *Gestures* is a piece of four images, forming a square, of Marclay playing turntables and records, and while it does not have much of a link to the others in that it is a collage but not of found footage, it does establish what will be an important approach – the use of four parallel images. In *Video Quartet*, these sit side by side in a strip, along one gallery wall. Ultimately, his piece *Crossfire* (2007) will dedicate a wall to each of the four projections. *Gestures* does reiterate something of *Telephones*, in that the materiality of the set of movements to accomplish soundmaking is brought to the centre – only then to be dispersed, in a pastiche of an inner sleeve showing four members of a rock group, each inhabiting one's own square. Personally, I find the rendering visible of the methods of making particular sounds panders to rock sensibilities, relieving the artist from the risk of not being taken seriously enough as he or she only uses 'pre-prepared sounds'. Nothing could be further from the truth in Marclay's audio work or the intermedial video pieces, but let's not presume that the display of instrumental techniques is different because the instrument is unfamiliar, or that it necessarily brings out the relations of the means of production. It would do so more if it used someone else playing turntables, but we also do not need to presume that this was a major consideration behind the piece. The display of playing in *Gestures* replicates the audio strategies of scratching and so on in video form, and rethinks how we take for granted that music can become whole through being made (recorded) in layers. Here, all the layers are there, parallel, in a way our ears cannot do, as they condense and recombine layers and sources into one single hearing.

Video Quartet imposes parallel sound and vision in a more strikingly dissonant way. It brings together many shots of music or sound (so the vocal segments extend to screams) from films – characters in musicals singing their dialogue, people playing instruments, performing traditional dances and music and showing shots of concert footage – with the whole adding to a dynamic conflation of *Telephone* and *Gestures*. The focal point is no longer the source music – what was diegetic loses its character of being the sound within a film, to be a segment of a rolling exploration of the *making* of music in films, and the four sets of sound or music merge (often cacophonously, certainly a-musically). The diegetic music is now an instrument in this new quartet – the sounds become the material for editing into a musical composition or something that occupies the space of a musical composition. The sight of music or sound makers on the four screens supplies the equivalent of the presence of the four players in an ensemble. However, here there are no performers, no score, no composed piece and no unity. That is not quite true – all of those things are there, but exploded into a collage instead of forming a realistic montage (i.e. such as that produced by the camera cuts in a filmed concert performance). Once again, it is music that has become the material, and that is made material instead of being a 'natural part' of films. Although it becomes a sort of composition, it is one made of pre-existing fragments (although maybe the same could be said of chords, melodies and notes on a scale). As Higgs notes, it has a sequential framework for things to happen ('*Video Quartet*', 89) and does follow a sequence from tuning to endings. Ultimately, it could be said to restore musicality to the music of cinema, as if the music in films was there ahead of its time of the film's assembly, awaiting de-fragmentation into a piece where it could be autonomous.

Marclay grows more 'tuneful' or compositional, I believe, in his edited large-scale video pieces, especially if we look at *Crossfire* (and also *The Clock*, from 2010, where a whole day is assembled anew from fragments of existing films). *Crossfire* takes only moments of shooting guns, along with the preparation and aftermath of those moments – aiming, holstering, safety catch releasing and spent cartridges tumbling all feature, as well as many variations on actual gunfire. The whole takes place over projections onto four walls of a room in a gallery and takes 8.27 to complete its loop. In the course of that time, we witness a vast amount of shooting – mostly from the perspective of the camera or of someone facing the gun that is being fired. The short clips are all taken from cinema films, many of which are well known, and, like in several of his other pieces, Marclay is not shy of showing very famous actors. This is not to set us a puzzle to work out which part comes from which film, but to emphasize the familiarity of source materials, and therefore the culturally established nature of what we are seeing. Of course, we do not usually see shooting in this way, even in the most robustly violent action film, as the narrative is reconfigured as a composed piece, playing in a sort of harmony across the four screens. Each act of shooting is isolated from all but its immediate background context, and lasts at most 3–4 seconds, usually less. Even the target, or purpose of shooting, is excluded from our vision (and hearing). The same goes for the results of the act – there are no bodies, no explosions, no escapes and no triumphs – just shot after shot, so the aspect of the skill of shooting is narrowed down and isolated into a small pocket of dexterity – in the manipulation of the gun. The immediate impact on the installation visitor is intense, as the four screens play off one another and the room fills with the sounds of gunfire. Marclay establishes rhythms through bursts of repetition, which flood the four screens, creating an illusion of narrative development (e.g. as a shooter walks across a screen firing) (figure 7.3).

There is a larger-scale rhythm – that is the structure of *Crossfire*: it begins with isolated explosive sounds, with single shots, interspersed with dark screens, and later a sense of tension mounts. Guns are loaded, cocked, picked up and removed from cases and drawers, primed, checked, safety catches are removed. As we near the two-minute mark, all screens show individual gun barrels being turned to camera centre, and at 2.03 a barrage of shooting begins, lasting until various calls to stop firing come in around 3.20. Casings drop, guns are holstered, but this is only a lull, because at four minutes, a series of salvoes, volleys, sprays and strafes opens up, and these last for most of four minutes. Much of the time, the screens show different clips, but there are moments they connect, stitching the shots into a sound and visual whole. The last thirty seconds are a moment of calming, but, just as with many suspense films, it is not quite all over, as a few shots pierce the

FIGURE 7.3 *Christian Marclay,* Crossfire *(2007). Edition of six; four channel video projection; eight minutes twenty-seven seconds looped. Courtesy White Cube.*

returning blackness. It is self-evident that sound is the core of this piece – the vast majority of the clips have sound, and the effect of massed firing sounds, whether from different clips playing at the same time or from the rolling of the same 'shot', is what creates a possible sense of being caught in a crossfire. It adds a locatedness that a silent version would not possess, as in that case it would seem to be a detached comment on the prevalence of gunfire in films. If this is a commentary, it is one that includes viewers, and includes them as listener, as embodied by the action around them. Part of the masculinity on show has been stripped away in the simple process of isolating the act of shooting from most of its context, but it is certainly possible to conceive of the piece as somehow dogmatic, forceful and brutal. I would not rule out such a reading, but it could not explain the full range of what occurs in *Crossfire*, not least because the piece could be some sort of commentary on macho gun culture and love of noisy sound in Western popular culture. The vast majority of people shown shooting are male, but they represent a broad global cross-section of humans. In addition, shooting itself seems to break out everywhere – urban or rural, domestic or public, it can happen anywhere. It is individual or group based and happens in many different terrains, different perspectives, with the full range of facial expressions and bodily gestures. So instead of the wish to limit its commentary or unwitting statement to one of masculinity, it is more effective to see shooting in *Crossfire* as a microcosm of all human life.

The viewer/listener is brought into a place structured by the sound and sight of shooting and its attendant acts (as with telephone conversations in *Telephones*, where we hear many other sounds that precede or follow the actual firing of guns). The four walls position themselves as a total perceptual world, brought into focus by a seemingly limited set of sounds. In isolating the clips from their effects, Marclay is not merely aestheticizing shooting, he is also re-focussing the attention of the installation visitor, such that questions of life play out in ways that are directly relevant to them – that is, the sequencing of shooting events into the structure of *Crossfire* takes shooting away from its targets and becomes a perversely self-contained point of reflection. As the guns turn to the centre of the camera/centre of the room/target/viewer/listener, the gun is revealed as a limit condition, a tool that can exceed human use in ending existence. While it would be a stretch to think of the piece as a reflection on mortality, it could be understood as a way of inducing a sense of presence on the installation visitor, one that is also aware that what induced this is precisely a tool designed to kill. Equally, it does not seem likely that *Crossfire* either celebrates or criticizes a violence-oriented mass media (absence of results of shooting, removal of context and repetition). But it does bring out the ubiquity of media – as we see the range of actions, settings and attitudes as something mediatized, something that occurs in structures of communication, not in isolation from them. This then reflects back on viewers/listeners, themselves doing their listening, hearing and judging, from a culturally defined position within a globally mediatized environment.

These multimedia reflections, which are properly *intermedial*, in Marclay's later video pieces, insist on the acoustic element of global culture that is too often sidelined. McLuhan had identified the heightened sound quality of the contemporary world as the essential part of its tactility, its proximity and its *allatonceness*. Marclay stands as a paradoxical example of how moving away from a sound-only focus enables a fuller, more engaged way of producing sound art. Only at such a point can the intermediality of sound operate as the key part of intermedia (or 'post-medium') work. His career mirrors the development of a viewer who is also an auditor, capable of processing large-scale installations and sound that is brought from existing contexts (e.g. original films) into new ones (original installation works), and so he is at the core of the developing conventionalization of the practice of sound being part of 'visual' work.

Notes

1   Jennifer González, et al., 'Overture', in *Christian Marclay* (London and New York: Phaidon, 2005), 22–81, in turn referencing 'Christian Marclay – Gary Hill: Conversation', *Annandale* (Spring 2000), 2–9 (2).

2   Alan Licht, *Sound Art: Beyond Music, Between Categories* (New York: Rizzoli, 2007), 9–11.

3   For accounts of major exhibitions that properly consider, for the most part, the role of extra-auditory factors in sound art, see David Toop et al., *Sonic Boom: The Art of Sound* (London: Hayward Gallery, 2000), *Sonic Process: Une nouvelle géographie des sons* (Paris: Centre Pompidou, 2002) and *Sons & Lumières* (Paris: Centre Pompidou, 2004). The 2013 MOMA (New York) show, *Soundings: A Contemporary Score*, managed this less successfully.

4   The connection to minimalism is heightened in the shape of Robert Morris' exemplary object *Box with the Sound of Its Own Making* from 1961, which is what it says it is.

5   See Alan Licht, citing a conversation with Marclay, where the latter says, 'we tend to think of music as this sightless thing because recordings have distorted our understanding of music', 'Mixmaster', *Modern Painters* (March 2005), 30–3 (30).

6   See Michael Hicks, *Sixties Rock: Garage, Psychedelic and Other Satisfactions* (Urbana and Chicago: University of Illinois Press, 1999). For more on the physical acts of destruction that antecede the piece, see Carlos Kase, ' "This Guitar Has Seconds to Live": *Guitar Drag*'s Archaeology of Indeterminacy and Violence', *Discourse* 30 (3) Fall 2008, 419–42.

7   See Hegarty, *Noise/Music: A History* (New York and London: Continuum, 2007), 63–4.

8   Georges Bataille, *Story of the Eye* (London: Penguin, 1979 [1929]).Translated by Joachim Neugroschal.

9   Christian Metz, *Film Language: A Semiotics of the Cinema* (New York: Oxford University Press, 1974 [1971]). Translated by Michael Taylor.

10   This may also apply to those who are discovering vinyl for the first time, amid the dying of the CD format. As opposed to the improved audio quality sought by older purchasers of consumer electronics, maybe new vinyl listeners find new re-assurance in the overt fallibility of the format, its seeming concern for its own appearance and packaging that goes beyond the undemonstrative CD or shared file.

11   Mark Higgs, '*Video Quartet*' in *Christian Marclay*, 83–91.

CHAPTER EIGHT

Pipilotti Rist, Immersing

Installation art is by definition an occupation and reconfiguration of space, even sometimes a construction of space. This space is never complete, though, as it exists as openness to perception on the part of the visitor (including where the installation denies access or makes it awkward). As Juliane Rebentisch comments, in *Installation Art*, installations structure a particular type of space that is fluid and operates as a comment on how space informs ontology and everyday activity alike.[1] Video installations extend beyond their screens to position viewers spatially. Even single-screen monitor pieces invite a spatialization of the artwork as a conscious decision. Where more traditional art forms present themselves as complete, implying a position from which to view, or indeed to listen, video art's fragmented and contingent temporality prevents such self-presence, except when insisted on in the form of an enclosed performance of set duration, from which visitors cannot exit until the end. The more cinema-like display of contemporary art, where start times and duration are posted outside the installation space, attempts not only to fix the spectator temporally but define their spatial attitude towards the work.

The space of video art is as improper as the temporal relation towards its public: it demands more attention, more reflection on positioning, and it is precisely these demands that open space – installed space – to speculation, reflection and affect (i.e. awareness of events occurring in time that are not reflective but the cause of movement within, towards or away from installations). Sound explicitly fills the space, while visual elements seem to have a clear source in the projected surface. Sound builds the space of an installation in ways that differ from the light, images, reflections, boxes and other objects that constitute the visual part. Both senses are addressed temporally, as they operate as separate dimensions of a unified installation time–space.

Many video artists have used these ideas, even if implicitly, in considering the viewing/hearing conditions of a piece. The location, size, number, technical support (film, Video Home System [VHS], digital formats) and screening surfaces are all important elements of a piece. Some artists explicitly deal with bodies and events in space – such as Dan Graham and Bruce Nauman, and these can be thought of as architectural artists (Vito Acconci having actually made the move into architecture) as they not only consider the placement of work in what would be considered a flexible yet pre-existing, newly determined space but also build or use spaces more explicitly as media. Later artists have also addressed the physical nature of buildings as part of works – not just as content but as support, as part of the medium or format itself: Alain Fleischer's projections on buildings would be one example, and even better would be Jane and Louise Wilson, who double content and form in installing works in the locations they have filmed, and also re-create environments for their video work that recall the source spaces/locations.

In the hands of Pipilotti Rist, space becomes malleable, porous and unpredictable, such that space becomes a dimension of the work, not a set of dimensions the work is simply placed in. Space operates in conjunction with partial temporality (partial like Freud's definition of fetishes as 'partial objects'),[2] to provide an unsettling, playful surrealization of the viewing and listening environment. Rist's relation to sound is crucial, particularly in her sense of the role of music in determining moods, messages and ambience of installation space, in ways that recall the multimedia environments of the late 1960s. She has done many pieces that work as disruptive commentaries on music video, or how video is used to accompany songs, such as in the glitchy *I'm Not a Girl Who Misses Much* (1986) (and *Blutclip* from 1993). *Ever Is Over All* (1997) also has some similarities to music videos. Overall, I think it best to conceive of Rist's connection to music video as one of *affinities*: music forms part of her pieces to a significant extent because this reflects the sonic component in much of our own 'non-art' spaces and movements outside of gallery settings. Music video is part of the backdrop, just as pop music is.[3] While Rist recalls the outside world through the inclusion of the 'everyday culture' of music, she also makes explicit the exclusion of that culture by the gallery/museum. Even as sound art infiltrates art institutions and concerts feature as part of exhibition events, still music is kept out, unsuitable for the contemplative demeanour that apparent aural stasis provides. So, Rist's spaces, use of music as well as sound make her work multiply intermedial – heightening the sense of 'a' medium (video art) that does not really hold with containment. Some of her environments, such as *Pour Your Body Out* (2008) among them, lead to extremely passive audience behaviours, which I explore below, but in brief, it may be that her installations recall other privileged yet total spaces such as playgrounds, zoos and homes, while removing the harsh demands of often modernist-inspired art institutions.

Rist projects onto many different spaces and surfaces, and constructs many chambers from which to view and hear. Screens can turn up amid objects, models or in the floor, as in *Selfless in the Bath of Lava* (1994).

This work is on a very small screen (with speaker) embedded in the gallery floor. The visitor to this piece may well miss it, and only the hint of sound from somewhere draws the attention so that listener can also become viewer. Peering into the circular hole reveals a woman surrounded by flames, calling out to the passerby, and demanding help in a range of languages. The flames and the lowness suggest a hellish environment, and the looping adds to this, signalling, perversely, the infinity of being caught in the absence of linear, forward-moving time. The isolation of the piece is illusory, requiring its hiddenness within a larger space to work – so it reflects, that is, bounces back from and into the space now made other – that is, that has become a self-reflective space rather than a space that merely exists as a location for the world to occur in. This piece stands as the paradigm for Rist's audiospatialization and for the mutual relation between piece and gallery room that may sometimes be swallowed in what seem to be more harmonious occupations of gallery spacetime.

Selfless in the Bath of Lava recurs in the altogether more aquatic *Sip My Ocean* (1996), briefly interrupting Rist's floating, swimming and dipping amid dropped toys and objects. This installation consists of two screens, showing reflections that join at the centre, as they mirror round the apex of an internal triangle. Rist rises in and out of the water, merging and separating from herself. Another woman features briefly, in a more static yet still concertinaing form. The video is playful, brightly coloured, almost hallucinogenically so, as are many of Rist's works. The audio track is a cover of Chris Isaak's 'Wicked Game', a stately piece of guitar-led music featuring Rist's vocals and her regular musical collaborator Anders Guggisberg. The most interesting part is the backing vocal, where we hear her screaming along to the lyrics, with the line 'I don't wanna fall in love' emerging loudest. The combination of voice and image leads to a reflection on the attitude of the carefree woman in shot for much of the time, specifically the thought that she is turned in on herself – moving from being one to two, or from being half and incomplete to being one. As she rejoins herself or subdivides or separates, she takes control of possible engagement with the world, herself and others. But the piece is far from closed in on itself – the music fills out in the room, and the two-projection format suggests opening, rather than inwardness or rejection of the installation visitor.

The woman's free movement, the evocation of the element of water, the sea and the fluidity – particularly when taken in the context of Rist's gleeful evocation of menstrual blood in other works (e.g. *Blutclip*) – strongly suggest a feminist aspect to her work. But any critic seeking to emphasize this has to struggle against Rist's post-feminist lack of interest in the question. Clearly, a video made by a woman, featuring a woman's body and the sea, does not necessarily mean a feminist argument is present, even if these things readily connote it to a reader avid for this dimension to be present. Rist has argued that we misunderstand feminism and her art if we presume a woman in a video symbolizes Woman and/or women, making the point that 'when there is a naked man – aha, it must be about the "human". But when there is a naked woman, the assumption is that it is to do with sexuality' (Patricia Bickers, 'Interview with Pipilotti Rist', 4).[4] In fact, Rist overstates her antipathy to feminism, in that whether she likes it or not, she regularly treads in the footsteps of French feminism based on bodily presence and difference. In *Sip My Ocean*, Rist may well be attempting to capture all of humanity's connection to the liquid world, but it does seem to be doing work very similar to philosopher Luce Irigaray, in emphasizing the connection between sea, woman's bodily structure and female sexual pleasure. The openness of the two screens suggests, in simple fashion, a possible genital openness, but, less stereotypically, we could see the joining and separating of partial Rist-bodies as an analogue, as an *affinity* with Irigaray's ideas about the multiplicity of women's sexual organs signalling a different relation to the world, one of dualities, of touching and coming apart and of an internal or autonomous kissing that signals dwelling in jouissance – that is, rolling, non-end determined, erotic pleasure:

> Two lips kissing two lips: openness is ours again. Our 'world'. And the passage from the inside out, from the outside in, the passage between us, is limitless, without end [...]. When you kiss me, the world grows so large that the horizon itself disappears. [Our pleasure is] always in motion: openness is never spent nor sated. ('When Our Lips Speak Together', 210)[5]

Whatever the issues with Irigaray's possible biological reductionism, it is at least a way of understanding *Sip My Ocean* as feminist due to how it is made, rather than how the content reminds someone of a set of clichés about women. I am not going to attempt to cover the full range of Rist's work and how it may or may not relate to, improve on, fail or ignore various feminist models – except where those pieces have a significant sound or musical element. So here, above and beyond a possible feminist fluidity, the music operates as a signal for subversive identity compared to superficial image, and also exists in and around the projections that join at 90°.

Even more akin to music video is the equally joyous *Ever Is Over All* (1997), again featuring a music collaboration between Rist and Guggisberg. Again, the structure is one of two projections on two walls, connecting at the apex. The left-hand screen shows a woman in blue dress and red shoes walking down a city street in slightly slowed-down motion, carrying what seems to be a 'red hot poker' flower. The right-hand projection is (mostly) of fields of that same flower, the colours of red, yellow, green flowing together, almost sickly in richness. This time, though, the projections are less labial, and more interstitial, or intermedial. The expected intermediality of video art migrates inward, into the piece, in how the sound works in relation to the images, but also in that the footage of the 'nature' screen bleeds into the other image – showing a transgression that is a formal echo of the content-based subversion of the left-hand images.

As the woman walks down the street, gently atmospheric pop (a near-relative of trip hop), including worldless singing, accompanies the woman's smiling walk. At regular intervals, as she moves along a row of parked cars, she reaches in to smash a window with her 'flower', at one point receiving the approbation of a passing female police officer, which to this later viewer strongly recalls the not-quite feminist video to Beyoncé's 'If I Were a Boy' (2008). The sound of the smashing window is dramatically loud – and acts both as diegetic sound and as part of the musical soundtrack, in that it alternates between these two possibilities, at different points in the piece. So, in one case, the smashing occurs alongside the music, while at another, it can happen in a moment of suspension of the extra-diegetic music. In fact, this variation makes the distinction between what happens in the video and what happens as extraneous soundtrack disperse. The distinction does not go away, as it is precisely the distinction that is being played with here. The soundtrack becomes properly intermedial, moving between layers 'in' or 'above' the content of the left-hand projection. The swaying fields of the other screen, meanwhile, might seem to provide a contrast of nature to urban environment, but as the flower is the tool of breakdown of the urban consensus, we have to see the infiltration of the field into the other image as the pressing of 'outside' (nature) onto conventionally controlled culture.

The reaction of the female police officer suggests feminist approval, because we see, first, the incorporation of women into what is generally suspected to be a traditionally male role; second, the institution is shown as changing, encouraging further free expression on the part of women – who could be seen to still need to metaphorically smash some windows to attain freedom and equality. My point is, again, that it is the formal work of *Ever Is Over All*, and not the presence of a woman smashing windows as such, that creates the possibility of these more political readings.[6] Peggy Phelan expresses this in terms of a subversion of traditional tropes that plays out across the screens in relation: 'the narrative works in the space between the two video projections as well. In that blank but fecund space, the associative links between nature, women, violence and beauty are all rearranged' ('Opening Up Spaces within Spaces', 62).[7]

The violence is certainly something that occurs in both narrative content, visual and aural form, and partakes of the ecstatic refusal of law, proper behaviour, rationality and so on, recalling Bataille's idea of the accursed share – the smashing of windows steps out of the restricted world of rules and, fleetingly, creates a kind of subjectivity based on loss and erotic fun that is deeper than mundane political statements. In a world less brightly coloured and less on video than that of *Ever Is Over All*, we could consider the actions of the woman as equating to the anarchist model of 'propaganda by the deed', which then forces the State to make explicit its repressive nature. Or maybe it is a very irresponsible advocacy of random destruction. Just in case one was tempted by such a simplistic reading, we can recall the second projection – the expanses of fields seeding rebellion, as part of longer cycles of nature, beyond the apparent solidity of manufactured goods such as cars and their over-regulated arrangement in 'parking'.[8]

Fields, flowers, bodies, meditative pop sounds and bright colours – all have traversed Rist's work over the years. From 1992's *Pickelporno* (*Pimple Porno*) through *Homo sapiens sapiens* (2005) and *Pour Your Body Out* (2008), projections have grown, become more immersive and expanded the human form to colossal proportions but without summoning ghosts of heroic statuary. *Pickelporno* attempts to use and subvert photographic tricks of pornography, portraying sexual activity but from odd close-ups, on hair, for example, or a finger. Both male and female bodies feature, and they drift over and through digital or digitally treated landscapes to the sound of Les Reines Prochaines (Rist's band) and Peter Bräker. The choice of close-ups, the endless bodily mobility and the colour separation overlay style of merging image tracks, and the odd angles make the experience very distant from pornography – but instead of being a critique of pornography, it is an attempt to inject some eroticism into the form, away from its conventions. It still shows every body part, much lithe movement and caressing, but the apparent scale of hands that touch other parts is unsettling – often seeming to be hands of a more giant type of human. The film does end climactically, with faster editing and music suggesting release – and this is what it is, as the screen fades down through the colours after larval explosions and then brings back in piano music over images of the sea. The video is about loss of self in the type of eroticism offered by Bataille, where the self gives way to its own emptying into the universe.[9] This eroticism is not just in release; it is in the entanglement of bodies, body and nature, body and digitalscapes, which all signal life outside of isolated monadic living. The music accompanies the sounds, structuring an ebb and flow as it tracks through a wide range of genres, never settling, even though it is always composed in every sense. In the sound of *Pickelporno*, we see the prototypical Rist soundworld for her immersive environments.

The use of building as screen, echoing the development of body as screen, develops in the form of *Homo sapiens sapiens* (2005), originally designed for the San Stae church in Venice as part of that year's Biennale, but removed due to 'technical difficulties', likely as code for someone realizing that the building was hosting an all-encompassing video full of naked femaleness. The video is projected on the ceiling of the building where it is installed, and visitors to the installation are invited to lie down and look up. Sound, of course, permeates the room (as does light from the ceiling installation), and the whole establishes a meditative yet still playful ambience. Again, the colours are hallucinogenic, with the detail now in much higher definition than the 1990s works. The dividing, labial opening of twin/double images still informs the piece, with the woman in the film doubling, joining and rejoining herself, separating into microscopic details shown on an immense scale. This woman glides through and within a lush landscape, while her bodies/body also become/s some other sort of scape. This then is some sort of emergence – even as the audience loses themselves in the crossings of nature/human/digital/self/other, this is humanity arising from nature, but still part of it, still physically anchored and still able to see the full spectrum of her habitat. The music fashions natural samples and digital musical sound into an inviting, unthreatening sound part. This is music as a device for heightening function, drawing installation visitors into spending time viewing.

The same can be said of *Pour Your Body Out (7354 Cubic Metres)* installed at MoMA in late 2008, in the colossal yet spiky atrium. Multiple projections filled the walls; natural, digital and vocal sounds combined again to complete (or act as supplement); and the cushions were positionally formalized into a round 'reclining area'. The scale of the piece is not only vast but also features in the title, in a sort of 'wow, it's this big' fashion that directly undermines the potentially epic or stadium potential of such a large installation. The space is restructured as sound and light habitat (other pieces have chosen to zone off areas, as in the London Hayward Gallery show, *Eyeball Massage*, in 2011). The music is absolutely functional; 'I'd like pleasant sounds', says Rist, while preparing the piece.[10] She specifies that the installation is to be a welcoming contrast to the city around it. We could take this as a sign that the piece is only there for relaxation, an epic New Age gesture, but it is also a utopian space, one that encourages a durational viewing through its very accessibility. Rist also talks of *Pour Your Body Out* bringing people together, and that their proximity will lead to conversation as a result of shared presence organized through the structure of the piece. It is not just backdrop but pivot for communication, and so it enters the risky terrain of relational work. The sound is very much designed to be backdrop, to be a way in to the piece, and the same goes for the reclining area (figure 8.1).

FIGURE 8.1 *Pipilotti Rist,* Pour Your Body Out (7354 Cubic Meters) *(2008). Video still from multichannel audio video installation. Courtesy the artist, Luhring Augustine, New York and Hauser & Wirth.*

This area seems unchallenging and safe, but it does help amplify the spatial completeness of the work, in that there is no set place at which to correctly position yourself. Being anywhere looking up or around will do, and walking around and talking is also fine. Its permissiveness is part of the immersion, perhaps unexpectedly. Nonetheless, and despite keeping visitors for longer than other simply wall-based works might do, I think of lying down, or reclining or scrunching into beanbags as likely to encourage passivity. There is the temptation to let pieces wash over you rather than being absorbed in a way that maintains or heightens attention. Even La Monte Young and Marian Zazeela's *Dream House* installations (first staged in 1969) flirt with this possibility but the sound and light of those are harsher and there is no sense of being asked to come in to merely chill out. Is being seated or lying down part of listening? Is it an attempt to isolate it, reducing vision (in the case of *Pour Your Body Out*, the visuals are designed to replace what is normally to be seen in the city, or in this part of the museum). To me, it is a reduction of the hearing aspect, a confirmation of the use value being accorded music in these installations, for all their good immersive qualities. It is the very opposite of the mobility accorded to the woman traversing the screens and her own body; it accedes to the completeness of the piece in wishing to dramatize the inclusion of the spectators.

And yet, the works do fill space into which the public pours, the sound and visuals of even the largest of the installations do not hold people at bay as do many black box rooms. So the pieces stretch across screens, from sound to visual and back, into and out of screens and/or separate projections – and this applies to all the above pieces, via which we can return to the question of how bodies and actions in Rist's videos operate as formal iterations of erotic crossings from within standard, isolated subjectivity, which includes or even partly consists of, the policing of gender as well as sexual action. The pleasure element of her works, whether in the content, form or audience reaction, is part of whatever commentary she does want to make about gender, sex and feminism itself. The approach is one of immersed involvement, of immersion as engagement.[11] By inhabiting something akin to what Rosi Braidotti terms a 'virtual feminine' – a history of women writers focussed on ideas of becoming rather than fixed identities (*Transpositions*, 184) – Rist is able to expand out from traditional symbolism, drifting over, glossing them bodily, visually and aurally.[12] This occurs without the need to re-introduce 'patriarchal' norms or stereotypes; instead these are ignored signposts, present in emptiness, that is, voided of their power. This means that Rist is not merely alienated from historical oppression, stereotyping or inequality, and is able to operate with sets of signifiers that do not remain in place as new, improved and cleansed symbols for a new order. Instead, the flows, both actual and metaphorical, of the large-scale installations, bring us back to an idea of a 'libidinal economy', devised by Jean-François Lyotard, in 1974 – part of the 1970s turn to talk of 'the body'.[13] Lyotard's libidinal economy does not assert either embodiment or identity. Instead, his body comes apart in a 'libidinal band', akin to the one-sided paradoxical shape of the Möbius strip. This new libidinized body is no longer genital, no longer even an isolated body – rather it stretches out beyond its extremities, to become intimately connected with all that is ostensibly outside, or that it produces, or that it encounters:

> Open the so-called body and spread out all its surfaces: not only the skin with each of its folds, wrinkles, scars, with its great velvety planes, and contiguous to that, the scalp and its mane of hair, the tender pubic fur, nipples, nails, hard transparent skin under the heel, the light frills of the eyelids, set with lashes – but open and spread, expose the labia majora, so also the labia minora with their blue network bathed in mucus. (*Libidinal Economy*, 1)

This is patently not some nice recovery of a true or idealized body – this is a taking apart that reconfigures, an improper deconstruction that, for all its clinical aggression, amounts to a loving expansion of a body that is no longer one, that is a contingency among intensities. Libidinal experience cannot be held within the standard body-container: like Rist's microscopic probing and stroking of eye and ear, Lyotard's understanding of bodies is that they are so much more than a containing device.

> And adjoining the skin of the fingertips, scraped by the nails, perhaps there should be huge silken beaches of skin, taken from the inside of the thighs, the base of the neck, or from the strings of a guitar. [...] Don't forget to add the tongue and all the pieces of the vocal apparatus, all the sounds of which they are capable, and moreover, the whole selective network of sounds, that is the phonological system, for this too belongs to the libidinal 'body'. (*Libidinal Economy*, 2)

As the body is explored and engages its own explorations, it touches continually on what lies outside it. Lyotard connects this all up in the infinite yet monodimensional strip of the 'libidinal economy'. This loop is what we see in the interactive element of *Pour Your Body Out*, specifically because the interaction is not an add-on part, but an internally constructed supplement – that is, the work itself is about intermingling, a physical intermediality that stretches beyond the projected surface. The sound, mostly in musical form, is secondary to this, in that it provides a function, that of easing the auditor in, but the presence of sound is part of the extendedness of the work, its attempt to be all-encompassing, remaining open and welcoming as opposed to being imposed. This body takes in all possible textures, and remains highly textured, in its own right, and in so doing, it can no longer want to take a critical, exterior position. Everything is now inside (*Libidinal Economy*, 3), and this 'insideness' is derived from

> the motion of pleasure as such, split from the motion of the propagation of the species, would be (whether genital or sexual or neither) that motion which in going beyond the point of no return spills the libidinal forces outside the whole at the expense of the whole. (Lyotard, 'Acinema', 171)[14]

It is as if Lyotard saw into the future to witness Rist's installations, as his libidinal loop describes the motion in and out from *Pour Your Body Out*. The title itself now takes on more meaning – instead of taking a self and letting it go, the self comes into being through action, through being part of pouring, a liquefying self that is resolutely utopian.

Notes

1   Juliane Rebentisch, *Aesthetics of Installation Art*, 240–4, addressing Heidegger's conception of the work of art, and also 251–8 on how installations alter the gallery space.

2   See Sigmund Freud, 'Three Essays on the Theory of Sexuality', in Freud, *The Essentials of Psychoanalysis* (London: Penguin, 1986 [1905]), 277–375 [297–8]. Translated by James Strachey.

3   For the structuring and patterning of urban spaces through sound and music, see Brandon LaBelle, *Acoustic Territories*.

4   Patricia Bickers, 'Interview with Pipilotti Rist', *Art Monthly* 350 (October 2011); available at http://www.artmonthly.co.uk/magazine/site/issue/october-2011

5   Luce Irigaray, 'When Our Lips Speak Together', in *This Sex which Is Not One* (New York: Cornell University Press, 1985 [1977]), 205–18. Translated by Catherine Porter.

6   We might be tempted to read the flower that becomes an avenging tool through stiffness as a subversion of traditional gendering of flowers and stiff rod-like objects. Rist is on her guard when asked about the 'phallic' flower, saying that she would call it clitoric, 'not everything nice is phallic!' (Bickers, 'Interview with Pipilotti Rist', 5). In other words, we do not need to presume that power is phallic, thus lending the phallus greater symbolic power instead of imagining another type of strength.

7   Peggy Phelan, 'Opening Up Spaces within Spaces: The Expansive Art of Pipilotti Rist', in Hans Ulrich Obrist et al. (eds) *Pipilotti Rist* (London and New York: Phaidon, 2001), 34–77.

8   See sculptor Arman's *Long Term Parking* (1982) for a commentary on how cars can achieve immortality in parking – it is a tall block of concrete full of cars.

9   'Love and life appear to be separate only because everything on earth is broken apart by vibrations of various amplitudes and durations. [...] From the movement of the sea, uniform coitus of the earth with the moon, comes the polymorphous and organic coitus of the earth with the sun' (Bataille, 'The Solar Anus', *Visions of Excess*, 5–9 [7]). First published in 1931, translated by Allan Stoekl.

10   Rist, *The Colour of Your Socks: A Year with Pipilotti Rist* DVD.

11   Dyson is critical of the drive to immersion in 'new media', arguing that this represents an over-simplified understanding of the utopian capacities of art to transform subjective perceptions (*Sounding New Media*, 130), and leads to a wilful ignorance of the extensive material technology required to make anything like 'immersive' spaces happen (114–15). Rist does not entirely overcome this problem (and Dyson's focus is not video art as such but virtual environments), but she does make the space in which her work is installed even more visible, so for all her wish for installation visitors to lose themselves in her work, the mediated aspect is always visible, tactile and audible.

12   Rosi Braidotti, *Transpositions* (Cambridge: Polity, 2006).

13   Jean-François Lyotard, *Libidinal Economy* (London: Athlone, 1993 [1974]). Translated by Iain Hamilton Grant.

14   Jean-François Lyotard, 'Acinema', in Andrew Benjamin (ed.), *The Lyotard Reader* (Oxford: Blackwell, 1991), 169–80. Translated by Paisley N. Livingston.

CHAPTER NINE

Pierre Huyghe, Repurposing Sound

Nicolas Bourriaud's reading of Huyghe's earlier works in *Relational Aesthetics* has proved influential, yet ultimately misleading. For all that Huyghe seems to engage with institutional structures before, in, during and after his work, the attention he pays to form and format as critical *methods* means that a strong flavour of modernism remains, or indeed, strengthens, in his work. In fact, modernism underpins his work as content, nostalgic utopia and working method. This may well occur within overlapping envelopes of something more relational, but my interest here is to look at the predominantly video-based installations that offer High-Definition, self-reflexive perspectives on contemporary living and visualization. A recurrent fulcrum of Huyghe's work is the passing of the modern, the passing of the recent past and indeed the precariousness of future potentials. For Amelia Barikin, his work can be seen as an ongoing dialogue with an ever-absent yet always potential utopia. The ideal space is there to be visualized, to be realized, even as it remains spectral. Following Huyghe, she notes that he consistently tries to 'extend fiction into reality. He starts from preexisting fictional elements, drags them out into the "desert of the real" and exposes them both *to* reality and *as* reality' (*Parallel Presents*, 95).[1] She also identifies in his work an amorphous '"and" space mobilized by the deferred movement of desire and law' (139).

Sound and music are essential components in many of Huyghe's works. From commissioned soundtracks through to field recordings to 'incidental' sound, if there is a utopian drive or drift, then it is spatialized, rendered as not contiguous with itself, through sound (and how sound plays off the visual part). As do many video artists, he draws our attention to sound as something other than the image, yet profoundly connected to it: something totally enmeshed yet retaining specificity, something that Derrida would identify as *différant*. In other words, this is a difference that is essential, tangled and, above all, part of a process, and it is the importance of process that must have drawn Bourriaud in, just as it does Barikin. For both, it is vital that Huyghe's works are not finished monuments to achieved projects; instead, they retain a capacity to change dimension, and to continue to affect their initial setting. In short, they remain in some way open. For me, sound is a vital vector in any such openness, as it not only draws attention to and from the visual but also spreads outward spatially, and also temporally (as the two parts of a piece do not offer the same kind of prospective closure), as both sound and vision mark duration as something interactive, and something experienced. Arguably this happens in many video works, and with Huyghe, it is very consciously done: sound separates off to return, continually, and this is one of the means by which 'other places' can be suggested, brought into being or shown as disappeared. The localization of sound, in spatializing differently to the visual, sets up the possibility of locatedness (as opposed to fixedness) of ideas. While these ideas may seem highly abstract, they are precisely grounded in sound and in its relation to image tracks, and will be addressed at their most complex in works such as those of the multiple work *Chateau de Turing* (2001), *Streamside Day* (2003) and *A Journey That Wasn't* (2005).

Sound is already functioning as *différantiel*, as splitting and rejoining, in the early works based on film dubbing – *Dubbing* (1996) and *Blanche Neige Lucie* (1997). Having tracked various sound strategies, we are by now familiar with strategies for defamiliarizing the processes of sound production, recording and transmission so as to make an installation visitor more than a simple viewer. Huyghe expands on this idea of the deconstructive connection of voice and all diegetic sound with the visual screen in referring us back to conventions in use in more narrative cinema, whereby voices are dubbed by professionals, into languages other than that of the original, themselves mirroring a process that most films have used internally to clarify some lines of dialogue or vocal sounds. In *Dubbing*, a room full of French dubbing actors perform to the film *Poltergeist*, and the video piece shows the mechanics of both a normal recording session and also the strangeness of what happens when you do not artificially separate out a film's soundtrack into individual performances to be replicated alone in vocal booths, but instead, all the actors speak together in one place and time. The original film now becomes the audio score for the video piece, the realization of which the installation-goer sees in the screened performance of the dubbers. *Blanche Neige Lucie* centres on actress Lucie Dolène, who voiced the character of Snow White in the French dubbed version of the Disney film of the story. She had just mounted and succeeded in a campaign to have the rights restored to her, thus cementing a perhaps traditional view of the personal possession of the voice as something essential to the person. Legally and financially, of course, it makes complete moral sense, and Huyghe tries to replicate that restoration in his video.

The video begins and ends with a shot of an empty filming studio, and the central part features Dolène, seated, looking directly at the camera. She does not speak – instead, subtitles convey her part of what we presume to be an interview about the story and process of regaining ownership of her voice. After the opening shots of the stage area, she sits silently as the subtitles roll. She sings *Un jour mon prince viendra* ('Someday My Prince Will Come'), a recurring song from the film, and then returns to silence. Shots of the empty room frame the whole 'narrative'. This time, Dolène is at the centre, visible, present, and her story restored. Barikin, following certain of Huyghe's comments, argues that Huyghe is mostly interested in the complexities of copyright and ownership of rights, even if he is not making a militant point about them (*Past Presents*, 100–4). But if anything, the use of sound in the piece only complicates the question, and far from merely bringing out the means of production or revealing the presence of the hidden workers, Huyghe's piece does something else. After all, Dolène is wordless here. Furthermore, the subtitles, it says on Huyghe's collaborative Anna Sanders site, are scripted by him.[2]

The incidental sounds reflect the wider scope of film-making, of producing works that require workers in many practical activities beyond the camera's view. The studio, though, in *Blanche Neige Lucie*, seems to prepare itself – perhaps referring to the machine-like status of mass media, but certainly not a revelation of all the hidden, poorly paid workers that make film productions happen. The presence of subtitles recounting the tale before Dolène's appearance on screen also heightens the process of her alienation from ownership of her vocal means of production. To counter this, she sings the song: in so doing, she reclaims her status as Blanche Neige, while repeating the somewhat 'pre-feminist' idea of being saved by a man of power.

In short, there are several obvious ways in which this piece cannot be construed as being primarily a deconstruction of the rights and wrongs of ownership where copyright is owned by circuits of production rather than individuals. It is in some way about that, but it is not what the piece *does*. What it does is raise wider questions of self-ownership and of voice as expression of self, and how these become tools or toys of the director using them. It would seem that Huyghe is aware of the ironies of his method of directing this actress and that they too form part of a long and almost paradoxical chain of connections that feature the more political critique as part of a broader formal project. The film closes with the subtitles (in the English language version) announcing, 'It's my voice after all!', and then moves to apparent silence, but we can hear the audio track and/or sound part of the film crackling as it continues to roll, but with no sound to record. The crackles also suggest the pops and clicks of worn vinyl – appropriately given the other separation of person from voice that is in play here is the nearly sixty years between recording of the French audio for *Snow White* and *Blanche Neige Lucie*. Huyghe is attentive enough to the sounds of music, and the sounds of machinery, to recognize these sounds as connoting not just the past but also nostalgia for the lost past. So if there is utopianism in this piece, it is one of reconnection, but also one that is not simply a resolution of a past problem. In fact, as the sound demonstrates, it is a keeping-open of the issue raised by 'taking' someone's right to his or her own voice.

In a further exploration of the border crossings between identity and ownership rights, Huyghe and Philippe Parreno bought the rights to a manga character called Ann Lee, and opened up the character for manipulation by other artists, and let the androgynous female figure appear as herself but always under the direction of others. Ann Lee would ultimately be given control of her own image rights and thereby ceased to be a functioning artwork. In the meantime, she ghosts in to Huyghe's *One Million Kingdoms* (2001). In this piece, Ann Lee is a spectral outline, her 1990s manga form recalling shapes from 1980s video games. She walks at steady pace, travelling through a landscape made from sound forms and from the voice of Neil Armstrong. Huyghe's script merges elements of Verne's 1864 novel *Journey to the Centre of the Earth* with fragments of Armstrong's actual mission communications and other more paranoid scenarios. This is then all recounted by Armstrong's sampled voice, complete with radio tonal effects, slightly blurring the edges of words, adding to an overall feeling of distance (spatial, due to the need to use machinery, temporal, due to use of now old technology) (figure 9.1).

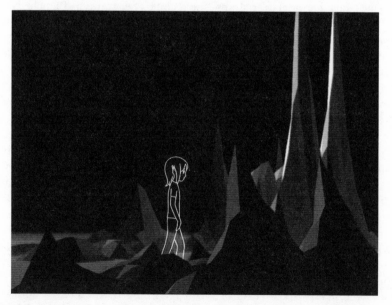

FIGURE 9.1 *Pierre Huyghe,* One Million Kingdoms *(2001). Colour video; six minutes fifty seconds. Courtesy Pierre Huyghe and Marian Goodman Gallery.*

As 'Armstrong' speaks, peaks rise and then fall away, and a mountainous moon appears, and disappears, and these are present only as words and other sounds occur, and as Ann Lee walks through them. The landscape is only sound, sound rendered in three-dimensional form, conveyed in two dimensions, via a sample of words written by someone other than the speaker, and the speaker is only a construct made from sampled fragments repurposed to speak new words, new configurations of cut-up textual sources. The two forms of Ann Lee and the landscape move along as if doomed to continue even though their mission is over – a 1969 astronaut and a 1990s animation both standing as futures past, non-places now. Part of Huyghe's text even refers to the shooting of moon landings as something fake, so Armstrong gets to undo his own utopian moment, a moment that was conveyed or even created through words (and the residual sounds of communications devices) as much as through the images of men on the moon.

Huyghe returns to the visually realized soundscape in his *Journey That Wasn't* (2005), and persists with the sound-heavy technological utopias of the past in other pieces from the same time, gathered in the form of his pavilion at the 2001 Venice biennale, *Le Château de Turing*. As many now know, Alan Turing was one of the central figures in the invention of modern computing, working on decoding machines in Bletchley Park in the Second World War. In addition to the technological reference, Huyghe is also surely thinking of the 'Turing test', which is a way of testing a machine to see if it can pass for human.[3] The building is also 'controlled' by another piece, called *HAL*, after the hubristic computer intelligence in Kubrick's film *2001*, itself a monument to utopias technical and spiritual/psychedelic. *HAL* operates the 'blinking doors' which appear opaque and transparent by turns (Huyghe uses this in other configurations of these pieces too). Presumably, then, it is the human visitors who are being tested to see if they match the conditions of artificial intelligence laid out by Turing, and installed by Huyghe. Only there is no answer, just a process of testing. The interactiveness of the piece is interesting to a certain degree, and well filmed on the DVD document of the pavilion, but it is the presence of humans inside the circuit that is interesting, that is, their incapacity to interact in ways other than following the limited pathways on offer.

Still in the pavilion, there is *Atari Lights* (1999), a ceiling-based rendition of the ultra-basic computer game Pong, a sort of abstracted tennis game. Anachronistic controllers are all there on the floor, and the room is dominated by the loud, crisp electronic pinging of the game. Joining in completes the circuit, but the game can play itself. In *Les grands ensembles* (2001), twin buildings play themselves. In this piece, Huyghe refers to the lost utopia of Le Corbusier, which gave way to stacking people in poorly built, ill-equipped tower blocks far from the centres of cities (in the case of France). As Mark Godfrey observes, '*Les grands ensembles* provokes the imagination of utopian communities *and* responds to the disintegration of utopianism' ('Pierre Huyghe's Double Spectacle', 41).[4] As with *Blanche Neige Lucie*, we need to note what actually happens before deciding the piece's attitude towards the utopian vision of modernist architecture. The piece consists of a film of two models of tower blocks (unlike architects' design maquettes, these are built after the event, observations instead of proposals), with a streetlight and some occasional wafts of smoke. The tower block windows light up in complex patterns as the music (by Pan sonic) builds. The residents, or the buildings themselves, are recovering the utopia thought to be destroyed by cynical and often-corrupt planning and building projects. The music is simple, a clean take on techno built from very minimal elements. When Pan sonic started (and when they were called Panasonic), their music was almost entirely based on residues of electronic machinery sounds. Over time, although the explicitness of this approach diminished, they continued to try to resuscitate machinery through unexpected potentials and also through overdriving electronic devices. In other words, the presence of Pan sonic here is very much as a selected soundtrack, but it meshes so precisely that it comes to have been an integral part of the piece (as the lights respond to it, perhaps operating as further Turing machines) or even the foundation of it. Modernism reshapes itself as the play of the more hopeful ideas of the postmodern. It is rejuvenated as if it always already had the capacity to be a joyous social location of community. But like many utopias, its loss (failure, passing or demolition) is carried as potential within it, and for all the pleasingly warm sound and festive lights, the landscape is bleak – devoid of signs of life. The lights and sounds fight against that fate, even if that destiny is already complete. *One Million Kingdoms* carries the same loss – manned spaceflight to somewhere beyond the Earth orbit abandoned for now – so it is entirely appropriate that a sampled Armstrong soundwalks forever through the mountains of the moon, alone except for Ann Lee's ghost.

The whole *Château de Turing* resonates, coding itself through sound – sound which has all been produced as data, via circuits, and then only later becoming analogue (in the reverberation of speakers and ears). The sound is not a unifier, though. Instead, it connects disparate moments and keeps them separate yet linked, *différantiel*. Different eras connect as mutual echoes, sometimes stretching back into the past, and at other times moving forward as very slow time machines from their 'proper' time. The utopianism is a constant; it is both cause and hoped-for effect of the various digital sounds in audition here.

In 2004, Huyghe produced the work *This Is Not a Time for Dreaming*, a playful and highly complex work based on Le Corbusier's utopianism – a utopia seemingly exposed as wrongheaded and dogmatic, fit only to be remembered through ironic nostalgia. Closer attention reveals that this is not at all the view presented in this piece, where Le Corbusier's building

(The Carpenter Center for the Visual Arts, Harvard University) forms the basis for Huyghe's piece, which is a puppet play, filmed in an extension to the Center devised by him, and then presented in a way that exposes the mechanisms of art and architecture commissioning and production. In one sense, then, this work is very much an exercise in relational aesthetics, using the process of developing work, the demands of commissions, the staging of work in cultural institutions, the existing building and the legacy of modernism, as material. What separates *This Is Not a Time for Dreaming* from the mundanities of self-reflexively looking at conditions of production is the way Huyghe makes the finished film incorporate an assertion of the validity of modernist architecture's utopian mission and modernism's capacity to be self-reflectively aesthetic and future-looking. This piece has no fear of being avant-garde, and so it succeeds in a merging of contemporary institutional critique with formalist work.

The framing of the piece is only gradually revealed, so it makes sense to summarize the progress of the main constituent part, the puppet play, even if some of it only becomes clear at the end. At the beginning, Le Corbusier is met at a metal gate in a desolate landscape by a large shiny black insect, who is gesturing for him to do something (no words are spoken, no text provided until the end). We later discover that this is the 'dean of deans' – in effect the head of Harvard, metonymizing for Harvard and, it will seem likely, also for the economic imperatives of commissioning. The Huyghe puppet is brought in by the curators to examine boxes of overflowing Le Corbusier papers, which are stirred up and whirl uncontrollably through the air. While Huyghe is overwhelmed, one of the papers seems to suggest a way forward. The space in both time frames, forty years apart, has as its only prop a sparse tree, on which the papers settle. Through the piece, both Le Corbusier and Huyghe encounter a red bird, usually carrying a seed, standing in for the possibility of creation. Both also fall asleep, against the tree, or elsewhere, and dream projects into existence. Le Corbusier dreams forms whirling through the air, geometrical objects as concepts as well as their visual rendering. As these shapes fly by each other, the space gives way to a grid structure – the frame of the prospective building. This will then be present when Le Corbusier presents his project to the insect dean. When Huyghe dreams, he sees a creeping green clump of indeterminate form, growing and almost pulsating amid a section of the building frame. This represents his first project to grow plants on the building, which ultimately failed. Huyghe then argues with one of the curators (Linda Norden), who is subsequently lifted and shaken by the insect dean, until she slumps to the floor while Huyghe looks on. This mysterious moment could be a way of visualizing the pressures of the funding part of commissioning work, or also that she had been taken over by the bureaucratic and ends-oriented ways of thinking induced by power relations and practices. Then we see the building being taken over by brambles, grown from a seed left by the bird, on the now-completed structure. This will then lead to a rethinking of the project, and a large Huyghe puppet manipulates smaller ones of Huyghe and Le Corbusier to put the new green-coloured structure into place adjoining the Center.

As we approach the end, shots of the actual building (surrounded by trees and greenery) and Huyghe's extension appear. Finally, having also seen shots of the audience in that extension, and watching the play, we hear and see a description of the work, written by Huyghe. I have described the elements at some length, because they all count, and they all contribute to the meditation on modernist formalism that is an extreme extension of that philosophy (or politics, or method). We still have the sound to consider. Huyghe takes music by composers Iannis Xenakis and Edgard Varèse, and turns them into a melodramatic soundtracking of the actions in both periods. There are also some moments where digital music occurs, skittering across the other music, as Huyghe and Le Corbusier join forces. Xenakis and Varèse worked with Le Corbusier on the Philips pavilion at the Brussels Fair in 1958, where the 400 speakers made the sounds a vital spatial structuring force (Xenakis also working on the project in a more narrowly architectural way). Early in the film, Le Corbusier dances to the sounds of Charles Trenet's song *La Mer* (released in 1946), with the tree joining in. While a central part of this work is the rethinking of modernism as something more than simply logical, this whimsical moment is not without its modernist referent, as Trenet built his own house (completed in 1950) in southern France very much in the style of Le Corbusier's individual homes.

Beyond the structural use of music, then, and its Corbusian connections, there are also some interesting incidental sounds – birdsong, the shifting of slabs as the building takes final shape (its components being capable of movement showing that modernism also knew about process, not just ends), the sounds of the puppets moving around or moving objects. Overall, though, and unlike in *Grands ensembles*, it cannot be said that the sound drives the visual. However, its strategic use of 'incidental', diegetic sound as well as a retooling of the highest of modernist musics, mean that the potentially solipsistic indwelling of a single form that modernism is associated with does not occur. The final sounds are of the reading of Huyghe's text and the revealing of the workings of the piece – the voice is a container of authority, a transmitter of the artist's intention, but it is too late, the piece too complex to be explained in this way. In any case, the speech suggests that it takes place before the play, and in presenting the talk in this way, Huyghe refers us back to the working of video installation, the time of the installation visit differing *dramatically* from a film viewed sequentially (the construction of the piece going against such clear linearity in its internal narration and merging of musics).

Sound is an important part of the intermedia nature of *This Is Not a Time for Dreaming*, but only part of an extensive play of forms, deformations, new formings, and some sort of process that can only be thought of as (Bataille's idea of) formless, that is, as occurring between, around, under, before or after forms. The temporal element of Huyghe's utopian exploration, as identified by Barikin, is prominent in the piece, and so is the spatial working out of the conceptual and ethical utopia of Le Corbusier. Built space is constructed and redefined through models, dreams, 'actual' buildings (still models, but diegetically real), actual buildings (the Center and extension), the play of viewing the play and the filming of it as if it was all done whilst an audience was there in the extension, and finally, in its relation to nature. Le Corbusier was a pioneering ecological architect, Huyghe affirms, as brambles cover the building in one dream, and as the tree dances with Le Corbusier, and inspires artist and architect alike. Le Corbusier's buildings, projects and urban plans all sought to maximize the space available for plants to grow, and to grow unimpeded by traffic, or humanity's tendency to sprawling over the spaces of nature. Huyghe's attempts to extend the Center back into nature are an acknowledgement, not a critique, of Le Corbusier's aims.

This brings us to the title. The exhortation to not be a dreamer is typical of corporate or any institutional instruction to society's more hapless members. But all creation, here, comes from dreaming, from stepping out of utilitarian and quotidian concerns. This, I think, is Huyghe nudging us towards the sense that modernist architecture is not just logic, efficiency and geometrically restricted structures, but that, even when it is, it plays off the irrational, the dream, the hope and the utopia of all possibility. So the title draws us to the value of a dream, a value that is generally non-quantifiable or saleable (hence the difficulties of both Le Corbusier and Huyghe in fulfilling their commissions). The time of the title refers to now. *This*, now, is not the time for dreaming, where the modernist past was a time for dreaming. For all the faults of the use (or abuse) of modernist architectural precepts in low-cost, low-grade mass housing, Le Corbusier's time (as defined by modernism) was a time for dreaming. It is not that modernist utopia failed here, crushed like the exploding Pruitt Igoe estate in St. Louis, symbol for both Robert Hughes and Charles Jencks of the failure and end of modernism; modernism's expression of utopia fails because utopianism is being denied any place in the time after modernism. Failure is not a sign of inherent badness in utopian projects, but the sign that utopianism, as mostly irrealizable potentials, is actually happening at all. Huyghe's own expression of utopianism in *This Is Not a Time for Dreaming* is a multiple, playful one, reminding us of utopia as something to dream, and so becomes more of a process, sidestepping potentially dogmatic parts of modernism's project(s).

The connection of nature and culture, as mutual others, is a recurring concern in Huyghe's video projects, and the focus on space, spatialization as well as defamiliarization of the place of nature as simple other to culture is part of the project to find 'other' spaces, and to bring them closer, or bring them into being. Two other projects take more explicitly locational projects as the material for video pieces. The first of these is *Streamside Day* (2003). Set in the recently built housing estate of Streamside Knolls, the piece documents the first commemoration of the inauguration of the estate, even though it is still not completed. Huyghe staged this celebration, an uncertain event in what seems like a contingent space, very much like a filmset of a lost J.G. Ballard story. The beginning alternates between a family making a car journey to the estate and shots of the borders, of still-not-removed nature, which gets its focus in the form of a young deer, seemingly captured (visually), unaware, while exploring the estate. The deer has already been seen as part of a community of animals (also including a hare and owl – all figures familiar from children's stories), and happily cohabiting a high-definition woodland.

From the beginning, Huyghe is positing a very mixed idea of coinciding utopian visions – on the one hand, the animal pastoral; on the other, a new beginning in a new human community. The two cross over, and, as Barikin notes, 'Huyghe's equivalences between humans and fauna, the forest and the town, break down distinctions between natural and artificial' (*Parallel Presents*, 168). It is not unusual for new human building to reclaim the bucolic, the utopia of simpler and more natural environments, in order to develop and sell real estate, but Huyghe's way of connecting nature and built society is more complicated, and not exactly critical of commercially interested evocations of nature. The first part of the film uses sound in highly strategic fashion. While we are with the driving family, their sounds dominate and represent a possible disruption to the woodland, whose sounds are, in their turn, to be heard when those scenes are shown. The sounds are often treated, but the sources remain identifiable, particularly as the piece cuts to a loud waterfall. This announces the sonic strategy of the rest of the first part (entitled 'The Score'), where rising sound carries a sense of portent, but also of the mutual crossing of the paths of nature and culture. As the deer approaches a house and goes in, the sound of hooves is clearly presented, but the entire journey it makes is guided by (or creates) a rising electronic soundscape. This is directly echoed in the shot of the car heading to the estate, at which point a loud electronic buzz announces their arrival, and fades down. A high-frequency tone accompanies the car circling around Streamside Knolls.

The first section ends with a scene over a minute long (from 9.00 to 10.13) within which the twin children from the car stand in front of two trees or bushes approximately shaped into human giant form, and as this happens, the electronic music rises again. The processing of natural sound into digital samples, along with the recurring presence of indexical nature sounds, indicates the crossing between nature and culture that is neither unidirectional nor about the simple subsuming of nature. Nature, in the form of its specific plants and animals at the edge of the estate, looks on with lack of concern, able to access the buildings and the children, and maintain freedom of movement. They are not so much a threat as a Romantic expression of Nature's immanence, and its ineffability.

The second part offers a very different sound strategy, as it charts, in documentary style, the progress of 'The Celebration'. This is a sparsely attended art event in its own right, much more of the relational genre than the finished video. There is a folk song played at one point, on a simple stage, but mostly the sound is of people talking, running around. It is left untouched, recorded simply (or presented as such), certainly not focussing much on any one thing. It seems very mundane compared to the first part, a celebration of the everyday, established on the basis of 'The Score' perhaps, but also despite it. Now the sound is more spontaneously generated, and the lack of aural focus is a sign that this estate is something of a community – that it coheres into something united, and something natural (sounds unprocessed). This estate is the proper environment for these humans. It too has its surreal-ish moments – most of the children have animal heads on, and towards the end a patently artificial Moon hangs slightly above house level.[5] These connect to the exploring deer in the first part as well as to the encounter of tree figures and human children. Above all, this video seeks to separate out different utopian visions (and hearings) in order to make them strange, and to connect them deconstructively. Barikin talks of a 'series of ruptures [*Streamside Day*] introduced within the construct of utopia itself' (*Parallel Presents*, 157), particularly when we take the differing sound strategies into account, along with the peaks of volume and complexity in the first part. So the utopia of *Streamside Day* is neither for nor against that of the Streamside Knoll estate. It is instead a maintaining not only of utopian concepts but also the outside of human culture, an outside that infiltrates regulated human environments.

A Journey That Wasn't (2005) covers similar terrain, in raising ecological issues, without definitively taking a position on them. I would argue that the complexity of these interrelated videos mean they also do much more than 'refer to' ecological question as content, but instead work through a series of displacements, at their most physical or material in this piece, to supply a very specific recasting of utopian, critical thinking. The work documented in the final video has several stages: a visit to an Antarctic island; sound gathering and filming there; presentation of topographical data to composer Joshua Cody; rendering of that in sound, by Cody with input from Huyghe, into musical notes suitable to be played by an orchestra; the playing of that work, with an outline of the island as well as rock diorama, in Central Park, New York; and showing all those activities.[6]

The video alternates between the Antarctic mission and the Central Park event, with narration of the first of those in the course of the second. In the Antarctic sections, the sounds oscillate dramatically between quiet and loud, reflecting the environment's rapid shifts between tranquillity and threatening meteorological havoc. This extreme variation is mirrored in harsh editing cuts in sound. That is the prime intervention as far as the final sound is concerned, but at one point a pulsing balloon sends out matching light to synthesized sound, and a group of penguins draws close to it (represented by an animatronic penguin in the park performance). The Central Park show begins with throbbing electronic sound, to be joined by other instruments, just as with the sounds shown in the Antarctic (and *Streamside Day*) analogue and digital sound processes intertwine. The island is reproduced in newly cultured sound form, both preserving the indexical quality of data while separating off from the sound of field recording and suggesting the loss of source material. As this loss occurs in sound, in fact presenting its loss in the change of form, from raw recordings to musicalization, so it is reinstated in light and also text. Barikin follows a different path through the soundscapes of the piece, and her conclusion holds good here, as she writes that 'in place of mimesis, Huyghe established a system that produced a "deformation of the same into the same" (a homeomorphism)' (*Parallel Presents*, 207). Godfrey concurs, in assessing Huyghe's reference to place as work that demonstrates 'that an elsewhere and an Other can be contacted but not represented' ('Pierre Huyghe's Double Spectacle', 55).

The sound ends on a blast, suggesting completion, but as with much of Huyghe's work, this ending is incorporated into a process where it too becomes material (for the film and installation). While the role of sound (and music) in Huyghe's videos play with levels, stages and ends of processes, it is much more important as a non-representational way of building a critical image of utopias, other spaces, and at each moment operating a defamiliarization that is properly uncanny. The cuts, crescendos and diminuendos also enact a re-presenting of the same that has changed – their use, in soundtracks, is primarily a way of imposing narrative structure or playing on pre-existing cultural associations, but nature too offers such changes, and without the one simply basing itself on the other, the two systems relate to one another as each other's opposite, all the while connecting as potential, as formless becoming form and vice-versa.

Notes

1   Amelia Barikin, *Parallel Presents: The Art of Pierre Huyghe* (Cambridge, MA: MIT Press, 2012).
2   http://www.annasandersfilms.com/archives/blanche-neige-lucie/. Accessed 4th February 2014.
3   See Alan Turing, 'Computing Machinery and Intelligence', *Mind* LIX (October 1950), 433–60. Note also that Turing specifies the people and/or machines to be tested need to be in separate rooms to the tester (434), a control echoed in Huyghe's use of *HAL* to visually open or close off rooms in the *Château de Turing*.

4   Mark Godfrey, 'Pierre Huyghe's Double Spectacle', *Grey Room* 32 (Summer 2008), 38–61.

5   Bataille notes that the cave art of Lascaux features no depictions of human features, but shows animals in great detail. His argument is that the beginning of humanity is partly a turning away from its own animality, but also a recognition of that turning away, the trace of which lies in the refusal to represent the human face. See his *Prehistoric Painting: Lascaux or the Birth of Art* (London: Macmillan, 1980 [1955]). Translated by Austryn Wainhouse.

6   The piece also has textual and verbal elements, and links to other works that work around similar material. For a detailed reflection on all those parts, see Godfrey, 'Pierre Huyghe's Double Spectacle', 46–55.

CHAPTER TEN

Steve McQueen,
The Destabilizing Ground

The first thing you encounter in Steve McQueen's video triptych *Drum Roll* (1998) is the sound – an almighty racket bleeding out of its installation space. Its twenty-two-minute duration is full of the clattering, rolling and bumping of the big steel can as McQueen rolls it down New York's 5th Avenue. Three cameras record its passage, one facing out in each direction from within the can, and another seemingly embedded in the shell, facing forward. So the first two present horizontally cycling windows, the other, presented as the central image, sets the sky, the people and street rolling vertically in front of us. That there is only one unifying soundtrack indicates the vital role sound has to play in organizing the piece, an organizational and centring capacity to be witnessed in many of McQueen's installation works. The initial effect is one of grounding – as in *Static* (2009), where the powerful sound of helicopter rotor blades places us concretely beside the camera that is circling the Statue of Liberty, where silence, or masking of that sound, would have offered an idealized or even Ideal, bird's eye view. First, sound locates the 'viewer' of the installation, with loud sound ensuring that the spectator of an installation also becomes a self-aware listener, and more and more present in all their senses. Second, the sound supplies information and directs perspective. But this is never simple. T.J. Demos, writing of McQueen's *Western Deep*, notes that sound estranges the view, opening up the possibility for further distortion and purposeful play between visual and political elements, with the opening of the piece being 'the first indication of a conspicuous refusal to represent in the visual register, which frustrates the documentary impulse to which the film is seemingly pledged'.[1]

Demos takes sound as an indicator, or index, of some other process that McQueen engages in (in all his work) – that of not allowing the purely visual to take over, nor to be beholden to film/video as a transparent medium of capture ('The Art of Darkness', 65). I agree, but I think Demos emphasizes only the explicit intention of McQueen – the purposely structured part of why sound is there in the first place, perhaps, whereas in fact the use of sound is much more detailed, and much more central than merely being a form of annunciation. In fact, if the beginning of *Western Deep* illustrates anything, it is the centrality of sound as organizing device, which centres only to deviate the 'viewer' from finding simple meaning and linear narrative. In this piece, the opening few minutes (up to 6.40) are loaded with abrasive machine sounds – something like a train – which turn out to be the sounds of a lift descending into a South African gold mine. Blurry shots of the miners alternate with darkness (recalling Debord's *Hurlements en faveur de Sade* [1952]), and then sound cuts abruptly as we and they arrive. Machines, bodies and silences alternate positions as the film takes on more of a narrative tone (but always in a self-disrupting way). The opening is more than an introductory device – it evokes the miners' condition as swallowed into the machine-ridden earth, themselves mineralizing into metal, gold and rock. Rather than constructing a message over-ride for his work, McQueen picks politically charged and oppressive political situations and 'lets' them do the work through rendering them in visually experimental form.[2]

It is hard to imagine an ancillary 'message' for *Drum Roll* in the same way. Its physicality (in the act on display, in the deformation of the visual and in the overpoweringly loud sound) stands forcefully as a bulwark against attributing a clear and final sense to it. Still, the location is not innocent – a wealthy New York thoroughfare, a trashcan rolled along it, suggesting the threat of the dispossessed (either as themselves waste or through their threatening mobility due to lack of homes). This is an act of intrusion. It is not aggressive – McQueen does not aim at people; he obeys traffic lights and can be heard apologizing if he is looking to get by or when he interrupts the passage of someone. In fact, it is a perversely polite interruption ('watch out', 'excuse me', 'I'm sorry'), perhaps suggesting a menial worker going about his task among the wealthy folks, aware of his relative class station in life.[3] The 'drum roll' is a military signal – it can signal reward, aggressive condolence or a call-to-arms, when it structures marching. While the three cameras maintain their discipline, the rolling can is like oil dripping into the otherwise-already rolling waters of New York – there is a structure, but it can only be arrived at chaotically. While not creating any sort of breakdown, it is the irruption of the generally hidden or denied 'formless' of urban life. If this is some sort of revolution, it is a revolt that unravels the fabric of the society it seeks to change, rather than being an open assault.

Like Georges Bataille's 'formless', it is not something that comes from outside, but something that lives in internal exclusion: the otherness of the rolling drum is a chaotic patterning that underpins and undermines the social structure around it: '*formless* is not only an adjective having a given meaning, but a term that serves to bring things down in the world' ('Formless', 31).[4] The drum brings a sense of form as lost form – not just formlessness, but a driver of the process of forming. It does this through the way it gathers the world around it: there is no outside view of New York here – the city, its inhabitants, businesses, traffic, demographic and even climate are brought into being only as, and exactly when, the drum rolls through them. And it arrives only as refracted into three, so the drum gathers, creates the space around it, like Heidegger's bridge, and brings space into being:

> [the bridge] does not just connect banks that are already there. The banks emerge as banks only as the bridge crosses the stream. The bridge expressly causes them to lie across from each other. [...] With the banks, the bridge brings to the stream the one and the other expanse of the landscape lying behind them [...]. The bridge *gathers* the earth as landscape around the stream. ('Building Dwelling Thinking', 354)[5]

More accurately, given the openness of this arbitrary builder, the *city* is brought into being through the drum, the drum when in movement, because when it is still, nothing comes into view, and nothing can happen. It is not just abstract space but meaningful features, connected cityscape and people as dwellers of the polis that are brought into (troubled) focus. Not only does the racketing drum bring a fractured city into noise-defined reality, but the smoother the passage of the drum, the more disorienting the visual effect.

If the drum acts as some sort of centring device for the city, then the drum too is centred through the noise of the recording. The city gathers only in a form refracted through the continuous clatter of steel on urban ground. The city intrudes into the intrusive sound of the drum, but only to merge with it. The explicit noise of the functioning of the 'drum roll machine', comprising drum, cameras, microphone and McQueen, is in turn a marker of the deeper noise the introduction of the machine represents: noise as intrusion. The sound is intrusion and noise, but also rhythm, however disjointed it may be. Like the drum, the noise is engaged in gathering, that is, melding the triple perspective into one – but not 'one' that resolves the multiplicity of views. It completes the fractured whole, but almost from outside, and so leaves the puzzling three-eyed view on show. The central image should combine with the sound, offering a safe centre from which to be mildly thrown, but it does not. Instead, the centre is an attack on stereoscopy, on finding a safe position – as it does not resolve the surrounding images (from the sideways – facing cameras). The combination of images in this way means we are not centred in the events seen, but *on* the visual and auditory narrative – the images hold us back, and the sound draws us in – thus we are caught up in the noise of multiple processes (sound, vision, bodily movement and material), where the spectator/auditor is specifically and awkwardly positioned, as if McQueen is there with you in the dark room, shoving you this way and that, while shouting.

McQueen continually redirects and deviates the perception of the person encountering *Drum Roll*, and this occurs in the defamiliarizing acts that cross between form and content, material and abstract and the shown and the showing. This occurs because of the presence of sound of such force, and its difference from or place within the visual parts. Lastly, the field recording, in so far as that is what we have here, is directly material – achieved not by standing back from the environment to capture it, but through total immersion and permanent touching of the ground by the resonant drum. So the drum is a device through and into which sound can travel due to its openness, but it is its unbroken surface that dominates, as it rattles and thunders like a colossal contact microphone. In so doing, *Drum Roll* reverts to being a sort of *arte povera*, or even minimalist land art, where the material is taken, only to be left as material, as opposed to abstracting it in any way (Koji Asano has done the same with the microphone rubbing the ground in his *Quoted Landscape* CD [1995]).

The same could be seen applying in *Static* (2009), where the airborne camera films the Statue of Liberty from a circling helicopter. The sound of the helicopter's flight is highly prominent – this is not a view from above, a view that would seal the statue into a triumphalist pose. Instead, the very loud sound of the blades brings us to the material basis of both viewing camera and the viewed object. In a strong hint at narrative purpose, there are two extended moments where the sound drops out (for 1.24 and 1.22 respectively, out of a seven-minute duration) – strongly suggesting the now-absent towers of the World Trade Center. A third, brief quietness that comes before the others could either stand for the third, smaller tower or even the previous attack in 1993, to impute direct, and literal referencing to historical events. Can we presume this meaning? It needs several presumptions about connotation, but as these are standard ones, all connected to self-representations of the United States, and the city of New York as gateway into that freedom, it would seem to be a likely possibility. That it is through noise that this meaning is generated is significant in that noise is a complexifying and intrusive force. The complex route into this first-level meaning ('something about 9/11') already shows that there will not be a straightforward message here. The perverse tranquillity of the periods where the helicopter sounds are absent might indicate a mourning, but also a reflective stillness.[6]

If the silences signal the destruction of the World Trade Center, then to display and linger on the Statue of Liberty runs the risk of either triumphalism ('our values still hold') or of stoic acceptance and resilience. But McQueen lures us into this possibility, only to take it away – *Static* ends amid helicopter silence and the sound of the wind – something that might make us more inclined to the tragic reading of the broken, beached statue as offered in the film of *The Planet of the Apes* (1968). If the threat of noise and its removal are ambiguous, then so is the display of the statue: the helicopter suggesting surveillance, or even military intervention. This could be to protect freedom, but the way in which freedom is protected can be, shall we say, overzealous, and lead to its opposite. The statue itself is not shown as a whole, so despite it being static, it becomes fluid, as the camera picks out the folds of clothing, the book, the crown and the face. Liberty is not a predictable unitary quality or thing, and its reality on the ground is as something variegated, possibly fragmentary. If we imagine McQueen bringing this all together, the attack of September 2001 creates a situation where the representation and defence of freedom have become very difficult – that is, they are deeply compromised even if a still beautiful object (freedom) warrants attention. The statue is also shown in its isolation from New York, and the sections we see of the city are functional rather than those that would stereotypically signify any values connected to freedom, wealth and democracy.

If the issue of freedom shows McQueen's will to engage with higher matters, then *Gravesend* (2007) takes the formalist critique of exploitation present in *Western Deep* to a higher plane, where labour itself is a device that connects humanity to the universe, and/or alienates it simultaneously. Rather than opting for either Marx or Aristotle here, who both argued in similar vein, I prefer to connect this work to Georges Bataille's idea of a general economy, where humanity's labouring is an epiphenomenal part of a universe in process, and one where destruction is at least as much a force as creation.[7] *Gravesend* also starts with the sounds of machinery – crisp whirring, the sound of compressors and loud throbbing introduce a robotic machine in a sterile environment, sorting and transporting. From there, we encounter silently working black miners. Unlike *Western Deep*, this piece does not stay in the work environment, but increasingly separates off sound from visual activity, ending in shimmering light over water, backed with the sound of chipping rock (which occurs at numerous points in the course of the piece). For all humanity's control over the mineral, and its (selective) economic benefit, the transformation of material into value is only a limited example of metamorphosis or stability in nature – water, rock and sound will remain beyond human control. The limits of rational control are also illustrated in the treatment of sound and image, unusually explicit for McQueen, for brief sections later in the video. Labour can be heard (before it can be seen) as alienation – the feasibly unalienated act of working of rock, generally seen as a pivotal act in original human culture, is the sign of the 'progress' into technical, economic and metaphysical alienation to come.

A more mysterious meditation on animality, humanity, sight and sound can be found in *Pursuit* (2005), a film that is mostly dark, lit by groups of moving dots, and where the sound is once more the organizing force. Scratching, shuffling sounds give way to the sounds of digging at earth, animal vocalizations, with the sounds getting 'nearer' in the second half. The dots of light can then be seen as an animal moving in the dark, reminiscent of the title sequence of BBC's music programme *The Old Grey Whistle*

Test. The feeling of the piece, especially in installation form, is somewhat worrying, with the sense that the sounds we hear are of something we cannot quite glimpse, that is hunting us and getting nearer. But as the piece goes on, it seems more like an anthropological or zoological documentary, with the mysterious object hard to grasp – literally and metaphorically. The 'pursuit' becomes the possibility of knowledge, with the creature evading us, just as we evade its questing. The relation then becomes the mirroring that occurs in a notional border of human and animal: the human looks back to the animal as other, to learn it, while 'the animal' haunts the human as a threat, or memory of transition. This happens through sound, and it happens through the uncanny animal voice:

> the animal voice is not truly 'empty' [...] but contains the death of the animal, [and this is how] human language, articulating and arresting the pure sound of this voice (the vowel) – that is to say, articulating and retaining the *voice of death* – becomes the *voice of consciousness*. (Agamben, *Language and Death*, 45)

The uncertainty of the film's sounds does establish an air of menacing uncertainty, but the ultimate location of this is to do with that edge of humanity, the edge of the town and the edge of where 'we' live, in a sense that is much more than there being a threatening creature beyond or within the screen.[8] Instead, the border of humanity is played out, with the menace being the threat of the returning animal voice (that always only returns for the human, which can distance itself from death). Humanity uses language to enact this distancing and the bringing into thought of death, as other, as separate.[9] So the threat remains. This threat is exactly what is brought into being as some kind of remnant in the moaning, patchily lit and shambling creature, which cannot take form, other than as voice and light. The pursuit then is that of the animal past that lingers on as the sense of death.

Access to these wider phenomena, how we perceive them and how they are represented, is achieved through sound, noise and silences in all of these works. Given the capacity of that sound to overload (in all senses) the visual, we can balance that by taking an example of McQueen's work where sound overloads sound – *Girls Tricky* (2001), which promises initially to be either rock video or fly on the wall music documentary about Tricky recording the song 'Girls'. Instead, McQueen is pressed into a glass-walled vocal booth with Tricky, in a claustrophobic shared physicality. From the start, the singer smokes deeply from a joint, which, as it burns down on his deep inhalations, crackles and glows (the booth is mostly in darkness). Tricky himself is seen in silhouette for much of the first half, an alien with huge protruding ears (he is listening in on himself and the band, who play facing the booth, through headphones). In the second part, where there is a full run-through of the eight-minute song, Tricky's face is shown 'full-frontal' but still almost pressed in by the camera, and in turn pressing back. The sound is close, too close, as extraneous sounds are blocked out to focus on the voice in itself, for the recording. Elements of recorded songs that are usually hidden, such as breaths, small adjustments, physical movements, are brought to the fore, estranging the sound. For all the proximity of the singer, in vision and in sound, it is too much and sounds false – we are entirely habituated to seek voice in its own right while knowing that we habitually encounter it mixed up with more frequencies, interruptions and noise. We therefore expect the sound, and then filter it out, unconsciously as much as consciously. Here, noise goes away for the voice, for the singer to become the noise of uncanniness. To sound and vision, we have to add the body as a further medium that is brought too close, that is, brought into a proximity that we sense alters the border between McQueen and Tricky, but also between them and us as viewer-listeners. As the singer warms to the role he plays in the song, shaking with continually modulating emotions, the song and even the sight fall into the background – the performance displaces the content of the performance. This works precisely through McQueen's search for the too-close, with sound as the vehicle, marker and outcome of this proximity, ending in a strange inversion of centre/periphery, where the outside is centred.

Here, though, sound is the primary content from the start – *Girls Tricky* is about sound, about music – about the place and production of it. So we have to search a bit differently for the meaning and/or grounding performed by sound in this piece. Ultimately, this could well have been used as a music video – the singer is central, and the band is there, near but elsewhere, perhaps suggesting the willed isolation of the lyricist-singer, with the others becoming his familiars. Tricky's investment in the song ostensibly feels more like a performance to be seen than part of a recording process that will live on only as trace in the finished object. But – the process has become too material for that to work – the physicality and materiality of the (now-doubled) recording process begin to overwhelm the song and the persona of Tricky (which is revealed as persona when he immediately 'comes down' from the angry repetitions of the song to calmly ask in his normal accent about whether it was ok). The recording process is shown as the precise opposite of authenticity – or at best, the place where authenticity goes to become transformed into something else, thus (hopefully) making us see that authenticity was the lure, the trick, and it was right for it to go away. Barthes' idea of the physicality of the voice we forget in imagining an idealized singing, sounding and breathing subject is here given full scope.[10] There is no more pure song and pure expression, and this realization plays out in the too-close, and the ecstatic charge of the threat to the viewer-listener's border with the singer builds – there is no room for resonance to signal the space between us. Tricky dissipates into his own bodilyness – the precision of what we see and hear leads to its paradoxical opposite – abstraction, a glow trail of sweat, smoke, breath and muscle. Through sound, we have arrived somewhere else, but yet again, McQueen has used sound as a destabilizing 'ground', a way in which that offers only entrapment. This brings us back to *Pursuit*, for with the video of Tricky, the spectator is brought closer to the being whose identity is sound based. Where *Pursuit* offers a mystery that shifts position, controlling what seems to be a wider acoustic space, Tricky is enclosed, so is McQueen, and so is the viewer/auditor, when the screen is large enough and dominates the very dark room. Just as the mobile and anonymous sound-thing of *Pursuit* uses space to identify the threat of a crossing of a threshold by the animal, so the animality/materiality of *Girls Tricky* recalls the culturally suppressed physicality of what it means to be a subject individual – which is to perform it, fleshily, sensorily and in too-close proximity to oneself.

This fleshy thing which does not house but *operates* a subjectivity is also historical. McQueen's own body is used as material in several pieces, and Tricky's exposed torso recalls miners in his other films – the black body is coded as closer to the material through the colonial history of Europe and the places it went to, the displacement and exploitation of one category of people by another. I am not sure we can say that in his video art McQueen is always or definitively offering a critical set of bodies as part of a postcolonial, critical mission, but the physicality of oppression is very significant in his work – hence the focus of the film *Hunger* (2009) on the physical effects of hunger striking – and its extreme presence in *12 Years a Slave* (2013). With Tricky he is showing us a hyperbolic sounding body that hints at oppression or, in more recent times, repression, in order to overcome these. This is a triumphant body, heavy with history, yet subtle and insinuating in its becoming-voice (as shown in the particular setting of *Girls Tricky*). McQueen, like Agamben, does not want to essentialize voice, or indeed body, but traverses these and other categories that suggest possible limits that enclose (the human), disclose (the human) and close out (death, animality, physicality and even history). Sound establishes and undermines these borders, creating a locatedness, a sense of dwelling or occupation (for subject and viewer alike), but it is not settlement. And so the grounding, the centring proposed in McQueen's use of sound is exactly what remains after phenomenology's attempts to understand being. It is a practical deconstruction.

Notes

1   T.J. Demos, 'The Art of Darkness: On Steve McQueen', *October* 114 (Fall 2005), 61–89 (61).

2   This applies even in his ultra-political (i.e. somewhere outside of politics, taking a position, but also commenting on it, and all this through the absence

of comment) work, such as the film *Hunger* (2009), or the stamps featuring British soldiers killed in Afghanistan and Iraq, *Queen and Country* (2010).

3   McQueen is extremely good at raising the question of race obliquely in his video art. To get to the political critique requires work and an initial piercing of a rebarbatively difficult visual exterior. Even when the infliction of power through pain occurs in *12 Years a Slave* (2013), the direct materialization of power creates a difficulty for the viewer, this time in terms of extremity.

4   Georges Bataille, 'Formless', in *Visions of Excess: Selected Writings, 1927–1939*, originally written in 1929. Translated by Allan Stoekl.

5   Martin Heidegger, 'Building Dwelling Thinking', *Basic Writings*, 343–63. First published in 1954. Translated by Albert Hofstadter.

6   Two sound pieces have acquired this meaning; first Stephen Vitiello's ten-inch record *Sounds Building in the Fading Light*. Recorded in 1999, this work used the apparent stillness of the World Trade Center to record the city through the glass windows. William Basinski has connected his *Disintegration Loops* (2002), a piece where the playing of his old tapes erases them, to seeing the towers fall.

7   Bataille first introduces this idea in the essay 'The Notion of Expenditure', in 1933 (*Visions of Excess*, 116–29), and develops it fully in the 1949 book *The Accursed Share* (Zone: New York, 1991), translated by Robert Hurley.

8   McQueen also explores the cosmological, in tandem with evolution in the more didactic *Once Upon a Time* (2002).

9   See Agamben, *Language and Death*, 96.

10   Roland Barthes, 'The Grain of the Voice', in *Image – Music – Text* (London: Fontana, 1977), 179–89. Translated by Stephen Heath.

CHAPTER ELEVEN

Jane and Louise Wilson, An Other Index

If video art's beginnings are in performance, minimalist sculpture, the exploration of media and the political potential of individuals being able to record events, then the spread of video into large-scale and/or multiple projections has brought a new emphasis on place, even as those early attitudes and contents persist. For Maeve Connolly, an interest in place proves fundamental to the operation, and therefore the understanding, of video installation art. She extends the scope of such installation to its being a commentary on museum/gallery space, and then on to contemporary notions and experiences of place in a more general way: 'the multi-screen video projection is implicated within broader institutional and political imperatives involving the staging of "publicness" in contemporary art museums' (*The Place of Artists' Cinema*, 63).[1] Processing through space enables the public to interact with memory (as opposed to retaining it) in ways that counter the drift of spaces into 'non-places',[2] and re-assert the value of the institutional practices that are on display as part of the viewing experience of multiscreen works. This interest in location also informs much contemporary political art, and very often the medium used seeks to assume a transparency in the face of its subject. With Jane and Louise Wilson, the places that feature are heavily loaded, genuine sites of historical signification, often of anachronistic modernity or military/political activity. The challenge for video art is to use this formally, and to be able to reflect on the use of place, site and location as content. If it does not attempt some sort of transformation, then all we would have is some sort of documentary, claiming the perspective of an impartial observer.

However a video installation attempts aesthetically to frame a place, and even if done with belief in the neutrality of the empirical, it still has to operate a transfer – first in being represented as images, and second, and more importantly, in the case of large- or multiple-screen installations, in bringing the place to the gallery, such that 'the multiscreen projection seems to have served as a privileged setting, if not conduit, for the experience of transportation to another time and place' (Connolly, *The Place of Artists' Cinema*, 72). The installation visitor is not there in front of the place being shown. Instead, the place is shown as *there*, not here and present. Connolly is glossing Peter Schjeldahl's comments on the work of Jane and Louise Wilson functioning as a 'transport vehicle' ('V.I.: Jane and Louise Wilson', 5)[3] – two sets of transfers happening at the same time: the viewer is removed from the here and now and the place being shown is now not present. As is often the case, we do not hear so much about the aural part of the works. It is certainly noticed, but it is sound that completes the potential for indexicality – that is, what you see is a representation of something, a sign of it, and therefore a sign of its existence.

The sound and visual parts of an installation do not just come fully formed as a combined reference point, but even where they seem to work that way, a space in which the transfer of place is to occur is established by the presence of sound or simply the non-removal of sensory output other than the visual. The presence of sound conveys more of a sense of being located spatially, so by extension, it can enhance the proximity of sites being shown. So it becomes even more complex when that sound separates off from what is shown, or connects selectively, or purposely establishes disconnection, as we have encountered in the work of many video artists. This is not a puzzle to be solved by the installation visitor, and it is generally signalled as a vital part of the work precisely in how it has an autonomous, or at least non-secondary, existence with regard to the visual part. The sound becomes a supplement that turns out to have been there from the start, at the heart of what it seemingly accompanies. It also turns out to be important in the question of the specific functions of the place brought into an artwork – in implicating the viewer in its spaces.[4]

When presenting the spaces of the Stasi headquarters and Hohenschönhausen in what had been East Berlin in the German Democratic Republic (GDR) in *Stasi City* (1997), Jane and Louise Wilson run the risk of aestheticizing the most oppressive part of a totalitarian regime. As is often the case in work that runs this risk, the end product is powerful precisely because of that 'danger' and in how it negotiates competing visual (and auditory) stories to be told and generated from those spaces. Buildings that had been abandoned become signs of a kitsch yet cold set of spaces. As the reality of the GDR fades, parts of its aesthetic are being reclaimed, precisely as emptied signifiers, and symbols of the ruin of that side of modernity. The same can be said for their pieces based on the Soviet astronautics programme, *Star City* and *Proton, Unity, Energy, Blizzard* (both 2000) and *Dream Time* (2001), even if that space programme has proved more reliable and effective, in the long run, than its US counterpart. *Stasi City* moves through the spaces of the police apparatus of the GDR, some of which look tidy, and ready to get to work; others look wrecked, and still other parts feel simply deserted and perhaps abandoned out of shame (i.e. they are neither broken nor ready for business). The installation consists of two sets of mirrored projections, where two screens face two others around an apex. Sound occupies the room, providing a menacing counterpoint (through the alternation of sound and silence). All images and sounds claim a certain level of indexicality, of connection to the real places, even the woman in a tracksuit who floats, on occasion, through one set of images.

Cameras take us through heavily edited visual labyrinths – this is no straightforward recall of the building, just as there can be no definitive truth in a realm where truth is State defined. The camera also echoes the surveillance element of the secret police, and as noted by the artists and Lisa Corrin ('In Stereoscopic Vision', 8–9) and Claire Doherty ('Awaiting Oblivion', 74–6), this surveillance extends to all bureaucracies, with these buildings being an oppressive pinnacle that also hid itself from view while watching and listening to as much of East German life as it could.[5] Paternosters move up and down, sometimes occupied, and a set of rotating filing drawers, now empty of files, turns to some effect but to no outcome, a post-Communist bachelor machine. Rooms lie idle, corridors stretch, but also merge into themselves, as doubled images compress and concertina back out again. These are buildings designed to capture, not reveal, and this is what the piece illustrates, or realizes formally.

Stasi City is also uncanny, as observed by Claire Doherty, Maeve Connolly and Lisa Corrin. This term is one often used loosely, to indicate something a bit strange, or a reference to unwitting surrealist-ish juxtapositions, but with Jane and Louise Wilson, this is both more direct and more an implicit part of the functioning of this and other works. For one thing, they multiply the doubling effects of screen positioning, editing and crossings from one screen to the next. While they must enjoy references to their own twinning, it is much more about creating a set of reflective surfaces for the installation visitor to work on, or be worked by. Grasping opposed sets of screens, while processing different images even in one set, as in *Stasi City*, and the first two of the three Soviet pieces noted above, creates a position of uncanniness for the viewer. The uncanny is never what is being shown, but in the sense or reaction it creates.[6] Without wishing to labour the point, the uncanny or *unheimlich* is precisely about location, about something unfamiliar occurring or displacing the familiar, and the homely, so in its own right it is a spatial idea.

The displacement extends into the sounds of the piece, which are more or less diegetic, in that they arise from recordings made in the building, but before addressing the actual sounds and rhythms of the sound part, the most prominent estranging device is in the visualization of the sound part of the work of the Stasi. For all the 'will to surveillance' of the East German state, most of this was conducted pan-aurally, through phone tapping, interviews, eavesdropping, reports and records of interrogations. This we see in the form of shots of telephones (and basic closed-circuit television [CCTV] screens at one point), but most strikingly, this occurs in the footage of a tape recorder spooling, for four seconds. Nearly inaudible, we are seeing the surveillance conducted by sound, transforming the work of the location back into itself – revealing it as fundamentally auditory work.

Sound provides the narrative, as the viewer/listener eavesdrops on the erstwhile spies' location and is structured in the piece in a way that suggests the structuring power of the overheard in the state/location/building on show/audition. Two moments repeat in sequence, which are the loudest parts. These are the four-screen-moving paternoster lift part, followed by the rotating file drawers. Each of these sounds has been recorded (or has been maintained as an audio choice for the final piece) to suggest an internal or inherent rhythm. Evenly spaced, this twin sequence is almost a familiarizing chorus, but the establishing of rhythms defamiliarizes the link between sound and space, thus undermining any presumed naturality of field recording as a sort of faithful rendering of a narrative of movement through a space. The piece begins with the switching on of lights, another rhythmical yet location-generated sound; it ends with a canister tumbling to the ground (the tumbling completed in one screen only). So in terms of sound, there is a narrative progression that replicates the estrangement of the multiple screens and the uncertain passage through uncanniness, without matching it in any way. Instead, the audio part operates the same way, in some way not quite parallel, also indicating the presence of the location, its history, the artists' presence and the implied attendance of the installation visitor.

The three pieces based on the Soviet/Russian space programme cannot help but also suggest surveillance – the global spying of satellites and Reagan's dream of Star Wars missile launchers in orbit being the defining moments in the Cold War's contribution to globalization through media. But the sounds of *Star City* or of *Proton, Unity, Energy, Blizzard* offer a more tranquil audiosphere, echoing the underwater spaces shown in *Star City*'s cosmonaut training centre. The two pieces are dominated by generalized machine hum, split by HAL-like announcements (though these are made by people). In the latter piece, there is a more machinic feel, as the camera floats over, towards and away from various stage activities in the space programme (at Baikonur). Functional and disused spaces intertwine, but only function produces discrete sounds – of machines in movement and of occasional large-scale clattering, droning hums. Both pieces use the structure of the twin sets of double screens in opposing corners of the space made by the installation, the whole filled with the estranged indexing of selective sounds. The sounds do perform something else, slightly unexpectedly: the two works, and particularly *Star City*, are very stately, very clearly defined in terms of forms and colours, adding up to a melancholic technological sublime – even the current machinery will join an aesthetic history of futures past. But the sounds ground the images – connect them (and the listener) to their status as functioning machines and working humans. Jane and Louise Wilson have not dematerialized the space programme into a merely beautiful set of images or actions, but have properly structured a sublime in the space between the gorgeous and fascinating images and the intermittent or dully continual sounds. In a way, this is the space through which *Dream Time* will take off.

Less visibly uncanny as a journey through the spaces of the Russian space programme, *Dream Time* establishes a visual complexity through the use of multiple images, converging into a single image track, all in the space of a single-screen projection. There is a clear narrative progression that makes this alternation seem less unusual than one might expect, adding up to a progressive montage that elucidates the passage towards the flight. It is the sound that returns us to the instability of such viewing, keeping it from just being a natural set of choices made by a news channel. The film tracks the build-up to take off of the first Russian flight to the International Space Station, and Jane and Louise Wilson note the play between documentary and purposeful montage, describing the work as a 'single screen installation edited so that the narrative collapses moving between single and multiple views of the preparations and rituals surrounding the launch, and culminating in the launch itself' ('Jane and Louise Wilson', 'Artists [sic] story').[7] The visual part of *Dream Time* passes from interiors at the space station, which we see empty as the rocket launcher is wheeled out, and into position. The sound shifts between clatterings, pre-recorded music heard through speakers, mission control announcements (later on) and electronic music reminiscent of 1960s experimental electronic music. This latter is almost in quotation marks, an established signifier of the time where manned space flight occupied a place as the marker of utopian human futures.

The sound is sometimes diegetic, but often out of phase. This phasing is heightened by moments where different sound tracks collide over four different images. One key sequence shows the astronauts, in military uniform, walking into a glass-walled room for a press assignation. Here, the sound is out of phase, I think slowed down at a slightly different speed to the slowing of the images and played back on a slight delay. This announces both the need for the reflecting power of media coverage and the imminent separation and distance of the astronauts from the Earth, echoing the communications delay their distance will induce. Throughout the piece, media coverage features heavily, their presence a part of the meaning of the programme. *Dream Time* captures the mission as integrated within the circuit of media transmissions – the three astronauts themselves acting as information in that circuit, and so standing in as representatives of all humanity (i.e. not just in their travelling into space).

The culmination is the launch itself, and this is where the sublime returns, within the blast-off. For most of a minute, the sound of the jet engines firing fills the sound part, and even heavily muted, it is a distorted sound of colossal volume and frequency range. Quickly, though, the ship and launcher go out of sight, and a clear sky is filled with noise. This is where the astronauts leave the standard human sphere behind: not in the physical leaving, but in the disappearance, in the separation of sound and vision that shows us the discrepancy between speeds of sound and light, earthbound and spacebound. Jane and Louise Wilson are not telling us something critical, but they are using sound analytically, in order to heighten the sense of something outside of the norm, a sensation much harder to achieve by the turn of the century when it came to space flight. At the same time, it is not just a dematerialized celebration, but one that is firmly rooted in the practical politics and mechanics of building and launching a space mission, and this is partly through what is shown in the film, but also in how *Dream Time* completes a tripartite and four-screen whole with the previous works also made in Russia and Kazakhstan.

Jane and Louise Wilson extend their narrative suggestiveness into something more formally straightforward in *Unfolding the Aryan Papers* (2008) and *Face Scripting: What Did the Building See?* (2011), in collaboration with Shumon Basar and Eyal Weizman. At least that is what the appearance of a voiceover narration initially promises. Both pieces tell specific stories, or, more accurately, build on them, through the use of what Michel Chion calls an *acousmètre* – voice that comes from outside the visual and aural diegetics, to pre-interpret, gloss or explain:

> [the *acousmètre*] is an invisible character created for the audio-viewer by means of an acousmatic voice heard either offscreen, or onscreen but hidden [...]. The voice must occur frequently and coherently enough to constitute a true character, even if it is only ever known acousmatically and so long as the bearer of this voice is theoretically capable of appearing onscreen at any moment. (*Film, A Sound Art*, 466)

The term suggests both mastery (sounding like 'maître' [master]) and the achievement of this mastery through being acousmatic – separated from unfolding events. In *Unfolding the Aryan Papers*, this will be further complicated by the actress who appears in the piece acting as an additional narrator. Stella Bruzzi has noted that while traditional voiceovers have often adopted this 'voice of God' position, many documentary works have taken a freer, more experimental attitude, whereby the voiceover is used consciously as an additional angle to narrative development, not as truth-giving judge.[8] *Face Scripting* departs from a real event – the assassination of Hamas member Mahmoud al-Mabhouh, in the Al Bustan Rotana Hotel, Dubai, by members of Mossad. The progression of the act was tracked extensively on CCTV, and subsequently made public by Dubai police. In the installation, this footage plays opposite that of Wilsons' film. In that

principal part of the work, cameras scan slowly around the largely empty
Al Bustan Rotana, occasionally alighting on cleaning staff, who, in this
context, come across as potential agents of one side or another. A voiceover,
read by Nadim Sawalha, recounts the events of the day, as scripted by Basar
and Weizman. To emphasize that this piece is about the documentation,
the recording of events, there is a sequence where Jane and Louise Wilson
have applied blocks of paint and possibly also tape to their faces, as devices
that would trick surveillance cameras, potentially thwarting the capacity of
recognition software to see faces as human. At this point, the narrator offers
some thoughts about the passage of people across cities, across the world
and across surveillance systems. The voiceover begins to suggest that a clear
position can be taken – that ultimately, surveillance can itself be observed
from outside, and the murder understood. The contrast between the
building's serene but disciplined emptiness and the use of verbal narration
to tell the story of the murder troubles the potential for documentary, and
its political intent moves away from the killing itself, or even the reaction
of the police, to reflect on how the real is adrift in the mass of 'intelligence',
like the scraps of the real in Baudrillard's vision of total simulation.[9] The
true events still occur, and these are in the voice, but they seem somehow
less significant than the version of non-surveillance or emptied surveillance
of the part filmed by Jane and Louise Wilson.

To emphasize the separation of image from the possibility of unmediated
reality, even as we see what is presumably the fatal room 230, we are told that
this is where the surveillance ended, and the murder itself was not captured.
As the narrator wonders about this part of truth evading cameras, a phone
rings in the bedroom and the piece ends. We could see this aporetic crime
scene (i.e. crime scene with no crime to see) as a return of a Lacanian Real –
that which stays outside the experience of living through representations – or
it could also work as a Baudrillardian resistance – death enacting a symbolic
violence in the totalizing simulation constructed through surveillance. Even
as the Wilsons' camera explores the room's interior, it just seems more
generic and bland. The sounds of the hotel, notably of slightly squeaking
wheels of trolleys being moved, are also the sound of all public spaces where
the public is mostly absent. Furthermore, and despite the second part of
the title, attempts to co-opt the building as witness fail. The central area
of the hotel, around which circle rooms and open hallways, offers jagged,
fractured lines, a modernist upping of the stakes of simple detective discovery
or a readably minimalist space. The interior of the building is not revealing,
but brought into a collaborative relation with concealment, echoing the face
camouflage seen earlier. After the ubiquity of surveillance, *Face Scripting*
develops a much more radical perspective, countering its own storytelling
in a vertiginous cover-up enacted by the building itself. As a result, the
spoken narration looks much less certain. Bruzzi identifies the possibility of
a narrational voice as something under threat, arguing that

narration could thereby be viewed as a mechanism deployed to mask the realisation that this mode of representation, and indeed its inherent belief in a consistent and unproblematic truth, are perpetually on the verge of collapse, that commentary, far from being a sign of omniscience and control, is the hysterical barrier erected against the spectre of ambivalence and uncertainty. (*New Documentary*, 52)

In the case of *Face Scripting*, it is not so much a mystery as to what occurred, but more the mystery of its status, its viewing, its locatedness and then its absence in the spaces of the hotel. It is the position to take on the event that becomes uncertain – from the clarity of selecting resistance to CCTV, we finish up in the much more uncanny position of the building itself, which is mute witness to recordings which offer obstructions to the detection of truths.

A further troubling of the security of images, and the reading of images, takes the shape of the mirroring of screens in both *Face Scripting* and *Unfolding the Aryan Papers* (2008). The literal mirroring extends the doubling within the works – of faces, of vocal and visual narrations and of past and present. *Unfolding the Aryan Papers* sees a coincidence of narrator and actor, as Johanna ter Steege partially re-creates her role in Stanley Kubrick's unmade film, *The Aryan Papers*, from 1993. The piece combines original stills of ter Steege and new footage of her wearing the same set of costumes, walking through sets consistent with the original wardrobe test stills. The story of the film focussed on the attempts of a Polish Jew, Tania, to evade the Nazis. Parts of that story are read by ter Steege, and these sections are interspersed with her comments on the process of getting the part. It is no surprise that this piece extends the problematic narratorial strategies of the later *Face Scripting*, in that the narrator is both inside and outside the frame, in past and present, in her playing of herself as the actress Johanna ter Steege and herself as Tania. The core story of escaping the Holocaust, even as it unfolds around Tania, is not overly emphasized in *Unfolding the Aryan Papers*, as it is much more about the making of a film, one that never gets made.

The seeming aesthetic elision of violent situations in the work of Jane and Louise Wilson does not remove or ignore the original horrific basis of the story, or of any of the stories they mobilize spatially, visually and aurally. Instead the story is suspended, hovering across the unmaking of the film itself, and directly shown in the many examples of physical turning away (by both ter Steege and the camera). Sound and vision double each other, but mostly out of phase – that is, both audio and visual parts reflect the doubling of then and now and of the actress as herself and as Tania (or, as it would transpire, Tania-not-to-be); just as the piece is about Kubrick's unmade film, or about the actress, it is also about the act of representation, and its persistence in the light of the event (in this case the Kubrick film) not occurring. It is the voice that provides this stability, even as it offers multiple perspectives and distances, just as the stills, tableaux vivants and moving shots do. It may work as a decentring device, but still it works as an anchoring presence, because for all the doublings, the voice doing the reading or being interviewed is the same.

Vocal narrations operate the same destabilizing as the image tracks in work by Jane and Louise Wilson. In other words, they develop the narratives of the pieces, and they also build a fragmented picture of the spaces at the core of the works (in turn reflected in installation form that brings into being a secondary, supplemental space for the spaces to exist in). When the narrations offer steadiness, they still react in contrary ways to the visual part, and not least of all, they are not scripted by the artists, and act as potentially other perspectives on the visual and diegetic sound parts.

Notes

1   Maeve Connolly, *The Place of Artists' Cinema: Space, Site and Screen* (Bristol and Chicago: Intellect, 2009).

2   The term coined by Marc Augé in his sometimes conservative *Non-places: Introduction to an Anthropology of Supermodernity* (London and New York: Verso, 1995). Translated by John Howe.

3   Peter Schjeldahl et al., 'V.I.: Jane and Louise Wilson', in *Jane and Louise Wilson* (London: Pale Green Press/Serpentine Gallery, 1999), 4–5.

4   This point is well made by Lisa Corrin, 'In Stereoscopic Vision: A Dialogue between Jane and Louise Wilson and Lisa Corrin', in *Jane and Louise Wilson*, 6–15 (8).

5   Claire Doherty, 'Awaiting Oblivion', in Jane and Louise Wilson et al. *Jane and Louise Wilson* (London: Ellipsis, 2000), 73–8.

6   Sigmund Freud, 'The Uncanny', in Freud, *Standard Edition*, XVII (London: Hogarth Press, 1955), 219–52. Translated by Ernest Jones.

7   Jane and Louise Wilson, 'Artists Story', available at http://www.a-n.co.uk/ artists_talking/artists_stories/single/61233. Accessed 20th January 2014. Original text is from 2002.

8   Stella Bruzzi, *New Documentary: A Critical Introduction* (London and New York: Routledge, 2000), particularly 40–65.

9   See Jean Baudrillard, *Simulacra and Simulation* (Ann Arbor, MI: University of Michigan Press, 1994 [1981]), 1–2.

CHAPTER TWELVE

Total Screen (Ryoji Ikeda, Carsten Nicolai, Granular Synthesis)

In his later works, Jean Baudrillard contended that the world had fallen into something he called 'integral reality', a successor to the idea of the 'total screen'.[1] For Baudrillard, reality is only ever a set of simulacra, and the history of humanity is a passage towards total simulation – in other words, the more simulated the world, the more perfect its reality. Increasingly, technology means that not only is there no visible gap between real and simulacrum, but this question itself is pure nostalgia, a wilful misreading of an era of total simulation. At the core of this descent (and Baudrillard himself also seems to be nostalgic for a lost reality, albeit one that was never real in the way most people understand it) is the digital. It is far from alone in creating simulation, but it is the development that hastens the end of anything being outside of simulated reality. For the most part, thinking about the impact of digital coding seems to be an outmoded question – Baudrillard himself addressed the ontological implications of the digital, of the belief in code that led to DNA and also binary computing, in his 1976 book, *Symbolic Exchange and Death*.[2]

On the one hand, we accept the ubiquity of the digital as if it were a force of nature that cannot be turned back and is simply present, or perhaps more accurately, it is treated like electricity or public water – it is there, is useful and enables other things to happen. On the other hand, it is also tempting to imagine that the digital has changed everything, as it has introduced fundamental social change through a supposedly novel interactive capacity. We can see both tendencies in art: in the first case, digital 'filming', recording, production, editing and formatting are all simply normal technical procedures, as well as allowing high fidelity 'sharing' of material. In the second, the digital, as basis for generative works, communications and participation, seems to signal a change in functionality of artworks – or, better, a change from purpose to functionality, where the end product is a process, a functional outcome. In the case of video art, the implications are mostly straightforward – the hard drive or 'cloud' stockpile replaces the physically impacted medium (e.g. tape); older works are routinely digitized for archiving and display alike (hence Tacita Dean's insistence on displaying her film works as actual films). In opposition to the pragmatic acceptance of digital formats and procedures, the perfection of the medium has been called into question, echoing structural film and early video art. Mostly this takes place in the form of musical or sound work, but it has crossed into the visual, into works that I still qualify as having the characteristics of video art.

In music, the development of the CD (as well as digital media that lost the format war – minidisc, DAT, DCC) furthered a belief in high fidelity reproduction and that the disc would outlast analogue storage methods. The history of the format has seen the meaning of this 'fidelity' developed and challenged: first, by record companies, who, every few years, bring out a 'new, improved' version of successful albums; second, by manipulation of the supposedly perfect disc, which could then be ironically displayed in triumphal accuracy on a finished CD (without the sanctification of the properly functioning finished product, glitching would be heard only as mistake); third, the very accuracy of re-presentation allows 'sharing' of music and visuals in ways that undermine the 'record industry' or its film equivalent.

The second of these methods, the most critically engaged, as it takes the form of intervention *in* the digital, is the most relevant in this chapter. Artists like Yasunao Tone and Christian Marclay would set about damaging discs, and then play back the result, using the new flaws as material. Others such as John Oswald, Oval, Farmers Manual and Pole would cut into digital recordings, scrambling the listener's expectations of music and format alike, but in fact not materially glitching at all.[3] In looking at flaws in the ostensibly smooth digital surface, even as potential failures, such artists were looking to deconstruct code as a device for listening – which we will see and hear in the work of Ryoji Ikeda, along with Carsten Nicolai (aka Alva Noto). Using the digital as material, in the context of video art, has potentially serious consequences: first, it could point to the redundancy of video art, as computers can generate infinitely or at least indefinitely changing work (see Brian Eno's 77 *Million Paintings* [2006]); second, there is the more positive outcome of developing, even exaggerating the multisensorial, intermedial character of video installation (as questioned by Dyson, referring to virtual and/or digital works, in *Sounding New Media*). If all can be code, and all code put into perceivable form, maybe the digital is the signal of video art's perfecting. Baudrillard argued that digital had actually ended art (*Le Pacte de lucidité*, 64), as it had abolished distance – everything can be constructed in code, perceived in it and accessed, hence the artwork would have no room to either communicate its message or be critically deciphered.[4] Ultimately, in this line of argument, perfection might also mean the end of the need to have a spectator, or listener. The installation could become self-sufficient or total, like the world built of data in *The Matrix*.

In practice, this vision also seems archaic – certainly galleries have insufficient interest, aesthetically or commercially, to dematerialize their collections, or have entirely digital works on display. How much can the digital actually be enough for an artwork? Is coding even that interesting, or specific to digital/binary programming? While coding and decoding were the prime drivers of modern computing, during the Second World War and the Cold War, much of the rest of computing has been about the speed of encoding and recoding, of packeting and unpackaging, such that speed and quantity merge as capacities. What is different about the digital realm of today is the simplicity of its constituent parts and its generative capacity. This can serve as the basis for permanent experimentation, but also comes with a strong dose of Late Romantic wonder at the world building that can emerge. Computer art has always had this, even in the early video experiments that used computers or machinery as content-generating material, and runs the risk of taking a technological sublime to the point where it is less about awe and more about the soothing spectacle of (machine) virtuosity, of technical ecstasy.

Artists Kurt Henschläger and Ulf Langheinrich, who go under the name Granular Synthesis (named after the process whereby information is reconfigured, remixed and restructured through media software), work through something like the sublime, in order to create forceful, excessive audio–video works, typically in the shape of large-scale projections with accompanyingly loud sound. Their work crosses between performance, installation, video art and sound art – with the images and audio parts closely associated and mutually reinforcing. The work *Modell 5* (1994–96) was initially a four-screen projection with eight massive speakers for parallel sound delivery (the version I am referring to is the 'remix' for single channel). In this piece, we see four projected images of performer Akemi Takeya, which, in a gallery situation, are each 4 × 3 metres in dimension. The idea is clearly to overwhelm. On the DVD version, the piece opens on four projections in line, and then focusses in on one close-up, with two parts of other projections visible at the perimeters. The image is of Akemi Tekaya's face and neck, with varying facial expressions. Sometimes all four faces are the same; at others, two or all go out of synch. Loops are made of sound and vision to create a jumpy, pseudo-glitchy work that has the momentum of a composition. Early on, the eyes are shut, the mouth is open and a high-pitch sound wave suggests a processed voice. The movement of the head matches the sound oscillations, and does so throughout – so sound acts as index for the visual and vice-versa. The disruption comes from cutting rather than defamiliarizing the link between sound and image, as, at 3.10 the heads move violently up and down, at four separate speeds, to the sound of a scream rendered rhythmical. Other sudden changes occur periodically, with the face looking more alien when the eyes are shown open, the mouth becoming a gaping vertical maw, recalling Bataille's 'Mouth' essay, H.R. Giger's alien and Bacon's screaming popes. It is not an image of contentment, then. Nonetheless, the overall piece, especially as it slows down later on, over its thirty-minute duration, is more ecstatic than grim, and in fact, it is increasingly hard to maintain the sense that the face on show is of an actual human. This is more than the dehumanization of technology, of digital rendering, as it seems to open up possibilities in something like a becoming-digital, where you would occupy a place between dimensions, as code is not restricted to the spatial group of dimensions we are used to.

Granular Synthesis look to work consciously at a very literal interface of human and digital, both in terms of their work on the material, and in how performer and viewer/listener interact with the machinery of coding. For most of *Modell 5*, the human vocalizing face seems to respond rather than cause the sound or image, as a result of the processing having defamiliarized the viewer/listener's expectations of a singing performance. The combined oscillation of image/face and sound/mouth would be very hard to achieve in the physical realm, so this face becomes uncanny, a proximate other. What we are seeing and hearing is only an epiphenomenon of code in any case, an accidental product (from the point of view of code), just as a lot of glitching in music is a phenomenological impression garnered through listening to what seems to be in some way broken sound. If we think in more analogue terms, the face and mouth are forms that emerge out of formless waveforms, moments of coalescent clarity, that in turn Granular Synthesis twist into troubling avatars of the human.

Ryoji Ikeda has no such interest in peripheral forms such as the human face/mouth. His project has expanded since the early years of this century into a massive display of the digital, brought out from being enmachined code, put into the realm of human vision, but still withholding any form other than the process of data becoming image and sound. Ikeda's 'audiovisual' installations go a large step further than Granular Synthesis, in offering a collapsing image of the same, as minimalism does, and as noted above in the case of Pierre Huyghe. Data becomes its own spectacle not just in being 'the spectacle of data' but in being the display of something happening as its own display, a kind of intra-minimalism. Ikeda's first digital explorations could easily be perceived or read as minimal, tiny electronic sounds barely reaching thresholds of rhythm, audibility and musicality, often designed to vary according to how the listener positioned his or her head in relation to the speakers (these works took form as installations, also as CD releases, such as *matrix*, from 2001). These works clearly used the digital as source and method, but not content. In other words, the digital was a means to an end, and these minimal pieces are much more about the experience of listening than they are about the functioning of code. When heard in any open environment (i.e. not via headphones), *matrix* summons the listener into physical presence amid sound, acting as resistance in the integrated circuit set up by the digital sounds of clicks, waves, pulses, beats, hisses and drones: '*matrix [for rooms]* forms an invisible pattern which fills the listening space. The listener's movement transforms the phenomenon into his ± her intrapersonal music' (*matrix* liner notes). The combination of different sounds – of different frequencies and wavelengths, generated by digital means and made analogue not only in the speaker broadcast but in the physical perception of sound – creates a space in which the installation visitor is aware of sound as air-deforming (like Bill Viola's extreme version of this in the sub-bass rumble of *Hallway Nodes*). The interaction that is offered to the visitor to Ikeda's sound installations is not a self-affirming involvement. Rather it makes the 'self' into a physical arena, as yet undefined until in contact with the sound. Once in contact with the sound, it is a process of auscultation – an audio testing of the analogue body, and an art echo of the ideas of Donna Haraway and Avital Ronell.

When Ikeda makes pieces that combine visual and audio in installation form, they are precisely not 'audiovisual' in that they are designed to be neither, and the very existence of either sound or image becomes a pleasing side-effect, a way for limited humans to see into the world of data, much as the scrolling figures of *The Matrix* (1999) tried to demonstrate. We might even wonder if Ikeda's installations, many of which come under the umbrella of the *datamatics* title, count as anything like video art, and yet they use all of the resources of that form, and actually expand the form through emphasizing a kind of formal synaesthesia, where not only are hearing and viewing called upon simultaneously but the distinction between them becomes porous and non-plastic. It could be that entirely code-based work qualifies as expanded video art, albeit without necessarily representing a step beyond, into a necessary future. If anything, digital-heavy art seems to be increasingly a product of a time now gone, a time where 'the digital' was in some way inherently futuristic, like, for example, plastic, margarine, hi-fi, orange household objects and maglev in an earlier era.[5] What remains to be explored is how human senses are not merely addressed in code, but how the presence of digitality and the present analogue body (i.e. encountering an installation) can be moved into a critical or quasi-ecstatic, and therefore externalized, non-objective, situation. As Herbert says, 'we all know for practical purposes, what infinity is. What Ikeda's art does is to make us feel something of it, to locate it in our own nerve endings: in intensely variable streams of visual or sonic information, in what floods the retina' (Matthew Herbert, 'Infinity's Borders: Ryoji Ikeda', 164).[6] He could, of course, have added the flooding of our residual gills, in the form of auditory stimulus, and also that this feeling of data as infinity is exactly only an awareness of the senses losing control, that is, losing the capacity to rationally process all that is in front of us.

The *datamatics* project is about the overwhelming power and brute empirical presence of data and digitality in the world. The digital is brought into sensual contact with the installation visitor, rather than being re-coded in human terms to be understood and manipulated by users. The project takes many forms – installations, concerts (some played live, others a scheduled performed runthrough of pre-prepared material) and albums. The installations can be sound only (*dataphonics*), displayed on walls and on floors, and projected outward, across floors and rooms, and in purpose-built plinths and so on. Data can take many forms, and the multiple modes of presentation are the physical realization of that subtler information. That complexity of form belies a fundamental simplicity of means – at one level, it is just variations on light and the sine wave; at another it is the display of yes/no, 0/1 decisions; and at still another, the material is data, its complexity arising from its mass, and its accumulation. Much of the information takes the form of numbers – either binary or decimal, and also the forms of sections of apparently infinite numbers such as ø, π or e. These numbers are 'irrational' and never complete, as their decimal precision spirals out of human comprehension or even savant listing. Other pieces feature colossal prime numbers, genetic coding sequences and star maps, but the irrational numbers have a specific purpose in *datamatics*. For all their unusual qualities, they are much more mathematically functional than standard everyday numbers, and seem to represent standard measures that work in the universe – and are all to do with proportions – geometric figures, relations of numbers to one another and proportional relations, and yet these are no more natural than any other number, despite their empirical successes. Instead, they are human creations, standardizations and forms, built out of a possibly real set of relations that exceed human invention. In other words, they have not been found, they are not objective, even in a posthuman perspective where the universe does not need to take into account human idealizations of universal relations. So these numbers are examples of mathematics exceeding the human, and then being understood as 'the numbers that exceed us', a classic iteration of Kant's version of the sublime. Ikeda renders this process in the scale of the works, which not only contain masses of data, of information at its most brute, but also are physically imposing, in order to bring out the infinitude of numbers, information, codes and processes that act as structuring devices, normally at scales too small or too hidden to be seen and heard, and in the *datamatics* series, they become too big to be consumed.[7]

The *data.tron* iteration of the idea starts out in huge wall projection form in 2007, presented on a 7 × 9.3 metre screen, and the spatial aspect of viewing is a vital part of the piece. As you back away from the piece (and all of Ikeda's data-based works), the mass of numbers fades into a solid, greying mass, such that 'the fact that the data is given a physical extension as information to be consciously administered to human perception gives rise to a blind spot both for the work and for the viewer' (Kazunao Abe, 'As "/"', 106).[8] This blind spot is not a failure as such, but a structuring phenomenon that we might say is always already there, like the massive dark matter seemingly structuring the rest of the visible material of the universe or the large black holes that occupy centres of galaxies. Some installation formats offer a clearer perspective, and hide this blind spot – such as the plinth grid *data.tron*, where a viewer can more readily browse the information, getting at least a sense of what lies outside of control ('known unknowns'), or the walkway format of *data.path* (2013). In this piece, the installation presents itself as a corridor of two projections, scrolling data/light, zeroes and ones. The proximity of the projections recalls Bruce Nauman's corridor pieces, with sound being the dominant way of locating the viewer/listener and the solid walls giving way to information, and so dislocating the person inside the installation. The floor comes into play with the *data.tecture* format, and here the illusion of control over informatics is replaced by a sense of being peripheral – the data continues to process and to be processed, with or without you standing on it, its seeming nothingness the revealing of a normally hidden architectural process here shown in impoverished (i.e. brute) form. Alternatively, maybe these pieces develop Yves Klein's idea of architecture built from air, water and fire, with code being the replacement for all other elemental imaginaries (figure 12.1).

FIGURE 12.1 *Ryoji Ikeda,* data.tron *[8K enhanced version], 1 January 2009–31 December 2010. Concept, composition: Ryoji Ikeda; computer graphics, programming: Shohei Matsukawa, Tomonaga Tokuyama; commissioned by Ars Electronica Center, Linz, AT; produced by Forma, UK. Image courtesy Ryoji Ikeda Studio.*

The display of the data as something spatial reflects its real-world spatial involvement – for example, in architecture, town planning, monitoring of population movement and flows – and sound is essential for this effect. The sound and light elements not only reinforce each other, they are dual expressions of the same material. Many visitors to one of Ikeda's installations, and perhaps even more so the concert attendees, will initially imagine the sound to be a soundtrack, a secondary and backing device to heighten the effect of the visuals, but the bifurcation of data into visual and aural form creates the properly intermedial nature of data within a fully intermedial installation, where sound draws attention to effects of the visual, and vice-versa. As noted above, the sound serves to locate your bodily presence inside a piece of *datamatics*, and reveals that the visual part is not separate, and is not to be viewed in isolation or from a position of solitary contemplation. You are inside data and too close to see it, but it is making you an audible device as it auscultates/palpates you.

The *data.tron* format is spatially expanded in *the transfinite* (2011, New York). This dual installation sets up an L-shape where the projection covers a screen of 15 × 20 metres and extends out on the floor by 30 metres. This layout is replicated on the other side of the screen. According to Abe, 'the L-shaped horizontal surface is aligned to be on the same plane as the body of the observer. This can only appear to us as an attempt to present us with a mediated space that goes beyond the Cartesian cut' ('As "/"', 106). First, the projection offers a type of surrounding effect that does not return to the domesticity of a room-like absorption; second, the viewer cannot remain separate or take in all of the visual plane as if it were designed for an upright seeing-mind to process; third, other viewers become incorporated into a three-dimensional space of rolling light and dark; fourth, this leaves us no space to take a position, even as co-ordinate data flood the space and the installation-visiting body is set adrift from locatedness.

Spatialization is taken to an extreme, to an almost empirical realization in *datamatics* performances (such as the concert event in Hobart, 2012). In this piece, star locations are developed in multiple form, and the ways in which location can be represented shift as this most universal of geographies is shown as a construct, as something continually in process. This process is one of changing levels of information – not just in terms of human understanding but in defining the material existence of the universe as one of information, and its exchange, use and dissipation (as identified by physicist Ludwig Boltzmann). As noise is a vital part of Ikeda's approach – as overload, but also in the use of white noise as sound generator, it is important to understand which part of this piece represents entropy. Counter-intuitively, it is not the moment of most noise (sound and highly complex fast visuals) that is the most entropic. It is instead the moment of *excess* information. The moment where stars are separated out into an equidistantly spaced grid (or absent, with only the grid in place). This is how entropy will happen at the universal level: the separation of every part, such that information exchange can no longer happen. If entropy is noise, then in this piece, the noise is the moment of least drama, not most.

The various manifestations of Ikeda's *datamatics* all point to a sublime, and to much more than just being something at which to marvel. The sublime is the content of Ikeda's project, a knowing reference to how the human idea of the sublime is precisely a reduction to 'that which cannot be understood' and thereby giving succour to the rest of human logic, order and reason. As Abe points out, Ikeda's is a properly Kantian exploration, akin to that of Barnett Newman, as theorized by Jean-François Lyotard (Abe, 'As "/" ', 107). The use of star locations (and characteristics) is a precise contemporary rendering of Kant's imagining of the infinite sea of stars all having planets, that is, that they were potentially knowable, but when seen in a mass, they dissipate the capacity for knowledge or 'knowability' through excess stimulation.[9] Even facts (for Kant), especially facts (for Ikeda), are the substance of the unknowable. Data is precisely the stuff of knowledge, or of information, and the more it is made present in its own form, rather than in its usable end products, the more the real is exposed as unknowable, and so ultimately Ikeda takes us out of simulation, through an excess of simulatedness.

Lastly, with regard to Ikeda's alternating of form and formless (sublime/unknowable), we can also consider the *cyclo* project conducted with Carsten Nicolai. In this book/software work, the two artists build a vocabulary of mobile forms that are sound and vision together, and while appearing to offer a reduction of the world into a number of forms (however large the number), the combinatory potential identified is colossal – shapes and sound waves come to make up a new set of parameters for computing: that is, computing not on binary forms (as such) but through letting forms interact as information exchange. They begin from the premise that oscillator screens are designed and used to map sound, and while they begin with sound, 'throughout our process, we abandoned the idea that image acts only as a functional accompanist to sound and instead subordinated the audio element for our desire for the image' (Ikeda and Nicolai, 'Preface', in *cyclo.id* vol I, np).[10] It is important to note that the visual is not being privileged other than in a zone where it is seen as secondary – the technical visualization of sound presented as guide for potential correction. The same could be done with audio waveforms in recording, mixing and producing software, and the use of sound as source would not change. This project sees Ikeda and Nicolai presenting themselves as authentic experimenters, not just making odd sounds but reverting to the classificatory models of science initiated in the early modern period – a period precisely where science and art were not entirely separate magisteria. The material they prepare in *cyclo.id* is a mass of usable audio and visual waveforms, mobile geometric code fragments, suitable for reassembly or even, logically, further breakdown. They thus also participate in the new mass observation/participation sciences of ecology and astronomy, given new detail and verifiability via digital devices and transmission of data. But the artists are not looking for some sort of remix project; instead the forms of *cyclo.id* are almost Platonic, a glimpse of a universe capable of being entirely rendered in form, via the total screen of connected computing, which will then go on to generate further form, like the old biosimulation programmes of the 1990s ('this open sourcebook invites users to activate and perpetuate *cyclo*' ['Preface']).

Much earlier, I drew a line between installed works and works designed primarily for personal access on TV, computers or other digital devices, but here it seems worthy of note that both Ikeda and Nicolai do not just represent a strand of neo-Romantic moderns, looking for a great sublime to be captured and brought back to display to the blessed gallery visitor, but cross multiple generations of world outlooks – once again, scale is what is at stake, but it is not always explicitly large scale. It can be a scale that is internally colossal, like that of the subatomic world or of the infinity of numbers between any two other numbers, and worthy of the reflections that accompany the sublime only to be lost and/or displayed as lost.[11]

Mutability is reflected in Nicolai's solo piece, *syn chron* (2005), a crystal-like pod (not very dissimilar to Huyghe's structure in *This Is Not a Time for Dreaming*), within, over and across which play digital renderings of test tones, sine waves and the like, with visual forms derived from the same material. The shell itself has speakers and projecting capacity, so the screen here becomes a Möbius strip, a libidinal band where sound, image (or framework for visual forms, more accurately) and physical planes coincide with installation visitors in a new circuit. For Nicolai, *syn chron* 'creates representations of the boundary between hearing and seeing that can be grasped directly by both the body and the senses' ('*syn chron*', 33).[12] In fact, Nicolai underestimates the functional capacity of this evolving object (cycling over twenty-one minutes in one version, forty-two in another). It no longer merely represents; it *simulates* – that is, it creates a replica, but one without an original. In intervening directly in space as well as in waveforms of light and sound, Nicolai has built an architecture that is not restricted to the built dimensions, let alone the flatness of 'representation'. It is, writes Barbara Barthelmes, 'a three-dimensional sculptural work whose specificity lies in its multiplication and refraction of the architectonic and spatial context surrounding it' ('A Symbiosis of Light, Sound and Architecture', 14).[13] So *syn chron* adds light and sound to the 'solid' dimensions of height, extension and breadth, and in doing so, adds its set of dimensions to those that pertain to the building in which it finds itself (originally, in 2005, the Neue Nationalgalerie in Berlin). The piece is not just doing what any object would do, nor is it doing what the space would ordinarily do (in terms of visitor perception). It doubles them, and it manages this not by copying the space, as, say an on-screen modelling of a spatial intervention, but by bringing the world of data into the morphology of sound, solid and light, For Abe, this means that the piece 'secedes from the gigantic and static modernist pressure system to generate a totally different emergent combination of space, time and information' ('syn chron | berlin | yamaguchi', 87).[14] Personally, I find this suggestion of a relational aspect a bit of a tired claim and would prefer we approach *syn chron* as a contemporization of modern projects. The mere use of the digital in making this happen has no bearing on a rejection of apparent rigidities of the modern – the dissolution of material suggested by data continually demands the recall of the physicality and materiality of the conditions of data to exist, function, be understood or perceived or take effect.

In *syn chron*, Nicolai moves away from the encyclopaedic nature of the *cyclo* project, and also the very specific experimental work of his sculptural sound installations, to create a space where the perception of the unfolding of the experiment becomes an experimental viewing, and also the visiting subject becomes an integral part of the development of the work, as they enter a test zone. As the world becomes more oriented to bureaucratization, best practice, quality audits, surveillance, DNA testing and the like, the totalization of this 'integrated' world will no longer be a subject for comment, but one to be divided up again, and in using code as form, content and format, Ikeda, Nicolai and Granular Synthesis show that emergent objects can be brought out of a fully digital realm even as listeners/ viewers are brought in, physically, perceptually and phenomenologically. So the digital work that pertains to video art is one of initial reduction into form, in order to comment on the flows and blockages that digitality sculpts in devices and access we 'possess'.

Notes

1   See Jean Baudrillard, 'Integral Reality', available at http://www.egs.edu/faculty/ jean-baudrillard/articles/integral-reality/, also *Screened Out* (London: Verso, 2002), translated by Chris Turner, the original title of which, *Écran Total* (Paris: Galilée, 1997), means 'total screen'.

2   See Jean Baudrillard, *Symbolic Exchange and Death* (London: Sage, 1993 [1976]), 57–64.

3   See Kim Cascone, 'The Aesthetics of Failure: "Post-Digital" Tendencies in Contemporary Computer Music', in Christoph Cox and Daniel Warner (eds.), *Audio Culture: Readings in Modern Music* (New York and London: Continuum, 2004), 392–8; Greg Hainge's corrective to it in 'Of Glitch and Men: The Place of the Human in the Successful Integration of Failure and Noise in the Digital Realm', *Communication Theory* 17 (2007), 26–42, and Caleb Kelly, *Cracked Media* (Cambridge, MA: MIT Press, 2009).

4   Jean Baudrillard, *Le Pacte de lucidité, ou l'intelligence du Mal* (Paris: Galilée, 2004). See also *Cool Memories V: 2000–2004* (Paris: Galilée, 2005), 101 on

digitization rendering the world extinct. Baudrillard's view updates Walter Benjamin's concern about artworks losing their aura once art can not only be easily reproduced but artworks can themselves be always already reproducible, like photographs ('The Work of Art in the Age of Mechanical Reproduction', *Illuminations* [London: Fontana, 1973], 211–44).

5   Maybe things are evolving quickly enough for the digital to already be a type of what Garnet Hertz and Jussi Parikka term 'zombie media' in 'Zombie Media: Circuit Bending Media Archaeology into an Art Method', *Leonardo* 45 (5) (2012), 424–30.

6   Matthew Herbert, 'Infinity's Borders: Ryoji Ikeda', in Kelly (ed.), *Sound*, 162–5.

7   This is a totally different process to the existential angst of Roman Opalka's painted sequences of numbers in *1965/1* – ∞.

8   Kazunao Abe, 'As "/"', in Ryoji Ikeda, *Datamatics* (Milan: Charta, 2012), 105–8.

9   See Immanuel Kant, *Critique of Judgement* (Indianapolis and Cambridge: Hackett, 1987 [1790]), 130. Translated by Werner S. Pluhar.

10   Ryoji Ikeda and Carsten Nicolai, 'Preface', in Ikeda and Nicolai, *cyclo.id*, vol I (Berlin: Die Gestalten, 2011).

11   C.f. Jacques Derrida, 'The Colossal', in *The Truth in Painting* (Chicago: Chicago University Press, 1987 [1978]), 119–47, part of 'Parergon' (17–147). Translated by Geoff Bennington and Ian McLeod.

12   Carsten Nicolai, '*syn chron*: Architectural Body as Interface. Space. Light. Sound', in Nicolai (ed.), *syn chron* (Berlin: Die Gestalten, 2013), 33–4.

13   Barbara Barthelmes, 'A Symbiosis of Light, Sound and Architecture. On *syn chron* by Carsten Nicolai', in Nicolai, *syn chron*, 11–5.

14   Kazunao Abe, 'syn chron | berlin | yamaguchi' in Nicolai, *syn chron*, 87–8.

CHAPTER THIRTEEN

Ryan Trecartin, Videocore

Digital technology does not have to just be about itself: it is neither fully formed nor modernist in aspiration; it is not unitary, nor is it an end in itself. Even though the implications of the digital for culture, for art or for further technological advance have been the subject of philosophical and sociological interest for fifty years, the mystery of code and of coding can never fully go away, as the object and process both develop, react to other developments and have effects of their own, and as they are integrated into circuits of other powers, processes, networks, cultural habits and acquisitions. Where an artist like Ryoji Ikeda does manage to critically open up the digital through its hyper-realization, it is not the only way to look at, use or criticize digital practice in art. We can also consider the practical functionality of digital technology: recording, editing, storing, manipulating, borrowing, messing up, producing and sharing. No doubt this has many interesting effects on the work of video art in the binary era, and many of these phenomena and practices are explicitly on show in the work of Ryan Trecartin, whose work is resolutely designed, produced, edited, shared and so on in digital format. Instead of exposing the way the digital works, he looks at (and listens to) the effects of digital culture (or more accurately, the culture within which digital is just one formatting option), in a way that avoids resolution into clarity, simplicity and narrative monomania. Kareem Estefan includes Trecartin as one of today's artists who are 'responding to the supposed openness and accessibility of digital culture with a poetics of opacity and illegibility' ('Deep Code', 123).[1] His installations include non-screen media and material, and certain of the videos take as their conceit the crossover between artistic forms and format of production. Here, I will focus on three sets of works that are screen based (even if there is a good chance that that screen will be in your hand, house or office) and where the principal method of colliding layers creates a multiple sensory field, within which sound play has a vital role.

Trecartin's videos illustrate something slightly threatening to theorizers of digital/IT/communications technology: while his works are partially about all of that, for him, digital technology is a given – it is just there – to the point where it becomes complicated to talk about how these videos are 'about' something technological. In other words, Trecartin's videos are so immersed in 'the digital' that they illustrate it, make a point of it, say nothing about it and almost let it fail – all at the same time. In the course of looking and listening to the work of Trecartin, it becomes clear that it is possible to be of the world of contemporary media and communications, comment on it and make work about it, while not having to rely on reading the functioning of machinery (including software) to do these things.

Trecartin has made a series of seven interlocked videos, entitled *Any Ever*, that splits into two series, one of three (*Trill-ogy Comp* [2009]) and one of four (*Re'Search Wait'S* [2009–10]). Within each of these, there are a myriad of characters it would be churlish not to label garish, who expostulate, make things, break things, argue and 'express themselves'. In *Re'Search Wait'S*, they come to stand in for a range of activities, personae, attitudes and creative practices. They do this in a non-linear fashion; that is, the narratives are highly complex, unresolved and overlapping. Where William Burroughs used to cut up sentences and recombine the fragments, Trecartin cuts up character, ideas, narrative, screens and sound in a play of surfaces where all complexity has been brought to the surface and can no longer return to depths nor surmount the plane of appearance to become meaningful as a 'commentary' on society. Linda Norden comments that his position is in some way post-critical: 'the operative apparatus in his production veers decisively away from deconstructive critique toward something a lot less tidy, without forfeiting any of its volatility, anger or critical edge' ('When the Rainbow Is an Option', 12).[2]

The first *Re'Search* film is *Ready (Re'Search Wait'S)*, wherein Wait, a girlish figure with poorly applied extreme facial tan colour, played by Trecartin, explores the possibilities of self-realization via a succession of moments where art, life experience, commerce and fulfilment merge, and also disperse, move away from one another.[3] Ideas of rebranding – which crop up in all four films – surface, and ideas about living through strategic identity development also appear. Many cuts disrupt any structured flow, the sound and image track cut continually; for all the talking, all the characters seem to inhabit non-mutual monologues, caught in loops of self-affirmation through talking, that is, through *communication*. The visual part is harsh, and so is the sound, which parallels the visuals throughout, especially when someone is talking. When people talk, it is in high-pitched processed form, sometimes more obviously in line with pop music uses of Auto-Tune. The effect of this is to strip vocal gender identification away. This is not the only outcome, though, as every voice is originally ridiculous, child-like or helium-driven, yet sloganeering in a weird combination of slang and admin-speak. It also disrupts the possibility of the viewer/listener enforcing narrative continuity, as the effect of voice takes over from its verbal content, particularly as we constantly cut from one speech to the next, even if staying with one character such as Wait. These non-harmonized voices make the pitch for their product (mostly in the form of themselves) amid a frenetic cut-up backdrop that is full of music, mostly occurring in very short blasts, often accelerated and/or pitchshifted, so that the musical effect is largely one of breakcore's ultra-rhythms that go against easy dance patterns. Visually and aurally, there is no attempt to display the latest technology, but instead a host of samples, presets, found sounds and musical styles from many recent decades all fight with images that are cut in highly visible style, and also give way to pop-up style windows or multiple windows, framed in preset borders, while text pontificates in monolithic yet disconnected patterns. Kevin McGarry puts it well:

> The projected image becomes fractal, a defined but extendable container for versions of itself from different times and perspectives. These divisions and multiplications of the screen articulate a logic that spirals open for more unruly, organic rhythms of character, text, and sound, a *mise en abyme* incarnating infinite optionality. ('Worlds Apart', 111)[4]

Into this mix comes the question of gender, but I think it would be lazy to say only that he plays with gender through dressing up or the pitch change of voices (everyone dresses up, clothes and pitch-wise, in the videos). For me, the formal collisions and the indeterminate content might suggest a critical rethinking of traditional borders, roles and so on, but this is only the beginning. Trecartin has gone beyond that phase to inhabit that world where to refer to critical play is almost to reduce its import – instead, as Norden has it, 'the aim here is to normalize *and* radicalize self-determination, not to insist on its otherness' ('When the Rainbow Is an Option', 14). Trecartin is interested in bodily mobility, role flexibility and the limits that need to be overcome to see this happen; it is just that the worlds on show are worlds of metamorphosis continually surmounting rule-bound thinking, whether in the guise of bureaucratic ideas or the notion that you can realize yourself by formatting according to focus-group-created programmes (figure 13.1).

The *Re'Search* series dwells in a world that is just parallel enough to the conservationist tendencies of the everyday to mean something, to suggest other modes of being, while taking critique as given, even over. Similarly, it could be imagined that the febrile crossings (sound, image, character, visual portals) are a critique of a society obsessed with self-image and facilitated by communications technology. This would probably be true – it does work as an angle, but it is not enough. Again, what we see in this series is a lateral twist on the 'problem' such that we are brought inside it to see its functioning.

FIGURE 13.1 *Ryan Trecartin, still from* Ready (Re'Search Wait'S), *2010. Courtesy of the artist.*

In the second part, *Roamie View: History Enhancement*, this extends into life as a sort of film-making as the character JJ revisits his past artworks, and screens open up in his studio. Meanwhile, Roamie and her gang set out to find new situations to please him and alleviate his anomie. It transpires that JJ does not need to receive his media through machinery, as images and situations arrive fully formed in front of him. So this meditation on mediation is media-free, except for a pure medium – one that is message only.[5] At the same time, it is another media overload, as the viewer/listener is bumped through locations, monologues, shouting, cuts between locations and jumps in individual scenes, as the audiovisual breakcore delivers another slice of a parallel, always-already cut-up space of sensory stimulation that has stopped trying to approximate anything real. In order for this emptying mediatization to occur, though, there is a very solid reflection on personality as something constructed phenomenologically, that is, through relations to the exterior – other people, objects, events and, above all, media devices and practices. The character of JJ, then, for all his slightly lost demeanour is only a cipher, as are all the characters in the series – ciphers that cannot even retain hold of the thing they are coding. They are only coding, the process of encipherment, where the code is always switching (reminding us of the gender characteristic exchange, mutation and hybridity occurring at some other level in the plane of *Re'Search*). Stepping outside of this plane or libidinal band, there is also some sort of playing with the idea of developing your character, your personality, through the mediated experience of others. Communication (at breakneck speed, cutting and falling in and out of musicality) is an end in itself; something happens and in happening is communicated, and this is enough. At no point does Trecartin slip into complaining about 'contemporary media'; nor does he celebrate them. What we have instead is an operation on the surface from within, like a hand rubbing another skin surface from inside and outside at the same time.

Music itself features as a somewhat limp attempt to reconstruct JJ's view of the world and restore his vim, as a group of drab and gawky indie boys play pop music with Roamie's invading girls, but more strongly in the third film, *The Re'Search*, which has at its core the 'dream' of making a success of being a girl band. Again, art and commerce monologues collide, as we cut from room to room, and also to the broadcast of Sammy B, a girl always threatening suicide and never living up to her fans' dreams of her death. On the face of it, and when not actually looking at or listening to the piece, its story and message seem clear, but it also takes in reality TV, the manufacture of all music, blogs, social media and communication in the real world that has been inflected out of existence by those media, at high speed and jitteringly. Like all the pieces in the overall *Re'Search* series, there is also the pathos of local TV, home-made media work and school projects, and this is crossed with lifestyle advice, undirected advice for the most part. The collisions of layers of screens, scenes, characters, sounds and the relentless pitch-shifted voices (that become one voice, so different views become internal contradictions) demolish young dreams of stardom or even self-identity as irrelevant, because all autonomous subjectivity is caught within competing sensory torrents. This absent subjectivity takes place precisely in the voices and bodies of what we imagine to be characters. Their merged voices, still lightly distinguishable one from another, are the sign of the becoming-multiple that informs Trecartin's universe here – they retain a semblance of individuality through possessing their own voices – only at the very end of this third film is there a voice unconnected to a visible mouth, and it makes the sound of crying. Only by this point, it does not raise any melancholy, it just seems inappropriate and foolish, and is therefore kept distant. If it represents a moment of reflection on the minimally tragic fate of being alive and under twenty in the United States, it is too odd to be heeded, and it is like a category mistake.

In both second and third parts, there are some breaks into music, as if it cannot be contained, restricted to being part of the becoming-multiple. Within the complexity of layers and parallel spaces (vaguely connected by a magical portable closet), the girl band persists, as if on a journey of discovery, even if in the shadow of Sammy B's ever-deferred death wish. The slowing down that is the final part, *Temp Stop*, is highlighted in the drawn-out drone that develops over more than eight minutes. This emphasizes in turn that the narrative has always been audible in the length of sound allocations (as well as in the units of speech produced along with movement as part of a 'character' focus). This piece reiterates some of the aspirations of the previous three, but as if shaking out all drama, and the more realistic its playing with stage sets or ideas about identities and living, the more it seems out of touch with the world to which it refers (the world of *Re'Search*). This is perhaps because this is the point of crossover or confluence with the other part of *Any Ever*, the *Trill-ogy Comp*.

If I were to ventriloquize a social reading, based on the politics of identity, I might say that this trilogy looks at issues, mobilizing them for aesthetic purpose, while developing identities for those that may have none or may have theirs removed. Any attempt to reduce to Trecartin to a politics needs to pay close attention to how questions of, say, gender identity become much more than issues and rejoin the realm of a world simulation that seeks to outdo the one everyone walks around in as if it was actually real. Where Burroughs sought to reveal some secret depth to the world, based on a communications cabal that both spread and collected information, Trecartin's world is more properly Foucauldian, but with added zest and a subtly malignant critique of processes, not of either power holders or power consumers – all of whom are at once stupid, scheming, in control and lost, as they haphazardly navigate the multiple flat spaces of the videos. The opening piece in the trilogy, *K-CoreaINC.K (section a)* 'explores' in straightforward, if twisted, form the question of national and gender identity in a globalized world. Clearly such a purpose would be too glib even for most of Trecartin's ciphers to mouth, but presumably that is part of what is in play with a bus load of similarly attired 'Koreas', who are all blond-wigged and with very pale face make-up, led by 'Global Korea', in a series of parties or 'meetings', where non-sequential conversations happen, featuring bureaucratic and business turns of phrase. They move from plane to mobile home (RV), trailing around a self-contained celebrity party. Meanwhile USA Korea (Trecartin) offers sing-song sequences of identity projections as business goals, a strategy based on rhythm and Blackberry use. Mexico Korea offers alternative business solutions, heavily based on a borderline racist 'Mexican' accent. This is not the only flirtation away from political correctness, with the 'Koreas' representing an empty vessel for all other national characteristics (few of which are brought out in the script, but are there in naming of characters).

'Global Korea' herself is a curious amalgam of genders and colours, basically in 'whiteface'. This might make us reflect a bit more on Trecartin's numerous female characters who are heavily covered in fake tan, but the play is much more than a means of creating offence or indeed of 'questioning identity' – it could only represent a minor part of the dissection of identity as a possibility that occurs throughout the seven films of *Any Ever*, and particularly in the *Trill-ogy Comp*. Throughout *K-CoreaINC.K (section a)* the screens and spaces alternate rapidly, but not as fast as in the other series – this is being saved up for the third part of this trilogy. For now, though, we already hear what will become an insistent use of the sounds of smashing, as Mexico Korea smashes up her office room by the end (figure 13.2).

In *Sibling Topics*, Trecartin plays all of the quadruplet sisters who get to watch a video made by their mother in premonition of her own murder.

FIGURE 13.2 *Ryan Trecartin, still from* Sibling Topics (section a), *2009. Courtesy of the artist.*

Two of these sisters take priority in what is the most linear piece of either series. The first, Ceader, is the 'rebellious' one, the one who also acts in a film within the film, a semi-musical set in a hotel and house. This one starts by smashing a bed up systematically, and will periodically break things through the video. Her enemy is Britta, who organizes realities, and is both highly successful and a bully. The other two sisters turn up occasionally in dual screen, playing to camera in adjacent spaces. All of the sisters (all of Trecartin's characters in fact) target the camera lens, and it follows them – the focus on the mouth and words – as if there is no subjectivity, no presence, without constant iteration, and this in front of a lens (or doubled in internal screens, on a wall inside the stage set, for example). Similarly, all words count to the point where it is very unusual to hear a voice without seeing those words being spoken by the emitting mouth and face (even if the words are often altered in speed, Autotuned). One of the drawbacks for this film is that, although it wants to run a central narrative and also undermine it, it also has sideplot and side scenes, and these feature a bit too much 'acting'. At one level, maybe this is the strongest aesthetic statement, a rethinking of Warhol's 1960s Factory films that actually engages individuals to reflect on the wider mission of what they are doing in the film, but more digestible because less inert, more narrative. The soundtrack is also very much a backing track for much of the time, except as the film nears the end, and with eight minutes to go, the video bursts into sonic life, with looped ball throwing, wandering through a house turned into a sequence of percussive moves. As if acknowledging that narrative needs to wind down as well as up, gentle electronic drones edge us from silently moving around a simulated house to Ceader's disappearance. *Sibling Topics* offers a strong dispersion of character traits, rather than an attempt to create characters, as even stereotypical roles do not hold steady here when put into event or situational form. At the end, we have one sister looking for complete reality control (the layer most akin to the real outside of Trecartin's piece, the most power oriented), the principal other sister loving inhabiting a house with no resonance, no dwelling, just affectless occupation – being inside simulation is the best, most therapeutic outcome.

Sibling Topics does try to 'tell' something of contemporary living, communications, relations and, in the distance, playing, power, guesswork and difficulty of shared living, let alone the impossibility of self-identical awareness. The key evidence that this piece is interested in storytelling is its relative formal restraint, with narrative disruption not going beyond the side stories' intrusions into the central story of rivalry, played out at levels of reality rather than emotional position-taking. This is not a tragic tale of alienation due to communications technology. Machinery is portrayed as props, and not as a driver of anything. Mostly, it is attitudes to the use and outcomes of technology that count. The audio part gives a strong clue here in never aurally conveying someone's voice as being transmitted by the endless handheld phones, Blackberries and so on. The machines, their wired networks, are not carrying anything. Instead networks are occurring between cipher individuals, beyond and beneath the range of the incidental phoneprops.

Depending on your viewing sequence you could regard *P.opular S.ky (section ish)* as the link into the more frenetic *Re'Search* series, or as the apotheosis of the approaches of both. Perhaps accidentally, I tend to the latter, in respect of its audio side, which ends in riotous cut-noise. The piece brings together elements from the previous parts of the trilogy and from the other series. This suggests it is the nearest thing to a conclusion that *Any Ever* is likely to have. It emerges with bustling noise over a black screen, giving way to intercut multiscreen shots and papery windblown tunnels. There is a multitude of ultra-short songs, which are not fragments as such, but come from a fragmentary realm where the microscopic is the norm. The film is also peppered with the sounds of things being smashed and bashed, and towards the end this escalates along with a moment of near-plot as Ceader is attacked in a car, clambering out through the smashed windscreen. A flurry of microsongs cedes to a sequence of screams, water sounds, sax, smashing, rising noise, bits of music and multiple fast voices, all speeding into one soundgyre to fall away in a creak, more water, and the crashing of cymbals. As this goes on, the visual side is no more tranquil, as the poolside seen earlier in the trilogy (and across in the other series) hosts a trashing of the set, as if a combination of narrative and edited multitracking (some sequential, some vertical) was the only way out.

The multilayered clash of genres, formats, references, monologues, characters and non-linear event development shows no sign of abating in the set of three connected videos made for the Venice Biennale of 2013, and like the vast majority of his work, Trecartin has posted the videos online. All three move into the terrain of 'scripted reality' TV, with an even heavier musical emphasis than in *Any Ever*, as songs break out on a continual if irregular basis throughout. *Center Jenny* takes as its theme the idea of developing identity in a focussed way through a televised and controlled environment, replete with bitching, streams of assertive monologue and a cast of many Jennies. *Comma Boat* takes the world of the 'center' and runs further with the idea of direction (Trecartin as tyrannical film director taking centre stage). *Item Falls* picks up on ideas and images of the other two pieces and takes as its 'plot driver' the idea of stunts, combined with animation taking over from the need for apparently unsimulated activity.

The enclosed environments of these pieces, like those of earlier series, may arise contingently, as practical filming locations, but they certainly become material for refraction of the sets of reality as shot for TV. Not only the space but the cast, through being asked to interact, and in ways that approximate that of reality TV, become set material as well as performers. Reality as shot and scripted for TV does not ignore the vast amount of time and energy spent on socializing via media devices, and it is curious that instead of mirroring this, as in earlier videos addressed above, where Trecartin extends the idea of people inhabiting a mediatization so full, these devices fall away. Instead of Blackberries, the cast is now 'making' reality, presenting reality the way it wants, through being given the means of production – that is, cameras. The point is twofold: first, any real is going to be consensually created or at least understood; second, there are limits on this, because Trecartin has framed this possibility, just as companies that develop software and hardware for media use have provided tools that in turn feed into their other products, while turning user-consumers into commodities.

Consumer-users have, of course, been embracing this for some while, and Trecartin is neither pointing to a social problem nor a utopian belief in the liberating power of machinery. But his capacity to structure a formally exploratory parallel where these developments are inherent is utopian, and does point to a freeing-up of individual and social potential – albeit potential that is always on the point of being corralled, redirected or brought under control. Both *Center Jenny* and *Comma Boat* feature the multisensorial effect of breakcore strategies – cut-up microsongs and beats sped up and slowed down to heighten the image track. Characters also break into song, crossing from one genre to another, but always with self-improvement or self-creation at the core. In *Center Jenny*, in which people learn to achieve self-realization as Jenny, or at least as a Jenny, Auto-Tuning features on several occasions to extreme levels, as a device for fixing identity and harmonizing voices in expectation of a world of sameness. Auto-Tune is not defined as an enemy, but is based on standardization and pretend harmony. Instead, it also allows for playing with identity, subverting its corrective mission. The constant use of the word 'bitches' in the song fragments needs no explanation as a connection to hip-hop mobilization of what used to be called 'slang', and here works as 'street', a short cut to gender and social identities, a verbal Auto-Tune, with the same problems and potentials. The world of *Center Jenny* is one of relentless musical shortcuts, and also of musicalization, to the point where music as standalone activity, let alone completed product, is dissipated into some totalized communicative 'experience' or maybe journey. Let's take two short phrases from near the end: 'I'm really into call and response' is the first: already a comment on what is being said, this phrase shows the transfer of the belief in interaction and communication beloved of politicians, into 'ordinary life' and also art; the second is 'I'm still in the club bitch' – possibly a reference to Jennifer Lopez's 'I'm still Jenny from the block', and how the block never leaves you, you never leave the club and it is just authentic dancing all the way, bitches. The club takes over social space; the amorphous, slightly military or medical institution in so many purposely verbally limited pop songs becomes the world.

The club is the place we can all express ourselves, even if directed, or in need of direction, and this is the lead in to *Comma Boat*, where Trecartin directs himself as the character of a difficult director, amid many others carrying cameras who sometimes take instruction, other times not ('why aren't you filming me', she says over and over). Like *Center Jenny*, there are moments where the full sound approach of either competing sound or heavily individualized focus falls away, and percussive sounds (or sometimes water) emerge as aural stumbling points, suggesting a change of direction but without content. There are more disjunctive moments in *Comma Boat*, with one of the most striking being the fight between Trecartin's voice (as the director character films in night vision), an Autotuned song and also a throbbing hum. As this video nears completion, the world of song takes over more fully, and the sounds race through various electronic dance music styles as singing and dancing take place alongside credits. The musical parts are not only a concurrent part of multilayering (all three pieces feature many overlays, internal screens and rapid perspective changes) but also a temporal guide to popular music, as in faithful replication of music-oriented scripted reality shows; all the recent past is there for the taking, because how best to express your emotional journey than through a song from someone else from a slightly different era.

The status of music is more significant then, in these three films, and it is curious to see that for all the participatory involvement of the actors in developing events and talks within the parameters of guiding scripts, and even in filming, the sound is controlled by Trecartin, and not just ultimately, but continually. When several cameras are in use (which we are regularly shown), the sound does not cut between microphones; there is still a unifying element, however cut-up, accelerated or undefined it may be at any one time. Where in many video works, sound serves to spread or disseminate the piece, Trecartin's pieces from 2013 use sound here as consolidating device (without reducing sound febrility). So sound tells us something interesting about Trecartin's methods, which are highly collaborative, not least with art partner Lizzie Fitch, who plays a major part in set design, acting, casting and provides all manner of contributions to the pieces. The actors too are kept *in situ* to develop the work live, which will then be worked on by Trecartin for editing and sound. But Trecartin warns us to be aware of the limits of this collaboration. His videos clearly define roles and who is in charge (all acting work is subject to editing) even if collaboration is valued as of the idea of a 'network culture perspective' ('Cindy Sherman Interviews Ryan Trecartin', 144). The organizing (and editorial, montaging) role of sound makes his videos an upgrade of McLuhan's view of television, where 'the TV image…is an extension of the sense of touch' (*Understanding Media*, 334), where touch, or tactility, is not literally touching, but the proximity of the thing being sensed, due to its synaesthetic power, such that it makes a 'seamless web of experience' (335).[6] What else do we see and hear but 'the total involvement in all-inclusive *nowness*' (335)? This newness is not something special for a digital age, but it is something that is normalized in this era, normalized to the point of totality. At that point, the only way to look at the totality is to hear as well as see it, to allow it a power to overwhelm instead of controlling it for consumption.

Notes

1   Kareem Estefan, 'Deep Code', *Art in America* (September 2013), 123–9.
2   Linda Norden, 'When the Rainbow Is an Option', in Kevin McGarry (ed.), *Ryan Trecartin* (New York: Skira Rizzoli/Elizabeth Dee, 2011), 11–15.
3   For some guidance on the content of the works of both series, see Kevin McGarry's notes, available at http://www.ubu.com/film/trecartin_ready.html. However, they should be regarded as parallel storytelling, akin to Marcel Duchamp's notes on his own *The Bride Stripped Bare by Her Bachelors, Even* (1915–23), in the *Green Box* (1934).
4   Kevin McGarry, 'Worlds Apart', in McGarry (ed.), *Ryan Trecartin*, 109–13.
5   See Trecartin in 'Cindy Sherman Interviews Ryan Trecartin' in McGarry (ed.), *Ryan Trecartin*, 143–6, where he states that 'there will be a point when cameras are so advanced that they disappear along with screens' (144).
6   Marshall McLuhan, *Understanding Media: The Extensions of Man* (London: Routledge, 1997 [1964]).

End: Elizabeth Price,
Noise Capture

Everyone thinks that they live in the most complete times – whether in terms of perfection, dereliction or just normalcy. Where we are now is where we will always be, even if they are the End Times, and even if everything was subject to change in the past. Evolutionists are tempted to tell a story of contingent physical developments, long sequences of chance incidents and perpetual change, and yet close that off by claiming that today's adaptations are the Goldilocks standard. Philosophers have long remarked on the closing down of culture as everything has been done, whether in the melancholy of Nietzsche or Gianni Vattimo, the premature celebrations of Francis Fukuyama or the superficially celebratory yet deeply pessimistic musings of Jean Baudrillard. The time 'after theory' is marked by returns to simpler ways of thinking, which are less critical, less inventive, yet still convinced of their timeliness.

The digital is the privileged site of this musing – a new world expands like an ever-opening flower, where we can either excite through new thoughts or transmute old ideas into new realms, monetizing all the way. In the previous chapter, I suggested that Ryan Trecartin *shows* us another way of being in 'digital times' – that we are not beholden to it, but dwell in it, and that we can best occupy its spaces by not allowing it to be thought of as the dominant Imaginary of 'our times'. Instead, the digital is a source, a method, a staging area and a set of practices and materials as much as it is an apparently dematerialized source of cultural wonder or fatigue. One route that video art could take is into the purely digital, appearing on your electronic device of choice. Beyond that, it could allow user interaction – at its best, this would be more along the lines of gaming. Beyond that, maybe we could all make art together, not only using game-style templates but remodelling them as we go. So, logically, video art would change its location just at the time it takes over the physical terrain of the gallery and other art spaces, visually and aurally. It could, but this would hardly be avant-garde – to me, it seems like a return to two periods at once – the late 1960s and the tech-optimism of 1990s posthumanism. Both were also high points in the history of critical theory, so I am not at all inclined to dismiss the immense philosophical and artistic imaginings of those times. But digital platforms are not inherently interesting and have not been for most of forty years. Yvonne Spielmann makes a strong case for video art's crucial connection to the development of digital visual technology, in two ways: first, the technical processes are very similar, and require parallel processing actions; second, video pioneers such as Steina and Woody Vasulka were heavily involved in both branches as inventors as much as artists (Spielmann, *Video: the Reflexive Medium*, 52). Neither do I wish to dismiss multiple realms of creativity in visual or auditory digital practices. The digital is not a conclusion to the story of video art, nor of art in general. However, it is widely used, in ways that even the most narrative of artworks take for granted – in terms of filming, editing and mixing. That this creates a different perspective on what 'material' is and what can be done to it cannot be denied. I have not tried to address the possible epistemologies of digital in comparison to cognate analogue activities in my tracking of formal structures of video work; nonetheless, the use of digital technology is a central part of not only the practical making of video pieces but also the developing of the medium through formal (as well as machinic) means.

The digital quotidian is one of high functionality: supposed perfecting of media, facilitation of communications and access to material and commercial connectivity. The pictures in this book are in digital form, sourced through digital platform communication systems, processed into appropriate digital format for publishing and then, in some cases, recirculated in yet another decoded form for consumption. This omnipresence is precisely what should not blind the maker of video art; in addition to the example of the critical immersion of Trecartin, I wish to close on a consideration of Elizabeth Price's 2012 work, *The Woolworths Choir of 1979*. This piece is a formally advanced work, emerging from digital methods, that illustrates strongly the use of 'new media' as something incidental, and also the persistence of sound as something now normalized in the gallery. The formalist exploration in *The Woolworths Choir of 1979* happens not at the level of 'the digital' but in terms of structuring the work.

What unites Trecartin and Price is the refusal of digital smoothness. When Deleuze and Guattari talk of smooth and striated spaces in *One Thousand Plateaus*, the smooth is associated with freedom, pliability and motion, whereas the striated is one of control.[1] While they write that the two types 'exist only in mixture' (474), beyond their categorization, or further in, if you prefer, smooth space is bland, unified and free from the jagged, the incursion. Moreover, it is precisely how 'the' digital operates – Google renders information searching smooth; social media smoothes communications and opinions; industry standard software, websites and machines plane choices into monopolistic runnels and circuits. This is not to criticize these activities, products or codings as bad. Instead, I want to strongly state that in the context of video art, perhaps also of art more generally, the digital should be made less smooth, less functional, perfect and ideal (this happens internally, of course, in the altering of what is desirable in terms of music definition in MP3, for example, or in automated stock market crashes). The digital is a realm where messiness can and will be introduced, so instead of embracing the enabling pacification of the predictable successes of code world, the more interesting artists are excavating the potentials of de-formation.

Where Trecartin plunges his hands in, rummages around and finds blooms of language/visual/sound in stuttering explosion, Price models an archaeology of forms and formats to produce a narrative that plays on the telling of a narrative as one more form. Again, this is not inherently interesting – it is after all the cornerstone of modernism, but it is also the fulcrum of art as critique (as opposed to the highly successful contemporary 'form' of critique as art). Price's work also marks the continued normalization of sound in the gallery, in terms of her 2012 Turner Prize success, following on from the award in 2010 to Susan Philipsz, for essentially sound-based work. *The Woolworths Choir of 1979* mobilizes sound as part of a multilayered piece that is properly intermedial – lying between media, maintaining the characteristics of digital imaging, sound, animation, photographs, diagrams and film, and also between abstraction and narration. 'Abstraction' might seem a perverse term here, but if we think in terms of abstracting as process, I think it has significant relevance in terms of this piece (figure E.1).

FIGURE E.1 *Elizabeth Price,* The Woolworths Choir of 1979 *(2012). HD video, colour, sound, twenty minutes. Courtesy Elizabeth Price and LUX, London.*

The video divides into three parts over its near twenty-minute duration. The first part addresses the meaning of the word 'choir', focussing on its architectural status as part of a built church (as well as its physical manifestation as a group of singers – thus 'choral singing' becomes a term to describe singers located in the choir). After thirty seconds of a silent black screen, the dark is punctuated by a handclap and simultaneous image burst of the doubled image of a girl clapping. A rhythm builds until finally the sequence of images and claps (as well as other sounds later, such as choral singing, and a high-pitched tone that rises in volume) coalesces into a more constant, if still chopped and montaged, narration. Photographs of church interiors, architectural features and digitally produced zoom shots overlay one another, alongside diagrams, added directions and text. The whole is like a fragmented modernist version of a children's documentary. The multiplicity of the images combines with the uncertain, interruptive quality of the sounds (mostly handclaps, but suggestive of slide carousels turning) to establish a fractal architecture that culminates in images of unexpected oddness in the church choir, in the shape of carvings of mythical and real beasts, sin, violence and sex. The profane has intervened and signals physical occupation, that is, the troubling of the apparent certainties of holy architecture by human physical presence. Gradually, shots of music videos intersperse, recasting the handclaps as promotion of these other choruses; a red screen interrupts visually, following on from the interstitial sound use; and at 7.20, the second section begins, a warped rebuild of Dan Graham's *Rock My Religion*, to the cut-up tune of the Shangri-Las song 'Out in the Streets', where the performers are not shamanic but joyfully ecstatic: part of groups, pop maenads dancing, singing, clapping, signalling life as continual process, interaction. Overlaying these cut clips are series of words, in red, notably 'we are choir', 'we are chorus'; the high-pitch tone raises higher than before, alarmishly, and then we cut to the third section, after ten minutes.

The dancers, singers, twirlers and groups give way slowly, living on as after-images and handclaps, mirrored now in the hand gestures of people being interviewed. The music builds again, 'we are choir' also returns and then smoke fills the screen to the sound of the high tone. Then there is silence, shots of firemen, the aftermath of a fire. This is where we finally arrive at the narrative core indicated by the title: the fire in the Woolworths store, Manchester, on the 8th May 1979, in which ten people died. The third section is largely made up of archive footage, of survivors, eyewitnesses and pictures of the events. For much of this sequence, images are twinned, and captions scroll across each one, or sometimes just one. In this way, the chorus seeps into these sections. The chorus is also made strange by moments where the image in one half of the screen is in colour, while its 'twin' is in black and white. This is particularly striking in images of the reconstruction of the spread of the fire that is interspersed with images of floor plans, drawings of the spread of the fire and more comments by those who were caught up in the fire. Price is in no way 'merely' formalist, to the detriment of affective interest. She is highly respectful of the situation and those involved, and also actually interested in the details of the event and its causes. She emphasizes that the furniture had been stored with little concern for fire safety, and that there was grossly inadequate further protection (including locked/inaccessible fire exits). So the cutting of film sections, the play with sound and light, is all purposeful – it is there to build a complex archaeology of an accident caused by negligence and at the same time pay homage to the prospect of community ('we are choir' comes back across the screen at one moment). The multiple sections, the overlaid imagery and discrete, less-than-predictable sound interventions all contribute not only to unearth the fullness of a story but also to comment on how we access the past, and how we envisage disaster scenes in ways that may merge with simpler (because older historically) documents. In short, the narrative power is strengthened by the formalist, intermedia approach. At the same time, narrative itself is subject to questioning.

After this wave-like process of interpretation and re-presenting, Price also leaves us with a reflection on 'the' digital. It permits the multilayering and encourages editing and the use of found sources, but it does not need to become a simplistic tool or unquestioned set of procedures. In fact, Price does not explicitly question the digital nature of the work at all. Instead, through interrogating the competing claims of documents, accounts and her own interventions 'in the style of' documentaries, the overall field of the piece becomes one of questioning, thus returning us to video as medium with potential to reflect on itself (Spielmann), or intermedial process that sets different media into relation with each other without having to resolve them into anything but a new intermedia. Price also allows (as does Trecartin) for the digital not to be a mute territory where the visual is consumed alone. Sound's nature as temporal, spatial, extensive and potentially unexpected allows it to play across and within layers of *The Woolworths Choir of 1979*, and then a clap gives way to smoke and credits, with only a final click to announce a rapid fade to black.

Note

1   Gilles Deleuze and Félix Guattari, *A Thousand Plateaus* (London: Athlone, 1988 [1980]). Translated by Brian Massumi.

BIBLIOGRAPHY

Abe, Kazunao, 'As "/"', in Ryoji Ikeda (ed.), *Datamatics* (Milan: Charta, 2012), 105–8.

Abe, Kazunao, 'syn chron | berlin | yamaguchi', in Nicolai (ed.), *syn chron*, 87–8.

Agamben, Giorgio, *Language and Death: The Place of Negativity* (Minneapolis: University of Minnesota Press, 1991).

Augé, Marc, *Non-places: Introduction to an Anthropology of Supermodernity* (London and New York: Verso, 1995).

Auping, Michael, 'Metacommunicator', *Bruce Nauman – Raw Materials*, 8–17.

Barikin, Amelia, *Parallel Presents: The Art of Pierre Huyghe* (Cambridge, MA: MIT Press, 2012).

Barthelmes, Barbara, 'A Symbiosis of Light, Sound and Architecture. On *syn chron* by Carsten Nicolai', in Nicolai (ed.), *syn chron*, 11–15.

Barthes, Roland, 'The Grain of the Voice', in *Image – Music – Text* (London: Fontana), 179–89.

Bataille, Georges, *Story of the Eye* (London: Penguin, 1979).

Bataille, Georges, *Prehistoric Painting: Lascaux or the Birth of Art* (London: Macmillan, 1980).

Bataille, Georges, *Visions of Excess: Selected Writings, 1927–1939*, ed. and trans. Allan Stoekl (Minneapolis: University of Minnesota Press, 1985).

Baudrillard, Jean, *In the Shadow of the Silent Majorities* (New York: Semiotext[e], 1983).

Baudrillard, Jean, *Symbolic Exchange and Death* (London: Sage, 1993).

Baudrillard, Jean, *Simulacra and Simulation* (Ann Arbor, MI: University of Michigan Press, 1994).

Baudrillard, Jean, *Screened Out* (London: Verso, 2002).

Baudrillard, Jean, *Le Pacte de lucidité, ou l'intelligence du Mal* (Paris: Galilée, 2004).

Baudrillard, Jean, *Cool Memories V: 2000–2004* (Paris: Galilée, 2005).

Baudrillard, Jean, 'Integral Reality', available at http://www.egs.edu/faculty/jean-baudrillard/articles/integral-reality/

Beckett, Samuel, *How It Is* (London: John Calder, 1964).

Benjamin, Walter, 'The Work of Art in the Age of Mechanical Reproduction', in *Illuminations* (London: Fontana, 1973), 211–44.

Bickers, Patricia, 'Interview with Pipilotti Rist', *Art Monthly* 350 (October 2011), available at http://www.artmonthly.co.uk/magazine/site/issue/october-2011.

Blanchot, Maurice, *Thomas the Obscure* (Barrytown, NY: Station Hill Press, 1988).

Bois, Yve-Alain and Krauss, Rosalind, *Formless: A User's Guide* (New York: Zone, 1997), / *l'informe: mode d'emploi* (Paris: Centre Georges Pompidou, 1996).

Bonnet, F. J., 'Noyade phénoménologique (Notes à propos de *Hallway Nodes* de Bill Viola), available at http://www.vibrofiles.com/essays_françois_bonnet02php.

Borthwick, Ben, 'Catalogue Entries', in Emma Dexter et al. (eds.) *Bruce Nauman – Raw Materials* (London: Tate, 2004), 130–41.

Bourriaud, Nicolas, *Relational Aesthetics* (Dijon: Les Presses du réel, 2002).

Boyle, Deirdre, 'A Brief Summary of American Documentary Video', in Hall and Fifer (eds.), *Illuminating Video*, 51–69.

Braidotti, Rosi, *Transpositions* (Cambridge: Polity, 2006).

Bruzzi, Stella, *New Documentary: A Critical Introduction* (London and New York: Routledge, 2000).

Buchloh, Benjamin, 'Moments of History in the Work of Dan Graham', in Kitnick (ed.), *Dan Graham*, 1–20.

Cascone, Kim, 'The Aesthetics of Failure: "Post-Digital" Tendencies in Contemporary Computer Music', in Christoph Cox and Daniel Warner (eds.), *Audio Culture: Readings in Modern Music* (New York and London: Continuum, 2004), 392–8.

Connolly, Maeve, *The Place of Artists' Cinema: Space, Site and Screen* (Bristol and Chicago: Intellect, 2009).

Cooper, Sarah, *Selfless Cinema? Ethics and French Documentary* (London: Legenda, 2006).

Corner, Stuart (ed.), *Film and Video Art* (London: Tate, 2009).

Cornwell, Regina, 'Gary Hill: An Interview', in Morgan (ed.), *Gary Hill*, 224–31.

Corrin, Lisa, 'In Stereoscopic Vision: A Dialogue between Jane and Louise Wilson and Lisa Corrin', in Peter Schjeldahl et al. (eds.) *Jane and Louise Wilson* (London: Serpentine, 1999), 6–15.

Crimp, Douglas, '*Our Kind of Movie': The Films of Andy Warhol* (Cambridge, MA and London: MIT Press, 2012).

Cubitt, Sean, *Digital Aesthetics* (London: Sage, 1998).

Daniels, Dieter, 'Video/Art/Market', in Frieling and Herzogenrath, *40YEARSVIDEOART.DE*, 40–9.

de Angelus, Michele, 'Interview with Bruce Nauman, May 27 and 30, 1980', in Kraynak (ed.), *Please Pay Attention Please*, 197–295.

Deleuze, Gilles and Guattari, Félix, *A Thousand Plateaus* (London: Athlone, 1988).

Demos, T. J., 'The Art of Darkness: On Steve McQueen', *October* 114 (Fall 2005), 61–89 (61).

de Oliveira, Nicolas, Oxley, Nicola and Petry, Michael, *Installation Art in the New Millennium* (London: Thames and Hudson, 2003).

Derrida, Jacques, *Of Grammatology* (Baltimore, MD: Johns Hopkins Press, 1976).

Derrida, Jacques, *The Truth in Painting* (Chicago: Chicago University Press, 1987).

Dexter, Emma, 'Raw Materials', in *Bruce Nauman – Raw Materials*, 18–23.

Doherty, Claire, 'Awaiting Oblivion', in Jane and Louise Wilson et al. *Jane and Louise Wilson* (London: Ellipsis, 2000), 73–8.

Dworkin, Craig, 'Fugitive Signs', *October* 95 (Winter 2001), 90–113.

Dyson, Frances, *Sounding New Media: Immersion and Embodiment in the Arts and Culture* (Berkeley, CA: University of California Press, 2009).

Eamon, Chris, 'An Art of Temporality', in Corner (ed.), *Film and Video Art*, 66–85.

Eshun, Kodwo, *Rock My Religion* (London: AfterAll, 2012).

Estefan, Kareem, 'Deep Code', *Art in America* (September 2013), 123–9.

Francis, Mark, 'In Conversation with Dan Graham', in Birgit Pelzer et al. (eds.) *Dan Graham* (London: Phaidon, 2001), 8–35.

Freud, Sigmund, 'The Uncanny', in Freud, *Standard Edition*, XVII (London: Hogarth Press, 1955), 219–52.

Freud, Sigmund, 'Three Essays on the Theory of Sexuality', in Freud, *The Essentials of Psychoanalysis* (London: Penguin, 1986), 277–375.

Frieling, Rudolf and Herzogenrath, Wulf (eds.), *40YEARSVIDEOART.DE: Digital Heritage, Video Art in Germany from 1963 to the Present* (Ostfildern: Hatje Cantz, 2006).

Genosko, Gary, *McLuhan and Baudrillard: Masters of Implosion* (London and New York: Routledge, 1999).

Gilroy, Paul, 'Soundscapes of the Black Atlantic', in Michael Bull and Les Back (eds.), *The Auditory Culture Reader* (Oxford and New York: Berg, 2003), 381–95.

Godfrey, Mark, 'Pierre Huyghe's Double Spectacle', *Grey Room* 32 (Summer 2008), 38–61.

González, Jennifer, 'Overture', in González et al. (eds.) *Christian Marclay* (London and New York: Phaidon, 2005), 22–81.

Groys, Boris, 'From the Image to the Image File – and Back', in Frieling and Herzogenrath (eds.), *40YEARSVIDEOART.DE*, 50–7.

Hainge, Greg, 'Of Glitch and Men: The Place of the Human in the Successful Integration of Failure and Noise in the Digital Realm', *Communication Theory* 17 (2007), 26–42.

Hall, Doug and Fifer, Sally Jo (eds.), *Illuminating Video: An Essential Guide to Video Art* (New York: Aperture, 1990).

Hanhardt, John G., 'Dé-collage/Collage: Notes toward a Re-examination of the Origins of Video Art', Hall and Fifer (eds.), *Illuminating Video*, 71–9.

Harbord, Janet, *Chris Marker, La Jetée* (London: Afterall, 2009).

Hegarty, Paul, *Noise/Music: A History* (New York and London: Continuum, 2007)

Hegarty, Paul, 'Hallucinatory Life of Tape', *Culturemachine* 9 (2007), available at http://www.culturemachine.net/index.php/cm/article/viewArticle/82/67.

Hegel, G. W. F., *Aesthetics* (Oxford: Clarendon, 1975).

Heidegger, Martin, *Basic Writings*, 2nd edition, edited David Farrel Krell (London: Routledge and Kegan Paul, 1993).

Herbert, Matthew, 'Infinity's Borders: Ryoji Ikeda', in Kelly (ed.), *Sound*, 162–5.

Hertz, Garnet and Parikka, Jussi, 'Zombie Media: Circuit Bending Media Archaeology into an Art Method', *Leonardo* 45 (5) (2012), 424–30.

Herzogenrath, Wulf, 'Video Art and Institutions: The First Fifteen Years', in Frieling and Herzogenrath (eds.), *40YEARSVIDEOART.DE*, 20–33.

Hicks, Michael, *Sixties Rock: Garage, Psychedelic and Other Satisfactions* (Urbana and Chicago: University of Illinois Press, 1999).

Higgs, Mark, '*Video Quartet*', *Christian Marclay*, 83–91.

Ikeda, Ryoji and Nicolai, Carsten, 'Preface', in Ikeda and Nicolai, *cyclo.id vol I* (Berlin: Die Gestalten, 2011).

Iles, Chrissie, 'Cleaning the Mirror, Marina Abramović, 1995', in Caleb Kelly (ed.), *Sound*, 187–90.

Irigaray, Luce, *This Sex Which Is Not One* (New York: Cornell University Press, 1985).

Jones, Amelia, *Body Art: Performing the Subject* (Minneapolis: University of Minnesota Press, 1998).

Jones, Caroline A. (ed.), *Sensorium: Embodied Experience, Technology and Contemporary Art* (Cambridge, MA: MIT Press, 2006).

Kahn, Douglas, *Noise Water Meat: A History of Sound in the Arts* (Cambridge, MA: MIT Press, 1999).

Kant, Immanuel, *Critique of Judgement* (Indianapolis and Cambridge: Hackett, 1987).

Kase, Carlos, '" This Guitar Has Seconds to Live": *Guitar Drag*'s Archeology of Indeterminacy and Violence', *Discourse* 30 (3) (Fall 2008), 419–42.

Kaye, Nick, *Multi-media: Video – Installation – Performance* (Abingdon and New York: Routledge, 2007).

Keith, Chris, 'Image after Image: The Video Art of Bill Viola', *PAJ: A Journal of Performance and Art* 20 (2) (May 1998), 1–16.

Kelly, Caleb, *Cracked Media* (Cambridge, MA: MIT Press, 2009).

Kelly, Caleb (ed.), *Sound* (London: Whitechapel Gallery/MIT Press, 2011).

Kitnick, Alex (ed.), *Dan Graham* (Cambridge, MA: MIT Press, 2011).

Krauss, Rosalind, 'Video: The Aesthetics of Narcissism', *October* vol 1 (Spring 1976), 50–64.

Krauss, Rosalind, 'Sculpture in the Expanded Field', *October* vol 8 (Spring 1979), 30–44.

Krauss, Rosalind, *A Voyage on the North Sea: Art in the Age of the Post-Medium Condition* (London: Thames & Hudson, 2000).

Kraynak, Janet (ed.), *Please Pay Attention Please: Bruce Nauman's Words* (Cambridge, MA: MIT Press, 2008).

Kraynak, Janet, 'Bruce Nauman's Words', in Kraynak (ed.), *Please Pay Attention Please*, 1–45.

Kroker, Arthur and Marilouise Kroker, 'Theses on the Disappearing Body in the Hypermodern Condition', in Arthur and Marilouise Kroker (eds.), *Body Invaders: Sexuality and the Postmodern Condition* (Basingstoke: Macmillan, 1988).

LaBelle, Brandon, *Background Noise: Perspectives on Sound Art* (New York and London: *Continuum*, 2006).

LaBelle, Brandon, *Acoustic Territories: Sound Culture and Everyday Life* (New York: Continuum, 2010).

Lageira, Jacinto, 'The Image of the World in the Body of the Text', in Morgan (ed.), *Gary Hill*, 27–55.

Legge, Elizabeth, *Michael Snow, Wavelength* (London: Afterall, 2009).

Lewallen, Constance M., et al., *A Rose Has No Teeth: Bruce Nauman in the 1960s* (Berkeley: University of California Press, 2007).

Lewallen, Constance M., 'A Rose Has No Teeth', in Lewallen et al. (eds.), *A Rose Has No Teeth*, 7–115.

Lewis, George, *A Power Stronger Than Itself: The AACM and American Experimental Music* (Chicago and London: University of Chicago Press, 2008).

Licht, Alan, 'Mixmaster', *Modern Painters* (March 2005), 30–3 (30).

Licht, Alan, *Sound Art: Beyond Music, between Categories* (New York: Rizzoli, 2007), 9–11.

Lock, Graham, *Blutopia: Visions of the Future and Revisions of the Past in the Work of Sun Ra, Duke Ellington and Anthony Braxton* (Durham: Duke University Press, 1999).

Lucier, Mary, 'Light and Death', in Hall and Fifer (eds.), *Illuminating Video*, 457–64.

Lyotard, Jean-François, 'Acinema', in Andrew Benjamin (ed.), *The Lyotard Reader* (Oxford: Blackwell, 1991), 169–80.

Lyotard, Jean-François, *Libidinal Economy* (London: Athlone, 1993).

Marclay, Christian and Hill, Gary, 'Conversation', *Annandale* (Spring 2000), 2–9.

McGarry, Kevin (ed.), *Ryan Trecartin* (New York: Skira Rizzoli/Elizabeth Dee, 2011).

McGarry, Kevin, 'Worlds Apart', in McGarry (ed.), *Ryan Trecartin*, 109–13.

McLuhan, Marshall and Fiore, Quentin, *The Medium Is the Massage* (Harmondsworth: Penguin, 1967).

McLuhan, Marshall and Fiore, Quentin, *War and Peace in the Global Village* (New York: Bantam, 1968).

McLuhan, Marshall, *Understanding Media: The Extensions of Man* (London: Routledge, 1997).

Meigh-Andrews, Chris, *A History of Video Art: The Development of Form and Function* (Berg: Oxford and New York, 2006).

Metz, Christian, *Film Language: A Semiotics of the Cinema* (New York: Oxford University Press, 1974).

Michelson, Annette, 'Toward Snow', in P. Adams Simey (ed.), *The Avant-Garde Film: A Reader of Theory and Criticism* (New York: Anthology Film Archives, 1978), 172–83.

Miller, John, 'Now Even the Pigs're Groovin', Kitnick (ed.), *Dan Graham*, 129–62.

Mondloch, Kate, *Screens: Viewing Media Installation Art* (Minneapolis and London: University of Minnesota Press, 2010).

Mondloch, Kate, 'The Matter of Illusionism: Michael Snow's Screen/Space', in Trodd (ed.), *Screen/Space: The Projected Image in Contemporary Art* (Manchester: Manchester University Press, 2011), 73–89.

Morgan, Robert C. (ed.), *Gary Hill* (Baltimore, MD and London: Johns Hopkins University Press, 2000).

Morse, Margaret, 'Video Installation Art: The Body, the Image, and the Space-in-Between', in Hall and Fifer (eds.), *Illuminating Video*, 153–67.

Murphy, J. J, *The Black Hole of the Camera: The Films of Andy Warhol* (Berkeley and Los Angeles: University of California Press, 2012).

Nancy, Jean-Luc, *The Inoperative Community* (Minneapolis, MN: University of Minnesota Press, 1991).

Newman, Michael, 'Moving Image in the Gallery since the 1990s', in Corner (ed.), *Film and Video Art*, 86–121.

Nicolai, Carsten, '*syn chron*: Architectural Body as Interface. Space. Light. Sound', in Nicolai (ed.), *syn chron* (Berlin: Die Gestalten, 2013), 33–4.

Norden, Linda, 'When the Rainbow Is an Option', in McGarry (ed.), *Ryan Trecartin*, 11–15.

Pelzer, Birgit, 'Vision in Process', in Kitnick (ed.), *Dan Graham*, 41–59.

Phelan, Peggy, 'Opening Up Spaces within Spaces: The Expansive Art of Pipilotti Rist', in Phelan et al. (eds.) *Pipilotti Rist* (London and New York: Phaidon, 2001), 34–77.

Priest, eldritch, *Boring Formless Nonsense* (New York: Bloomsbury, 2013).

Quasha, George and Stein, Charles, *An Art of Limina: Gary Hill's Works and Writings* (Barcelona: Ediciones Poligrafa, 2009).

Rebentisch, Juliane, *Aesthetics of Installation Art* (Frankfurt: Sternberg, 2012).

Rieser, Martin and Zapp, Andrea (eds.), *New Screen Media: Cinema/Art/Narrative* (London: BFI, 2002).

Riley, Robert R, 'Bruce Nauman's Philosophical and Material Explorations in Film and Video', in M. Lewallen et al. (eds.), *A Rose Has No Teeth*, 171–89.

Rodenbach, Georges, *Bruges-la-Morte* (Paris: Flammarion, 1998).

Rogers, Holly, *Sounding the Gallery: Video and the Rise of Art-Music* (Oxford: Oxford University Press, 2013).

Ross, Christine, 'The Temporalities of Video: Extendness Revisited', *Art Journal* 65 (3) (Fall 2006), 82–99.

Rush, Michael, *Video Art* (London: Thames and Hudson, 2003).

Sarazzin, Stephen, 'Surfing the Medium', in Robert C. Morgan (ed.), *Gary Hill*, 62–90.

Schaeffer, Pierre, *A la recherche d'une musique concrète* (Paris: Le Seuil, 1952).

Schmidt, Sabine Maria, 'At the Right Place at the Right Time?: A Brief Report on Current Video Art', in Frieling and Herzogenrath (eds.), *40YEARSVIDEOART. DE*, 34–9.

Schjeldahl, Peter, 'V.I.: Jane and Louise Wilson', in Schjeldahl et al. (eds.) *Jane and Louise Wilson* (London: Pale Green Press/Serpentine Gallery, 1999), 4–5.

Sciarra, Lorraine, 'Bruce Nauman, January 1972', interview, in Kraynak (ed.), *Please Pay Attention Please*, 155–71.

Serra, M. M. and Ramey, Kathryn, 'Eye/Body: The Cinematic Paintings of Carolee Schneemann', in Robin Blaetz (ed.), *Women's Experimental Cinema* (Durham, NC: Duke University Press, 2007), 103–26.

Sharp, Willoughby, 'Interview with Bruce Nauman', in Kraynak (ed.), *Please Pay Attention Please*, 111–54.

Sherman, Cindy, 'Interviews Ryan Trecartin', in McGarry (ed.), *Ryan Trecartin*, 143–6.

Sophie, Dupleix et al., *Sons & Lumières* (Paris: Centre Pompidou, 2004).

Spielmann, Yvonne, 'From Technology to Medium', *Art Journal* 65 (3) (Fall 2006), 54–69.

Spielmann, Yvonne, *Video: The Reflexive Medium* (Cambridge, MA: MIT Press, 2010).

Sturken, Marita, 'Paradox in the Evolution of an Art Form: Great Expectations and the Making of a History', Hall and Fifer (eds.), *Illuminating Video*, 101–21.

Todoli, Vicente, 'Foreword', *Bruce Nauman – Raw Materials* 2004, 7.

Toop, David et al., *Sonic Boom: The Art of Sound* (London: Hayward Gallery, 2000).

Torres, Francesc, 'The Art of the Possible', in Hall and Fifer (eds.), *Illuminating Video*, 205–9.

Trodd, Tamara (ed.), *Screen/Space: The Projected Image in Contemporary Art* (Manchester and New York: Manchester University Press, 2011).

Turing, Alan, 'Computing Machinery and Intelligence', *Mind* LIX (October 1950), 433–60.

van Assche, Christine et al. (eds.), *Sonic Process: Une nouvelle géographie des sons* (Paris: Centre Pompidou, 2002).

Viola, Bill, *Reasons for Knocking at an Empty House: Writings, 1973–1994* (London: Thames and Hudson, 1995).

Viola, Bill, 'David Tudor: The Delicate Art of Falling', *Leonardo Music Journal* 14 (2004), 48–56.

Wilson, Jane and Louise, 'Artists story', http://www.a-n.co.uk/artists_talking/artists_stories/single/61233

Young, Lisa Jaye, 'The Elemental Sublime: Bill Viola, *Fire Water Breath*', *Performing Arts Journal* 19 (3) (1997), 65–71.

Youngblood, Gene, *Expanded Cinema* (New York: Dutton, 1970).

INDEX